The Love of Wisdom

An Introduction to Philosophy for Theologians

Andrew Davison

scm press

Published in 2013 by SCM Press
Editorial office
3rd Floor
Invicta House
108-114 Golden Lane,
London
EC1Y OTG

SCM Press is an imprint of Hymns Ancient & Modern Ltd
(a registered charity)
13A Hellesdon Park Road
Norwich NR6 5DR, UK

www.scmpress.co.uk

British Library Cataloguing in Publication data

A catalogue record for this book is available
from the British Library

978-0-334-04384-3

Typeset by Manila Typesetting Company
Printed and bound by
CPI Group (UK) Ltd, Croydon

For Catherine

Much better to deck oneself out in truths that others have handed down . . . than . . . refuse to do so and go naked.

Étienne Gilson, *Methodological Realism: A Handbook for Beginning Realists*, San Francisco: Ignatius, 2011, p. 106

Contents

Acknowledgements

From the ancient philosophers we learn not only ideas but also method: that philosophy is inseparable from the spiritual life and that it is a communal enterprise. In the Church I have found traditions of thought, going back to the ancient world, renewed and expanded. I have also found the ancient emphasis on friendship as the crucible of thought and the connection of philosophy with prayer and worship. My debt and gratitude, therefore, are not simply to individuals, for having read a chapter, or put me right on this point or that, nor even to particular teachers, although all of that remains. My debt of gratitude is most of all to a community of people – many of whom know one another, but not all – who have lived, eaten and drunk with me, who have travelled, prayed and disputed with me. I thank all those who have set before me the example of Aquinas: who have both contemplated and passed on to others the fruits of their contemplation.

Introduction:
Why Study Philosophy?

The Scriptures warn us not to be 'taken captive' through philosophy (Col. 2.8; cf. 1 Cor. 1.20–5). As an aid to achieving that end, this book makes a counter-intuitive proposal: our theology is less likely to be hijacked by philosophy if we pay attention to philosophy. We can be *more philosophical* in order to be *more theological*.

We all operate within a philosophical framework. Philosophy, in this sense, is the position a person, culture or school of thought takes over what reality looks like and how its aspects fit together. Define philosophy this way, and every last person is a philosopher, and every last person has a philosophy. Everyone has a sense of how to think about time, knowledge, causation, justice and so on. There is an 'architecture' to the mind. As John Stuart Mill put it, the mind has 'furniture'.[1] We may not be able to articulate these assumptions in any systematic way, but we have assumptions nonetheless. By and large, English-speaking cultures do not provide much space for us to think about these matters. It would be different if we lived in France or Iran, two countries where philosophy is prized and philosophical books sell in large quantities.

The Christian theologian will want his or her framework to reflect a Christian vision of the world, and unexamined philosophical presuppositions determine our outlook even more than examined ones. Unexamined presuppositions are the ones that it does not cross our mind to question. Fergus Kerr has described the consequences:

---

1 *System of Logic*, New York: Harper and Brothers, 1882, p. 21.

if theologians proceed in the belief that they need neither examine nor even acknowledge their inherited metaphysical commitments, they will simply remain prisoners of whatever philosophical school was in the ascendant 30 years earlier, when they were first-year students.[2]

'When the existence of metaphysical commitments is ignored or denied', as Kerr goes on, 'their grip only tightens.'[3] I can think of two theological books, whose titles I shall pass over, where the clinching move in the argument comes straight from Hegel. The author's conclusion, ultimately, does not rest on theological sources but upon Hegel's conviction that a cycle of tension and resolution lies at the heart of things. Neither author wrote 'as Hegel would say' as part of his argument. Indeed, if either had, he might have questioned whether Hegel's metaphysics should be given such sway.

This book takes a historical approach. Familiarity with the history of philosophy is useful, if only as a reminder that ideas have a history. However much an outlook today appears obvious to us, it has a heritage. At other times, people thought otherwise, and because we each receive our philosophical heritage in a different way, other people will think otherwise even in our own time.[4]

We cannot take ourselves outside of philosophical tradition, if for no other reason than that we cannot get outside of language. In the words of Michael Polanyi: 'The practice of speech in one particular language carries with it the acceptance of the particular theory of the universe postulated by the language.'[5] We can, however, think critically about where we stand and what we take

---

2 *Theology After Wittgenstein*, London: SPCK, 1997, p. 1.

3 *After Wittgenstein*, p. 187.

4 Similarly, even thinkers who are vigorously opposed to one another on many points will share philosophical convictions in common. In the words of Alasdair MacIntyre: 'The warring partisans on the great issues that engage our culture and politics presuppose, even when they do not recognize it, the truth of some philosophical theses and the falsity of others.' *God, Philosophy, Universities: A Selective History of the Catholic Philosophical Tradition*, Continuum, 2009, p. 1.

5 Michael Polanyi, *Personal Knowledge: Towards a Post-critical Philosophy*, Routledge, 1998, p. 295, and see pp. 266–7.

for granted. Polanyi's comment need not be fatalistic. 'Language' here means something more specific than English, French or Lithuanian. We can all 'learn to watch our language', so that 'our metaphysical inclinations are laid bare',[6] to quote Kerr again, and start to refine it where necessary. We will do that when our philosophy is prayed through and considered alongside study of the Bible, alongside readings from the great theologians, mystics and activists of Christian history. Theology can bend our philosophy into new shapes. This is part of taking 'every thought captive to Christ' (2 Cor. 10.5).

The Uses of Philosophy

We all have a philosophy; it may as well be a good one. The thought of Thomas Aquinas will unashamedly provide the fulcrum of this book. His provides two good angles why philosophy is useful for the theologian: it provides tools for clear thinking, and it helps us understand people who think differently from us, as we talk to them about God. The first approach urges us to pay attention to good philosophy; the second urges us to pay attention to bad philosophy, so as to be able to explain why it will not suffice as an alternative to the theological vision.

The first use for philosophy is a consequence of the fact that we think with words and ideas. If we have to use concepts, they may as well be good concepts. Taken this way, philosophy does not provide theology with its ideas but it can help theologians to articulate the faith clearly. Gregory of Nyssa encouraged his readers to make use of the best philosophy available. He likened the Church's use of philosophical ideas, wherever they came from, to the Israelites carrying off the treasures of Egypt.[7] If the Israelites could put the gold of Egypt to holy use, why can we not do the same with the treasures of thought?

---

6 *After Wittgenstein*, p. 187.

7 *Life of Moses* II.115. Augustine wrote that Christians can 'claim' good philosophical ideas from pagans, who possess them unjustly (*On Christian Doctrine* II.11).

Sometimes philosophy is helpful at its most sober, and sometimes at its most provocative. In the philosophy of the twentieth century, those two options have sometimes been taken to extremes, the sober option being called 'analytic' philosophy and the provocative option being called 'Continental' philosophy. (We will return to this distinction in the final chapter.) If we take the sober option, we had better think that the philosophy in question is *right*, since sobriety does not have much to offer beyond its clarity. When philosophy is of a more edgy variety, it can inspire us to be creative even when we think the philosophy is very wrong, by way of provoking us to think otherwise.

The setting for Aquinas's second account of the usefulness of philosophy is in discussion with those who differ from us over how to think and understand the world. As he puts it, if we are talking to someone who does not accept the authority of the Scriptures, he or she is not going to think within the same scheme as the Christian. What counts for us as the best place to start will carry little weight for them. In this case, philosophical discussions come into their own: positively, since we can work towards God in terms of 'what they concede' and defensively, in seeking to 'answer his [or her] objections'.[8] Our interlocutor might be an individual, but this process is also played out on a far larger scale, for instance in the media, when we are in dialogue with an entire culture. This is an apologetic use of philosophy, in relation to those outside the mind of the Church, just as the first use was theological, in relation to those inside the mind of the Church. The apologetic use of philosophy does not only involve answering objections; it can also involve showing flaws in positions proposed against the faith. This often works by showing that a scheme is contradictory[9] or by showing the undesirable consequences – moral, perhaps, or political – that follow from a particular position, when its logic is allowed to run its course.

As an example of these two uses for philosophy, in theology and apologetics, take our understanding of death. In the first category,

---

8 *Summa Theologiae* (hereafter *ST*) I.1.8.
9 Aquinas discusses this *In I Phys.*, lec. 3.

we are looking for the best ideas and terminology with which to talk about death from a perspective born of Christian wisdom. Classically, Christians have used the language of the soul here. To get there, they have sifted among rival perspectives and chosen the best: Plato has something to offer, Aristotle has more, but Christian theologians have not been happy to stick exactly with either. Nothing in this process was accepted uncritically; philosophical traditions have served as a quarry for ideas and parts of ideas, all the while serving the biblical tradition. The result, when it comes to the soul, articulates both our sense that human beings are bodily creatures and our sense that something essential about the human person is graciously preserved by God between death and the general resurrection.

To aid in the second, apologetic, task, we ask philosophical questions about the understandings of death pervading the culture in which we live, minister and bear witness. That might involve reading philosophical books, but just as likely it will involve listening for the implicit philosophy of death that lies behind what our peers say and do. We might also turn a philosophical eye to literature and film, to our common turns of phrase, and to practices and secular rituals. Our response may then be both positive, pointing out how implicit half-theological assumptions cry out for proper theological foundations, or it may be gently critical, pointing out that secular beliefs and practices cannot justify the consolation they purport to offer, while the nihilism to which they truly tend is not convincing in face of our sense of human dignity.

Philosophy and Human Consideration

Philosophy is *practically* useful for the study of theology. Philosophy is also worth attention in its own right. Paul instructed the Philippians to sift out all that is noble and excellent and to meditate upon these things:

> whatever is true, whatever is honourable, whatever is just, whatever is pure, whatever is pleasing, whatever is commendable,

if there is any excellence and if there is anything worthy of praise, think about these things. (Phil. 4.8)

Parts of the world's philosophical traditions fall under these descriptions.

God has made us as rational, reasoning creatures. We are made in the image of God and, while this has many facets, being rational plays an important part. Rationality is a natural endowment, but it is also a talent that we can improve with due care (to echo a hymn by Bishop Ken and Christ's language in Matthew 25). For his part, Paul urged us to seek the 'renewing' of our minds (Rom. 12.2). He began that particular chapter with an injunction that our worship is to be 'spiritual' (Rom. 12.1). The Authorised Version has '*reasonable* service'. The Greek is *logikēn,* with its root in *logos* or reason. Human beings are rational and, while there is more to being human than developing our rationality, we should seek that as best we can. In the words of Pope Benedict XVI, God is not pleased when we act without reason, since to reject reason is to reject God's own nature.

> God does not become more divine when we push him away from us [into irrationality . . .] rather, the truly divine God is the God who has revealed himself as Logos [reason] and, as Logos, has acted and continues to act lovingly on our behalf. Certainly, love, as Saint Paul says, 'transcends' knowledge and is thereby capable of perceiving more than thought alone (cf. Eph. 3.19); nonetheless it continues to be love of the God who is Logos. Consequently, Christian worship is, again to quote Paul – *logikē latreia,* worship in harmony with the eternal Word and with our reason.[10]

In all of this we should take the Fall seriously. Not all of every philosophical tradition will be true or honourable, just, pure or commendable, to use some of Paul's criteria. The problem is not

---

10 'Faith, Reason and the University: Memories and Reflections', delivered at the University of Regensburg, 12 September 2006.

so much that sin has changed the metaphysical structure of reality. Rather, sin darkens the human intellect. That intellect is dimmed but not extinguished. Fallenness means that nothing is as good as it should be, not that everything is as bad as it could be. An evil will goes with a degraded intellect, but even the most abjectly wicked person retains the power of thought: honed, even, in certain unbalanced ways.

Mention of fallenness alerts us to the moral dimension of human knowing and a balance we should strike. Even those traditions of Christian theology and spirituality that have most celebrated the intellectual quest for truth, and seen it as intrinsic to the spiritual life, have cautioned humility before the things of God and spoken severely against idle curiosity. There are intellectual virtues, and vices, just as there are virtues and vices for other elements of human life. One intellectual vice is presumption to know things beyond human knowledge; another is dishonesty; wisdom, keen judgement and perception are intellectual virtues. A healthy intellectual life also rests on virtues associated with action, such as moderation. We can be intellectually brave and diligent, restrained and fair. Moreover, thought involves acts: practices of reading and note-taking, for instance, or the discipline of getting out of bed and into the library.

An Historical Approach

As we have noted, this book is ordered historically. We start in the mists of philosophical pre-history and conclude with the second decade of the twenty-first century. We could have taken a different route, but the historical approach makes sense.

This is, after all, the order in which things happened. A historical approach does not free an author from choices, but a historical order is one of the least arbitrary ways to order the material. Second, most readers will have a sense of history and that might provide a scaffold for the ideas recounted here. This is an introductory book, and if the reader is new to philosophy then titles such as 'The Early Church' and 'The Late Middle Ages' are more likely to make sense in a table of contents than 'Epistemology' and 'Ontology'.

Third, the historical approach ends where we might want a book to deposit us: here and now. The story of philosophy is a fascinating one but it is not told for its own sake. It is a tale recounted to show where we are today, and why. The aim is to put our present and future theological thinking on a more secure and more theological philosophical footing.

Thomas Aquinas and Confidence

Erudition is said to involve knowing everything about something and something about everything. Neither this book, nor its author, can hope for either, but we can all seek to live by this principle as a goal. In this book we will survey the history and principles of Western philosophy with an eye to their significance for theology. We will do that broadly, as a gesture towards 'something about everything'. We will also look in more detail at a certain theological account of philosophy, as presented by Thomas Aquinas, drawing on Plato and Aristotle. That is our gesture towards 'everything about something'.

This book will be a success if it inspires confidence in the deposit of Christian thought that we have received, and gratitude for it. We today live in an intellectual culture that assumes that our Christian traditions of thought are spent and disappointing, defensive and claustrophobic. I hope that what you encounter here will demonstrate that this evaluation is extraordinarily mistaken. The Christian intellectual tradition is ever-renewing not spent, magnificent not disappointing, unafraid not defensive, and expansive not claustrophobic. Christianity is the guardian and synthesizer of a treasury of thought elaborated down the centuries and millennia. Christian theology, and Christian mission, has everything to gain from celebrating this intellectual heritage. As Benedict XVI commented:

The courage to engage the whole breadth of reason, and not the denial of its grandeur – this is the programme with which a theology grounded in Biblical faith enters into the debates of our time.[11]

Here we do no more than to celebrate, with Paul, everything in thought ('*think* about these things', he wrote) that is true, honourable, just, pure, pleasing, commendable, excellent, and worthy of praise.

Reading On[12]

Two other historical surveys of philosophy for theologians should be mentioned, *Christianity and Western Thought* published in three volumes, the first by Colin Brown and the others by Alan Padgett and Steve Wilkens together (Downers Grove: InterVarsity Press, 1990–2000) and Diogenes Allen's *Philosophy for Understanding Theology*, now in a second edition with additions by Eric Springsted (Louisville: Westminster John Knox Press, 2007). From a topical, rather than historical perspective, a slender volume from Kelly James Clark, Richard Lints and James K. A. Smith deserves a place on the bookshelves of anyone with an interest in the field: *101 Key Terms in Philosophy and their Importance for Theology* (Louisville: Westminster John Knox Press, 2004).

Among works of theological reference, the *Encyclopedia of Christian Theology*, edited by Jean-Yves Lacoste, stands out (Routledge, 2004). The English translation is expensive, but it can be found in reference libraries. For those who can read French, a related volume costs a fraction of the price: the *Dictionnaire Critique De Théologie* (Paris: PUF, 2007). On the other hand, from the philosophical side, the *Stanford Encylopedia of Philosophy* (http://plato.stanford.edu) is free. It is run from the Stanford University in California and articles are commissioned from experts.

---

11 Regensburg Address.

12 Locations are not reproduced in each case for the following publishers: Oxford for Oxford University Press (hereafter OUP) and Wiley-Blackwell, Cambridge for Cambridge University Press (hereafter CUP), London for Penguin (but Harmondsworth for earlier books), SCM Press, Routledge, Continuum, SPCK, T&T Clark and Verso, Indianapolis for Hackett, Washington, DC for Catholic University of America Press (hereafter CUA), San Francisco for Ignatius, Grand Rapids for Eerdmans and New York for Paulist Press.

I

Before Plato

Human thought and culture have flourished in bursts, whether with the burgeoning European universities of the High Middle Ages, the artists of the Renaissance, or physicists hammering out quantum mechanics in the twentieth century. We find such a burst at the dawn of Western philosophy, in a remarkable flowering of thought in the sixth century BC, centred around Miletus in Ancient Greece (modern-day Turkey). These are the 'Presocratic' philosophers: all the Greek philosophers before Socrates.

The earliest figure we know much about is Thales (c.624–c.547 BC), author of the striking proposition that everything proceeds from water. His question here is more significant than his answer. Like those who were to follow him, he was searching for the ultimate principle that lies beneath everything else. Water was a reasonable choice, and is echoed in 1 Peter 3.5, where we read that everything that exists was 'formed out of water'. In the past century and a half, scientists have added their confirmation to this idea, at least in the sense that all *life* emerged from water. Thales probably based his assertion on the observation that water is required for life.

Ultimately, Thales' proposal about water does not get us very far. The philosophical spark, however, was to wonder how things are constituted, and attempt to make sense of a complex world in terms of something more basic. With water, Thales gives a material answer, and in this sense Thales is hardly a philosopher at all. His scheme is almost more science than philosophy, although at this stage science and philosophy can hardly be separated, nor can either be separated from theology. Thales was an astronomer and is credited, perhaps spuriously, as being the first person to have predicted an eclipse successfully. His scientific interests tip into theology – he wrote that 'the world is full of gods' – but this theology also tips into science: these 'gods' may be more like forces of nature than anything a Christian would mean by the word 'God'. It is worth noting that nothing comes down to us from Thales intact. We know about him, and other philosophers of this period, only through quotations by later writers.

The Presocratics are intriguing not only for what they have in common but also for the stark contrasts between their ideas. From one to another, opinions swerve this way and that. Anaximander (610–546 BC), for instance, paralleled Thales in his combination of philosophical, 'scientific' and theological speculation. He taught that the Earth floats freely in space and that the world as we know it arose by something like evolution. In contrast to Thales, he did not look for a single first principle, either in water or anything else. For him the most basic feature of the world is not unity but the tension between opposites, for instance between hot and cold, or wet and dry. He is significant for theology as the first thinker to write about infinitude. He brought the Greek word *apeiron* to prominence, meaning infinite, formless, unbounded or indeterminate. In as much as anything is his ultimate principle, it is this *apeiron*.

Next we have Anaximenes (585–525 BC), who lighted upon *air* as the single substance that stands behind all that we can see, and Xenophanes (570–480 BC), who elaborated both a philosophical theology, in quite a lyrical style, and a rather dispassionate assessment of religions viewed from the outside: what we would today call 'religious studies'. He studied a variety of religious traditions and noticed their local features. This included what we would call 'projections' of local traits onto local deities. As he provocatively put it:

> If cattle and horses or lions had hands, and were able to draw with their hands and do the works that human beings do, horses would draw the forms of the gods like horses, and cattle like cattle, and they would make their bodies such as they each had themselves.[1]

---

1 Trans. G. S. Kirk and J. E. Raven, *The Pre-Socratic Philosophers*, CUP, 1957, p. 168.

This observation did not lead Xenophanes to reject belief in God but rather to press beyond local variations towards a more abstract conception of God. He proposed that God is really 'a simple, unchangeable being, who needs no bodily organs for particular purposes but who perceives and wills acts as a whole and in the same instant'.[2] Here, Xenophanes illustrates an ongoing tension between Greek *religion*, which was polytheistic and worked out in stories, and Greek *philosophy*, which was largely monotheistic and conceptual. His description of God as simple, unchanging, immaterial and eternal may seem a little bloodless, but it is a significant advance. Christian theology was to make use of each of these divine attributes.

The next figure in our procession of the earliest philosophers is the first whose name will be familiar to most readers: Pythagoras (570–495 BC). With him we move away from Greece, to Southern Italy, but not from Greek culture, since the southern portion of Italy was a Greek colony at this time. Nor have we moved away from the town of Miletus entirely, since Pythagoras was born and grew up there.

With Pythagoras we encounter a host of ideas that would recur throughout subsequent centuries. He considered the relation of human existence to a time before birth and after death, and came up with something close to reincarnation: the 'transmigration of souls'. The soul was an important topic for Pythagoras, and in his treatment it is divided sharply from the body. This would be influential on Plato, and through him on Christian theology. Equally illustrative of his desire to think in abstraction from matter is his love of mathematics. While any particular geometrical diagram will be drawn on physical matter (on the ground for instance), it nonetheless represents an entity (the triangle, for instance) which was for Pythagoras prior to any particular, physical triangle. There is an otherworldliness to Pythagoras and his followers. Unlike the earlier philosophers, whose ultimate principles were material – air or water, for instance – for Pythagoras, ideas were ultimate.

---

2 Christopher Stead, *Philosophy in Christian Antiquity*, CUP, 1994, p. 7.

Mathematics provided the core of Pythagoras's brand of mysticism, alongside music, which he treated in rigorously mathematical terms. He discovered that musical features such as harmony have a mathematical form, and took this as confirmation of a fundamentally mathematical structure of reality. It seems to have been Pythagoras who first observed that pitch jumps an octave when a string is halved in length. From our school days we no doubt associate Pythagoras with a rule about right-angled triangles: the square of the length of the hypotenuse is equal to the sum of the squares of the lengths of the other two sides.

Pythagoras did not work alone, nor was he the only one of his band to think about right-angled triangles and come to profound insights: it is recorded that when one of his colleagues discovered that the square root of two (the length of the hypotenuse of a right-angled triangle whose other sides have a length of one) is 'irrational', which is to say that it cannot be expressed as any ratio of whole numbers, Pythagoras had him drowned. This is disturbing but illuminating. Pythagoras sought for a harmony to nature through mathematics. He was shocked to the core to imagine that these lengths (one and one) were in relation to a length that could not be described harmoniously (as he understood harmony).

This revulsion at the square root of two also shows how involved these philosophers were in one another's lives (and deaths, if this story is to be believed). Whereas earlier Milesian philosophers seem to have worked alone, Pythagoras formed a philosophical and religious community. They functioned rather like a group of monks, together seeking transcendent truth. Our understanding of Greek philosophy was much enriched when we came to appreciate the central importance of this religious and communal aspect.[3]

Next in our procession come a pair of philosophers who are all the more interesting when taken as a pair: Heraclitus (535–475 BC) and Parmenides (flourished early fifth century BC). Heraclitus was another Ionian. His thought is somewhat obscure and, indeed, he picked up the nickname 'Heraclitus the obscure' in

---

3 This rests significantly with Pierre Hadot and his book *Philosophy as a Way of Life*, trans. Arnold Davidson, Blackwell, 1995.

subsequent discussions. Like Anaximander, Heraclitus put the emphasis on tension: the fundamental structure of the universe is the tension between opposites. Also like Anaximander, he elevated change over stability.

Heraclitus expressed these points in both static and dynamic terms: at any point there is tension, and over time there is change. His most famous saying is that one cannot step into the same river twice. Everything is in flux and by the time we take another step, the river is a different river.[4] Contrast Pythagoras, for whom timeless harmony was so important. Against Pythagorean metaphorical peace, Heraclitus expounded a philosophy of metaphorical war.[5] True to this destructive mood, the nearest Heraclitus came to proposing a single principle behind all things was to call the cosmos *fire*. As part of that discussion, he wrote that the *logos* is a spark of this fire. As far as we know, he was the first philosopher to use this word: *logos*, word, or reason. It was fated for some heavy lifting in Christian theology.

In contrast to Heraclitus, with his love of change and conflict, stands the other great philosopher of this period, Parmenides. Like Pythagoras, he called Southern Italy his own and was a lover of stillness and underlying unity. Like Xenophanes, he stressed the unchanging nature of the highest and truest being: an idea which was embraced but transformed by Christian theology. In many ways, Parmenides prepares the ground for Plato, not least with his sense that what is most real is unchanging and in his contrast between what is true ('being') and what merely seems to be true ('appearing'). In this, he forged the closest of links between 'being' and 'thought'. That too was to have profound theological consequences. At its best, this relation bears witness to an intelligibility to things that comes from God, in whom being and reason coincide; at its worst, it has undergirded an unfavourable contrast between materiality and thought which has sometimes evacuated the concrete, tangible world of value. If we approach this tradition, stretching

---

4 Plato, *Cratylus* 402A.
5 Colin Brown, *Christianity and Western Thought*, volume I, Downers Grove: InterVarsity Press, 1990, p. 23.

from Parmenides, in the company of 'the Word made flesh', we can rejoice and not disparage.

Among the immediate disciples of Parmenides was Zeno of Elea (490–430 BC). He came up with arguments, in the form of paradoxes, to show that the world involves neither multiplicity nor movement, despite appearances to the contrary. These paradoxes are clever but easily defeated with later mathematics. His method is more significant than his conclusions. We have it from Aristotle that Zeno invented the 'dialectic method'. In the hands of Zeno, this meant reducing one's opponent's arguments to rubble by leading them to absurdities. More positively, it is what friends do when, in discussion, they each build upon the arguments of the other.

Next in our survey come the atomists, another group whose ideas pre-empt modern science (as with evolution and the earth as a body in space) even though they had little *scientific* reason to think as they did. The most famous atomist is Democritus, who held that the world was composed of tiny parts. The qualities we perceive, such as colour or texture, do not belong to these 'atoms' (literally, 'unsplittable' things) themselves but to what comes into existence by the agglomeration of atoms. Colin Brown's interpretation is sensible, that the atomists sought in this way to reconcile the unchanging matter of Parmenides with the experiences of the senses, where things do change.[6] The atoms are unchanging, but their combination allows for development and diversity. According to Democritus, the world emerged out of chaos, and its order was imposed by a cosmic mind (*nous* in Greek).

The atomist Empedocles enumerated the elements, listing the four that have become familiar: water, earth, fire and air. He added love and hate as principles of movement. These four elements were accepted as part of the furniture of the universe by Christian theologians until the end of the Middle Ages (although with deference to Aristotle over a fifth element, the quintessence – literally, 'fifth element' – from which the imperishable heavenly

---

6 Brown, *Christianity*, pp. 26–7.

bodies were formed). When the sixth-century Christian poet Venantius Fortunatus wished to stress the breadth of Christ's redeeming work, he subtly listed all four elements:

> He endured the nails, the spitting,
> Vinegar, and spear, and reed;
> From that holy Body broken
> Blood and water forth proceed:
> Earth, and stars [fire], and sky [air], and ocean [water],
> By that flood from stain are freed.[7]

On the face of it, the earliest Greek philosophers present a riotous variety of positions: the universe is made of fire, or of water, or air; the deepest truth about reality is variety and change, or unity and stillness. In another sense, however, they each set themselves a similar, twofold task. Brown draws attention to the quest to discover stability: 'what it is that underlies everything'.[8] Anthony Meredith sees them as 'fascinated by the problem of change'.[9] Both writers are correct, since these concepts go together. Change makes sense against the background of what does not change, and therefore undergirds change. Unless *before* is in some sense tethered to *after* we do not have change; we have meaningless flux. Change and stability are good topics for investigation even if – as Aristotle also writes – the Presocratics tended to satisfy themselves with materialistic explanations (such as atoms) rather than pressing on to more ultimate, metaphysical categories (to which we will soon turn).[10] They were more like philosopher–scientists than philosopher–theologians.

This question, as to what makes for change and what for stability, has haunted the human mind since these earliest philosophers. We will come across it again and again in these pages, worked

---

7 The hymn *Pange Lingua Gloriosi*, still sung throughout the Western Church at Passiontide.

8 Brown, *Christianity*, p. 20.

9 Anthony Meredith, *Christian Philosophy in the Early Church*, T&T Clark, 2012, p. 21.

10 *Metaphysics* I.3.

out in terms of form and matter in Plato and Aristotle and then in striking, even bizarre, accounts from Spinoza, Kant and various postmodernists, to name but a few.

We have already mentioned the soul. One reason we speak of the soul is to name something that joins the various stages of a person's life together: in face of all the changes that life brings, the person has continuity. The same dynamic (and a similar answer) applies to different individuals of the same kind: the quest for that which is common to all frogs, or to all chairs, despite the differences between individual frogs or chairs. Similarly, sacramental theologians will turn to this vocabulary when they ask of the Eucharist what remains and what changes at the consecration.

Socrates and the Sophists

The Presocratics were often materialists (expect for the otherworldly strand represented by Pythagoras and Parmenides). As Meredith points out, these materialistic explanations began to pale, and to loose ground, when faced with two new forces.[11] On one side we have the pragmatic approach of the Sophists, for whom the earlier questions were of little value in the battle to win influence and money, and, on the other, that of Socrates (470–399 BC) and Plato (427–347 BC), which was more religious and more principled.

We will not go far wrong to think of the Sophists as the self-help writers of their day. They were driven by goals rather than ideals. Rather than pursuing the truth for its own sake, they offered techniques to people wanting 'to win friends and influence people', and earn money in the process. Imagine modern politics; there is nothing new under the sun.

Socrates was their nemesis. He is one of the towering figures of philosophy. We have, after all, summed up all of the preceding figures under the title 'Presocratics'. To his band of followers, he described himself as a midwife of thought, being to ideas what his

---

11 Meredith, *Philosophy*, p. 21.

mother had been to babies. Socrates was Plato's teacher, and Plato was the teacher of Aristotle. That makes Socrates the hand that rocked the cradle of Western thought, the midwife of the intellectual tradition for two and a half thousand years. Søren Kierkegaard, usually inclined to destroy philosophical idols, likened Socrates to Jesus for the purity of his message and his willingness to die for it. Justin Martyr, during the first flowering of a distinctively Christian philosophy in the second century AD, concluded that the only way Socrates could have said and done what he had was that he had an intimation of Jesus 'through the Logos'.[12] For all his importance, we know about Socrates only through the reports of others. This is appropriate for a man whose method was elliptical and whose preference for questions over answers can keep his own opinions out of the script.

Throughout philosophical history, we will see a recurring *sceptical* motif. Often this has been quite destructive. With Socrates, the seemingly sceptical move of preferring questions to answers served the very positive purpose of drawing others on in the search for truth (which is where we get our word *education*, from the verb 'to draw out'). Another significant strand to Socrates' educational method was to stress that growth in wisdom involves greater and greater awareness of our ignorance.[13]

Socrates was an athlete of the mind. In his *Symposium*, Plato has fun with the idea that Socrates had the sort of mesmerizing effect on a college crowd more to be expected of an athlete. Put another way, Socrates was a virtuoso. The two ideas are united in the Greek word *askêsis*, meaning both exercise and practice. From *askêsis* we get the English word 'ascetic' and the name – 'ascetical theology' – of what used to be a significant branch of theology, not least in theological colleges and seminaries. It has fallen out of fashion, no doubt in part because the English term 'ascetic' has become debased in comparison with the Greek *askêsis*. 'Asceticism' has become a miserable and shrivelled denial of the world. *Askêsis* is more positive, a

---

12 *Second Apology* 10.
13 *Apology* 23B.

form of training in all that is excellent and beneficial. We might benefit from a little asceticism; we would certainly benefit from *askêsis*.

In recent years, the American James K. A. Smith has written perceptively on the shape that *askêsis* might take for twenty-first-century Christians. He has paid particular attention to forms of life that refuse to be shaped by consumerism. In this territory, Christians find a pre-Christian ally in Socrates. Diogenes Laertius reports that, on looking into the window of an expensive shop, Socrates was heard to exclaim, 'How many things there are that I can manage without!'[14] Socrates also put an emphasis on recollection and critical self-awareness, which chimes with many Christian traditions. Among his most penetrating comments, reported by Plato, is that 'the unexamined life is not worth living'.[15] This is profoundly true, although in light of Jesus, and in particular his saying that he had come 'that they might have life, and have it abundantly' (John 10.10), we might add that the un-lived life is not worth examining.

Finally, Socrates seems to have made the controversial but ultimately highly significant point that 'no one willingly does wrong'.[16] The grounds for this point will become clearer when we turn to the Neoplatonists and their account of the nature of evil. It involves taking the idea very seriously that evil is always a *mistake*. In that sense, if we understood fully what we were doing, and if we were in our right minds, we would not make the choice – stupid on the face of it – of evil over good.

Reading On

Penguin and OUP have each produced an excellent anthology of Presocratic writings: Jonathan Barnes (ed.), *Early Greek Philosophy* (Penguin, 2002) and Robin Waterfield (ed.), *The First Philosophers* (OUP, 2009). Catherine Osborne's *Very Short Introductions*

---

14 *Lives of the Eminent Philosophers* II.25.
15 *Apology* 38D.
16 Plato, *Protagoras* 345D.

(OUP, 2004) is particularly good, as is *The Hemlock Cup: Socrates, Athens and the Search for the Good Life* by Bettany Hughes (London: Jonathan Cape, 2010) and Pierre Hadot's *Philosophy as a Way of Life: Spiritual Exercises from Socrates to Foucault* (trans. Arnold Davidson, Blackwell, 1995).

2

Plato

'The safest general characterization of the European philosophical tradition', wrote Alfred North Whitehead, 'is that it consists of a series of footnotes to Plato.'[1] Another significant twentieth-century philosopher, Bernard Williams, began his short book on Plato with the words 'Plato invented the subject of philosophy as we know it'.[2] Plato is central to Western philosophy. As far as we can tell, he is also the earliest philosopher whose works have come down to us complete.

Christian theologians in the early Church ran the full gamut of reactions to Plato.[3] Some were extremely respectful, praising Plato for having been on the right track, for instance over creation. When Christians say that everything was 'produced and arranged into a world by God', wrote Justin Martyr in his *First Apology*, they risk being told that they simply parrot Plato.[4] Plato was also admired for his sense of God's transcendence. Both transcendence and creation, or something like it, are found together in his *Timaeus*: 'now to discover the maker and Father of the universe were a task indeed; and having discovered him to declare him unto all men were a thing impossible'.[5]

Plato seemed so theological that some early Fathers charged him with plagiarizing Moses. Numenius held that Plato obtained his

---

1 Alfred North Whithead, *Process and Reality*, New York: Free Press, 1979, p. 39.

2 Bernard Williams, *Plato*, London: Phoenix, 1998, p. 1.

3 See Paul Ciholas, 'Plato: The Attic Moses', *Classical World* 72 (1978–9), pp. 217–25.

4 Justin Martyr, *First Apology* 20.

5 28c, quoted by Anthony Meredith, *Christian Philosophy in the Early Church*, T&T Clark, 2012, p. 24.

idea of God from the Pentateuch: he was simply Moses speaking Athenian Greek.[6] Justin Martyr proposed that Plato only failed to acknowledge his important Jewish source out of fear for his life.[7] When Plato wrote that an 'old tradition' describes God as including the 'beginning, and end, and middle of all things', Justin saw a veiled reference to God being 'I AM WHO I AM' from Exodus 3.14 (or 'being itself', as the Greek translation had it). That 'old tradition', Justin wrote, is 'obviously the law of Moses'.[8] Ambrose of Milan supposed that Plato had met Jeremiah in Egypt at the end of the sixth century BC. Augustine wavered on the question.[9]

Plato's Writings

Plato is important not only for *what* he wrote but also for *how* he wrote, which was almost entirely in the form of a dialogue. Plato typically engineers a scenario to bring a group of characters together for discussion and his text then proceeds more like a play script than an essay.

The dialogue form reflects his sense that truth is real but difficult to attain. We pursue it through argument. This task requires clear thinking, and the best way to think clearly is to think together. Philosophy is best carried out between friends, not least because mutual respect drives us to think as well as we can, and to submit our ideas to each other for criticism: 'after long partnership in common life devoted to this very thing does truth flash upon the soul, like a flame kindled by leaping spark, and once it is born there it nourishes itself thereafter.'[10] For Plato, lively discussion, without antagonism, is the ultimate act of friendship, and even of love. Augustine, ever the Neoplatonist Christian, cast some of his

---

6 Quoted by Eusebius, *Preparation for the Gospel* XIII, 12. Clement of Alexandria uses a similar phrase.

7 *Hortatory Address to the Greeks* 20.

8 *Address* 25.

9 Ambrose, *Epistle* 34. Augustine, *On Christian Doctrine* 2.28; *Retractations* II.4; *City of God* VIII.11.

10 *Seventh Letter*, 341e, in *Phaedrus and Letters VII and VIII*, trans. Walter Hamilton (Penguin, 1973), p. 136.

early works as dialogues and nothing in literature sounds quite as much like what we have just read from Plato as the moment of ecstatic insight that Augustine shared with his mother in the town of Ostia following a long discussion. It is recounted in his *Confessions*.[11] Friendship lies as close to the theological endeavour as it does to the philosophical endeavour. We grow as thinkers at least as much by talking as by reading.

Plato's dialogues themselves often fail to live up to these high ideas. There is rarely much real exchange between the characters. As an example, take the presentation in the *Republic* of 'the analogy of the cave', which has become the most famous image in all of Plato's writings. (We will discuss its message below.) Ostensibly, it is a dialogue between Socrates and the young man Glaucon. In reality, Socrates speaks in paragraphs and Glaucon merely interjects a few words here and there, either of puzzlement or agreement: 'Yes . . . True . . . I agree, as far as I am able to understand you . . . What do you mean? . . . Certainly.' If this is a dialogue, it is a very shallow dialogue. The same could be said of Augustine's dialogue works or those of Aelred of Rievaulx. Plato's *Symposium* is an exception. In that work, a variety of figures make lengthy contributions and the turning point is a speech delivered not by Socrates but by Diotima, a seer or priestess.

Perhaps we are asking too much of the dialogue form. After all, the average meeting between Socrates – among the greatest thinkers in history – and a group of keen but somewhat green youngsters would have been an unequal affair. Even a vestigial dialogue form reminds us that thought is communal and founded on friendship. For a full and forceful defence of dialogue we should turn, paradoxically, to one of the few works of Plato not written in that form, a piece called the *Seventh Letter*.[12] There, Plato is ambivalent about writing – ambivalent at best – because we cannot trap the truth in written sentences, and it is foolish to try. The most important truths

---

11 *Confessions* IX.10.

12 Most of the other numbered letters bearing his name are thought not to have been written by Plato.

are more to be glimpsed than spelt out. We pursue them on the wing but cannot expect to catch them and truss them up.

The dialogue form also serves to bring an ambiguity to the surface: Plato is not speaking in his own name. In the early dialogues, he was probably reporting what he remembered Socrates to have said. By his middle period, he was likely putting a great deal into the mouth of an increasingly fictional character called 'Socrates'. This, however, is never clear and, with the author occluded, we are encouraged to ponder for ourselves. More than saying 'think this . . .', Plato is saying 'think!'

This stands in marked contrast with the approach of the Sophists, whom we encountered above. They were little in the business (and that is the right word) of provoking anyone to think; they offered superficial techniques for winning arguments. In contrast, neither Socrates nor Plato thought anything worthwhile revolves around technique (the Greek is *technē*). What matters is virtue or excellence of character (*aretē*). The dialogue form and, even more than that, the principle of *dialogue*, to which it might no more than gesture, makes all the right points against the Sophists. It points to a journey not a product; it invites us to open ourselves to the truth and expect it to surprise us, since it is out of our control; it conceives of the philosophical endeavour not as an exchange of money for skills but as an exchange of time, life and love within relationships of friendship. 'Imitate me', urged Socrates to his friends as he was dying: copy me; don't copy a text.[13] Jesus was to say the same ('follow me' and 'I have set you an example' – Matt. 4.19; John 13.15), as was Paul ('Be imitators of me, as I am of Christ' – I Cor. 11.1).

Vitality of the Dialogue

Dialogue forms return throughout philosophical history. David Hume's *Dialogues Concerning Natural Religion* is a lively example. Hume no doubt wrote this way because he wanted to criticize

---

13 Plato (most likely), *Alcibiades* 108B.

the theology of his time with some degree of safety. He would have invited greater censure to have written unambiguously in his own name.

Philosophy also proceeds by dialogue in other ways. There is the *internal* dialogue, for instance, of which the supreme example is Augustine's *Confessions*. Here, Augustine is in dialogue with himself through constant questioning. Even more, since the questions are posed to God, he is in a dialogue with the Almighty. Rather than ventriloquize 'replies' from God, the 'replies' come from the Scriptures and from examples drawn from the providential ordering to Augustine's life.

A dialogue can also take the form of an exchange of letters. Notable epistle-writers include Augustine (with Paulinus of Nola and Jerome), Descartes (with Isaac Beeckman and Princess Elizabeth of Bohemia) and the Cambridge Platonists (with Anne, Countess of Conway). Sometimes whole books were written in reply to one another. Anselm's *Proslogion* so provoked and infuriated Gaunilo of Marmouters that he penned his *Pro Insipiente* (*On Behalf of the Fool*) in reply. Anselm answered with his *Reply to Gaunilo*. Sometimes the dialogue was between entire schools of thought, over an even longer timescale. In the eleventh century, the Arabic philosopher Al-Ghazali (known in the West as Algazel) wrote *The Incoherence of the Philosophers*. Here he took on Ibn Sina (known as Avicenna) and his school, criticizing its Neoplatonist philosophy from a theological perspective that is rather too hostile to reason for comfort. *The Incoherence of the Philosophers* provoked a response from Ibn Rushd (known as Ayerroës) entitled *The Incoherence of the Incoherence* (written itself, as it happens, as a dialogue), in which he defended the philosophers attacked by Al-Ghazali and criticized his arguments. A further, though less significant turn of the wheel comes with Mustafa Ibn al-Bursawi, who turned on Ibn Rushd. He missed an opportunity by not calling his contribution *The Incoherence of the Incoherence of the Incoherence*.

Ultimately, the whole history of thought is one of dialogue with what has come before. For Hegel, as we will see, this theme of tension and development became the basis for his account of the entire nature of being. The principle of dialogue reached its high-water mark in the scholastic method of the Middle Ages, which we will discuss in Chapter 7. For an excellent recent example of dialogue, consider Rupert Shortt's interviews with leading theologians entitled *God's Advocates: Christian Thinkers in Conversation*.[14]

The Forms

Having looked at *how* Plato writes, we can turn to *what* he writes. Of all Plato's ideas, the most influential concerns entities that are themselves sometimes called the 'Ideas', but more often the 'Forms', which is what we will call them here (with a capital letter). He proposed that behind whatever we encounter in the world lies a deeper reality: this world rests on one that is even more real. Depending on your position, Plato was either putting into words, better than ever before, an intuition common to many before and since (we have seen it in Parmenides, for instance) or he was sending Western philosophy down a cul-de-sac from which it has made only fitful attempts to escape.

Christians might take it for granted that something (or Someone) lies beyond this world, not least as its origin. This chimes with Plato, although that role was taken not by God but by these 'Forms'. They stand behind created things, in all their fragility and mutability, as the source of their existence and order. The Forms are also the ultimate standard of truth and the proper objects of human desire. Underlying all goodness in the world, Plato would say, is the *Good*; animating all beautiful things is the true and eternal *Beauty*; every example of justice is an expression of *Justice*; when a carpenter makes a bed he consults the perfect plan of the true *Bed*.

The Forms are the bedrock of Plato's philosophy and he advances several arguments as to why we should look at the world this way: as rooted in perfect, eternal and immaterial forms. First, although we never see two identical trees, we know what we mean

---

14 London: Darton, Longman & Todd, 2005.

by a tree in general, which is our intimation of the Form of the tree. With this observation, Plato touched on one of *the* perennial topics in philosophy: the relation of universals and particulars. Philosophers keep coming back to the question of how several particular things of the same kind relate to one another, and to their overarching kind. We might be talking about five cups and the idea of the cup, or six flowers and the idea of the flower. Many suggestions have been put forward over the centuries, but they fall into two basic groups: realists think that the cups share something in common, and that this is something *real*; in contrast, for nominalists, the cups share nothing in common beyond the fact that we give them the same name (which is where the term 'nominalist' comes from: *nomen,* the Latin for name).

Place five cups on a table, ask the nominalist 'how many things are on the table', and her instinct will be to stress the number five. She might then add that we recognize certain similarities and can therefore group those five objects under one heading. In that loose sense, there is one kind of thing on the table. All the same, belonging to a 'kind' happens in our mind and language; it does not inhere in the cups themselves. Ask the same question of the realist, and she will be far happier than the nominalist with the answer 'one', although she will answer 'five' in another sense: 'there is one kind of thing on the table, a cup, and there are five of them'.

For the nominalist, belonging to a kind called cup comes after the existence of cups and it does not go much further than being called a cup. For the realist, belonging to the kind called cup is everything for the cup. At the heart of every cup is certain foundational cup-ishness or cup-hood or cup-dom. This cup-ishness makes it a cup. These might seem like petty squabbles, but there is scarcely a topic where one's assumptions make more of a difference. More of that below.

Plato stands at one extreme. He thought that cup-ishness makes the cup a cup, and indeed that cup-ishness exists eternally and separately from any physical cup. This 'Form of the cup' is even more a cup than any cup made of clay. We can call this position 'strong transcendent realism'.

Another argument for the Forms would be to notice that the world is always in flux, and yet certain features remain, forming the background for change to occur. Something, Plato thought, must lend stability to the world amid time, change and decay. That something is the realm of the Forms. The relation of change and stability was as important for Plato as for the Presocratics. Aristotle reports that Plato got his interest in what holds fast among the changes of sensible things from having come across the thought of Heraclitus, and another Presocratic called Cratylus, as a young man.[15]

Plato also got to the Forms by thinking about the business of thinking and knowing. His guiding principle was that 'like knows like'. Our minds are immaterial and what our minds know is therefore similarly immaterial. I can know material things, but what I know about them I know immaterially. I can know a tree, but what is in my mind is not the tree itself but a thought of the tree. Plato took this as an argument that the truest objects of knowledge are immaterial, namely the Forms, and that it is these that lend intelligibility to material things. I can know a tree because it partakes of the Form *Tree*. This may not seem particularly convincing at the moment. It will come into its own once it is related to the Judaeo-Christian God: Plato's intuitions about the Forms are like seeds waiting to sprout in biblical soil.

Plato approached this question of knowledge from another angle. The process by which we come to understand something, he claimed, resembles a sort of 'drawing out', as if of something that we already know. (We have seen that this provides the root of our word 'education', from *ē-*, 'out of' and *dūcō*, 'I lead' – as in 'duke', meaning 'leader'.) From this, Plato surmised that to understand is to be *reminded* of what we once knew, before our birth, when our immaterial soul dwelt with the Forms and we beheld them face-to-face. Human knowledge in this world involves remembering what we once saw. In the *Meno*, Plato developed this idea with a thought experiment concerning how an uneducated slave would come to understand geometry. He would not be making mathematics up; he would be discovering certain facts about

---

15 *Metaphysics* 987a32-b1.

mathematics that are already eternally true. In a similar way, for Plato every encounter with the truth is an encounter with eternal truths, namely the Forms.

Whether or not this is a good justification for the Forms, it is significant in its own right as the first discussion in the Western tradition, at least according to Bernard Williams, of a certain sort of knowledge.[16] Access to the truth is sometimes divided into two categories: *a posteriori* and *a priori* (with the example from Plato belonging to the latter). We can know something through experience, by some particular encounter with the world. This is a posteriori knowledge, just as an argument that starts with facts or observations about the world is an a posteriori argument. A priori knowledge works differently because (it is claimed) it is not based on experience. Usually this means that what we come to know or argue is already lodged in the meaning of the idea from which we start. Statements that are true by definition fall into this category: all swans are birds; all spinsters are unmarried. As soon as we go beyond this, the topic gets both interesting and contentious: not perhaps with 'the whole is greater than the part' (which is relatively uncontroversial, somewhat interesting, and potentially useful) but certainly with 'every effect has a cause' (whether you are a physicist wondering about what causes radioactive decay, or one of the legion of philosophers after David Hume who think that most common-sense notions of causation are wrong).

The distinction between a priori and a posteriori stands as a useful shorthand for categorizing approaches. Arguments for the existence of God, for instance, are often grouped this way: some start with observations about the world (such that it possesses order, or that things move) and others do not (such as the proposition that the very idea of God shows that God exists). Those arguments about the existence of God also show a problem with the a priori / a posteriori distinction. Even reflection on what follows from 'the very idea of God' does not happen in a vacuum. I only have the word 'God', and all the other words I need in order to think about God, because of a prolonged series of experiences and an emersion

---

16 *Plato*, p. 17.

in human culture in all its detail. I can sit in a darkened room and think about existence, or what follows from the meaning of the word 'God', but I would not be able to do that if *all I had ever done* was sit in a darkened room (and not only because I would have died from vitamin D deficiency). Even Plato's imagined slave got to knowledge of mathematics by drawing shapes using material implements. Similarly, a posteriori arguments tend to rely on something like a priori assumptions at every turn. I can only make sense of anything in the world because I have *concepts* about the world. There is a message here: distinctions can be useful but questioning their watertight separation is also important.

Seeing the Forms

Few of the presentations of the Forms we find in philosophy textbooks make them sound believable. That leaves a significant deficit compared to the electrifying effect they have in the writings of Plato. This rather speculative section considers where we should look in order to catch a glimpse of them. The secret is that Plato's Forms point to God as the origin of all created things.

We can begin with Plato's suggestion that there is only one Form that itself approaches visibility, which is the Form of beauty. This cautions us not to be despondent over not seeing the Forms particularly clearly. The most we can hope for are intimations. It also suggests that beauty is a good place to start.[17]

By beauty we mean 'beautifulness'. Notice that is an adjective. With beauty, and other Forms such as good, truthful or whole, we are on different territory from more concrete, worldly and noun-like Forms, such as that of a bed or a tree. We are more likely to have an intimation of the Forms from an adjectival (or even verbal) observation than a noun-like one. One of the classic examples of a Form, in Plato's *Republic*, is the Form of the bed, which carpenters consult in making a physical bed. This is not likely to be convincing or inspiring for any but the most convinced Platonist.

---

17 *Phaedrus* 250.

To explain this, imagine a visit to an art gallery. We would find relatively few paintings of beds. They do not capture our imagination, nor do they represent anything particularly profound about God. We may, however, find paintings of someone sleeping on a bed, and there are likely to be even more pictures of a child sleeping on its mother's breast. (Most of them will be of Christ and Mary.) That is because here we are drawing close to something more primordially significant for human life and – which is not unrelated – to something primordially significant in God. We read in the Prologue to John's Gospel (1.18) of the Son who is 'in the Father's bosom' (the Greek could even be translated as 'nestling into', since it has the sense of 'towards'). This is why repose is more vivid and revealing for us of a Form than a bed. The idea of 'repose' participates more directly in God than does 'bed', although 'bed' might share in God at arm's length, *through* 'repose'.

To take another example, wandering round the National Gallery in London we might stumble on Albrecht Altdorfer's painting *Christ taking leave of his mother*, of 1520. This is an image of departure, which is a vivid idea or category. This moment of movement marks a decisive point in Christ's earthly mission. It is theologically respectable to say that this earthly mission is a working out in time of the eternal coming forth of the Son from the Father in the Trinity. Christ's earthly leave-taking is an image of his being sent from the Father, which itself rests upon the eternal coming forth of the Son from the Father. With leave-taking we are again onto something primordial in human life: ask any parent who has taken a child to school for the first time or faced a house newly quiet after the departure of a son or daughter to university. Again, here we are on to something primordial in God. The 'Forms' of repose or leave-taking are the sort of Forms likely to arrest us. We will leave this discussion for now but pick it up in the section on realism and nominalism in Chapter 9.

The Forms in Some Platonic Dialogues

Having spoken about the Forms in general, we turn to look at how the Forms function in a few of the Platonic dialogues. Most of the arguments we have seen for the Forms come from a relatively early dialogue: the *Phaedo*. The example of carpenters consulting the Form of the bed is from the *Republic*, which contains long passages of discussion of the Forms more widely, and particularly of the prince among the Forms, the form of the Good. Here we also find the allegory of the cave, where Plato compared the things of this world to shadows cast on the wall of a cave. Since they are all we have ever seen, we mistake them for the truest reality. In contrast, the philosopher is like one loosened from the chains that keep him looking at the wall, who is now able to see not only the shadows but also what cast them. As these shapes stand in relation to the shadows, so are the Forms in relation to the things of this world. Changing the metaphor, the philosopher then ascends from the cave to see the sun for the first time. The sun functions as an image of the principal Form, the Form of the Good, which somehow gives being to all the other Forms.

Elsewhere in the *Republic* (especially with the image of the 'divided line'), Plato discusses the Forms in terms of an ascent from opinion to true knowledge, from appearances to reality. Rather like Pythagoras, for whom Plato had great respect, study of mathematics leads us on here. Mathematics is useful because various different triangles, drawn materially, represent the very idea of the triangle, rather like things in this world represent the Forms. With mathematics we are halfway there. Ascent to the Forms through dialogue, however, is even more perfect. In mathematics we have to take our axioms, or assumptions, for granted, whereas in dialogue we are able to question our assumptions and therefore make an even more significant ascent.

The example of geometry is significant because even if we are seeking an immaterial truth of 'the triangle', we get to it through the materiality of chalk and slate, or pencil and paper. Physicality is also under discussion in the two principal dialogues about love and desire, the *Symposium* and the *Phaedrus*. These are important texts for the theologian since they present the pursuit of the Forms as both more spiritual and more physical, even erotic, than in other dialogues. Christianity – at least Christianity at its best – has no trouble associating what is most 'spiritual' with what is most material, nor is it surprised by the suggestion that the spiritual quest can seem like romantic passion (or that romantic passion holds intimations of the quest for God).

According to the argument of the *Phaedrus*, we have all seen the forms. Plato believed in reincarnation and that, between lives, we behold the Forms. Now, however, we are 'trapped' in the body and forget them. The sight of material things, however, can remind us of the Forms, especially the sight of beauty, which appears more than any other Form as itself rather than as a copy.

For all Plato's language of being 'trapped in the body' (and in the *Phaedo* the body is a 'prison' – a mistaken position according to Christian theology), the *Phaedrus* represents a better angle on materiality, according to which the beauty of things in the world play a part in our journey back to the Forms. Plato writes that we ascend almost 'in pairs', the beauty of the beloved giving us wings. This dialogue is one of the world-affirming dialogues, imagining a place for love, sociality, and the beauty of the world as a revelation of the Forms. It is the sort of dialogue from which one can argue for a reading of Plato that sees this world as the arena for the Forms' appearing, not their obscuring veil. It also helpfully stresses the interweaving of knowing with transformation of who and what we are.

The Forms in the Christian Tradition

The reader might wonder why we have given the Forms such attention. After all, Christian theology is unlikely to warm to separate and eternal exemplars of justice, heat or trees. The Forms are not promising in themselves but they capture an intuition which was to flower in a religious setting: first within Plato's thought itself, in an inchoate fashion, then in Neoplatonism, and most of all in Abrahamic monotheism. The topic is significant in its own right but it also offers an example of the theological assimilation, and elevation, of philosophical ideas.

From a Christian point of view, it will not do to imagine that there is any source of reality that stands eternally over and against

God. The Forms do that in the creation myth of the *Timaeus*, which is why the creating god of that dialogue – the demiurge – is only a weak shadow of the true God. Elsewhere, Plato's scheme comes closer to speaking about God, when he describes a source from which all the other Forms seem to proceed: not 'god' for Plato, but the 'Form of the Good'.

This goes some way towards a theological vision, but in as much as the Forms are still external to the Good, they are still intermediaries between the ultimate source and the world. Augustine of Hippo deserves particular credit for finding a way to relate the Forms to God in such a way that they are not external to God. His formulation is brilliant: what Plato called the eternal Forms are in fact *ideas in the mind of God*. With this simple move, Augustine secured a place within Christian thought for all he had found wise and perceptive in the Platonic tradition: a tradition he had studied in great detail, and which was instrumental in leading him towards Christianity.

Augustine's thought is shot through with a mystical sense of God's presence and transcendence woven together. In his *Literal Commentary on Genesis*, he puts it like this: God 'is both interior to everything because all things are in Him, and exterior to everything because He is above all things'.[18] Augustine was able to express *how* or *why* this is true by adopting the Forms, recast as ideas in the mind of God. The innermost being of everything comes from God and is related to God, being God's handiwork and an imitation of a divine idea. At the same time, God is not domesticated, since any created thing is more than a distant imitation, and is but one idea among limitlessly many ideas.

Augustine provides a particularly brilliant and succinct discussion of this in his *On Diverse Questions*.[19] Every 'religious person imbued with true religion', he wrote, would surely accept that 'everything that exists [. . .] was produced by God as its maker' and that 'all things were created in accordance with reason'. Where

---

18 VIII.26.48, trans. Erich Przywara, *An Augustine Synthesis*, London: Sheed & Ward, 1945, p. 106.

19 *Responses to Eighty-Three Questions* 46.2, in *Responses to Miscellaneous Questions*, trans. Boniface Ramsey, Hyde Park: New City Press, 2008.

then 'should these reasons be thought to exist if not in the very mind of the creator?' It would be 'sacrilegious' to say that God was guided by anything outside him when he fashioned the world. So, 'the reasons for all the things that will be created and have been created are contained in the divine mind' as 'eternal and unchangeable'. This is why Plato 'refers to these principal reasons of things as ideas'. Whatever exists in the world then exists by *participation* in these ideas. We will return to the idea of participation below.

Transcendence

Plato met a formidable critic of his doctrine of the Forms in his student Aristotle. We will turn to him below. Plato could also be a penetrating critic himself, and never more so than in the dialogue *Parmenides*. The past few centuries have seen particular criticism of Plato. The issue at stake could not be more significant for theology. The charge is that understanding the universe in relation to a transcendent reference, origin and goal sucks the value out of the world. At the head of these critics stands Friedrich Nietzsche.

The objection can be phrased in several different ways: eschatologically speaking, does the hope of a future recompense encourage injustice now? Does expecting a cataclysmic end of the world followed by a cosmic renewal make us indifferent to the degradation of the environment here and now? For the doctrine of creation, the question is also about the relation of the world to God now, as much as it is about its origins in the past. The poet Yeats wrote that 'Plato thought nature but a spume that plays | Upon a ghostly paradigm of things'.[20] Does Plato reduce the material world to a 'spume': a mist that imitates something itself no more substantial than a ghost?

According to Nietzsche, 'Plato's invention of Pure Spirit and the Good in Itself' must 'certainly be confessed [. . . as] the worst, the most tiresome, and the most dangerous of errors'.[21] Even to imagine the Forms is bad enough, but then to take them as the origin

---

20 'Among School Children'.
21 *Beyond Good and Evil*, trans. Judith Norman. CUP, 2002, Preface.

of everything is to give primacy to the 'most general, the emptiest [of] concepts, the last fumes of evaporating reality'. The 'last, thinnest, [and] emptiest is placed as the first' and most real. Nietzsche despaired that 'mankind should have taken seriously the brain-sick fancies of morbid cobweb-spinners!'[22] Any talk of 'another world' is a slanderous and disparaging accusation against this life, whereby we '*revenge* ourselves on life by means of the phantasmagoria of "another", a "better" life'.[23] Plato was a 'coward in face of reality' who 'flees' to the ideal.[24]

For Nietzsche, Christianity perpetuates Plato's error down the centuries: Plato was 'morally infected, so much an antecedent Christian'.[25] In our own time, Martha Nussbaum has taken up the criticism, claiming that 'directing our aspirations towards a "true world" has led to a denigration of our actions and relationships in this one'.[26]

Alongside Nietzsche and Nussbaum belong various post-Christian theological voices of a previous generation, such as Don Cupitt and his 'Sea of Faith' movement. For them, too, Plato, along with transcendence and metaphysics more generally, represents all that is wrong with Christianity. Others, however, have defended Plato, transcendence and metaphysics. Charles Taylor, for instance, has argued that an understanding of the universe in terms of relation to a transcendent source and goal 'can turn us towards this life with a new attention and concern, as has undoubtedly been the case with the Judaeo-Christian tradition, with decisive consequences for our whole moral outlook'.[27]

22 *Twilight of the Idols*, trans. R. J. Hollingdale, Penguin, 1990, 'Reason in Philosophy', p. 4.
23 *Twilight*, 'Reason', p. 6.
24 *Twilight*, 'What I Owe to the Ancients', p. 2. Other examples are 'How the True World Finally Became a Fable' in *Twilight* and 'On the Other-Worldy' and 'On the Virtue that makes Small' in *Thus Spake Zarathustra*.
25 *Twilight*, 'Ancients', p. 2.
26 'Transcending Humanity', in *Love's Knowledge*, OUP, 1992, p. 370.
27 Review of Martha Nussbaum, *Canadian Journal of Philosophy* 18 (1988), p. 813, quoted by Nussbaum, 'Transcending Humanity', in *Love's Knowledge*, p. 370. See Henri de Lubac, *Paradoxes of Faith*, Ignatius, 1987, pp. 93, 114.

Among the principal current Christian defenders of a transcendent reference to life and the world are the authors of the
1999 collection of essays, *Radical Orthodoxy*. They argue that
our choice is not between either the world in all its value, understood on its own terms, and the world in relation to a transcendent source, drained of value. The real choice is between a world
understood on its own and thereby rendered meaningless and a
world whose value is undergirded by relation to its transcendent
source. Cut the world free from transcendence, they argue, and
we are far from preserving the world:

> the great Christian critics of the Enlightenment [. . .] in differ-
> ent ways saw that what secularity had most ruined and actually
> denied were the very things it apparently celebrated: embod-
> ied life, self-expression, sexuality, aesthetic experience, human
> political community. Their contention, taken up in this volume,
> was that only transcendence, which 'suspends' these things in
> the sense of interrupting them, 'suspends' them also in the other
> sense of upholding their relative worth over-against the void.[28]

These writers recognize that there are world-denying forms of
Christianity, but see them as inauthentic. A 'bad Platonism' in
Christianity deserves the criticism it has received, but such criticism leaves a proper Christian Platonism untouched, according to
which a transcendent reference to the world teaches us that the
world is the arena in which all that is most valuable can appear.
The *Radical Orthodoxy* authors call us to explore a Christianity
that, in being more Platonic than ever, is also 'more incarnate,
more participatory, more aesthetic, more erotic, more socialized'
than ever.

They suggest that one must either see the world in participatory
terms, with everything proceeding from God, or see the world as a
brute fact, a decision which they think can lead only to nihilism:

28 John Milbank, Catherine Pickstock and Graham Ward, *Radical Orthodoxy*,
Routledge, 1999, p. 3.

it might seem that to treat of diverse worldly phenomena such as language, knowledge, the body, aesthetic experience, political community, friendship, etc., apart from God is to safeguard their worldliness, in fact, to the contrary, it is to make even this worldliness dissolve.

In contrast, a 'theological perspective of participation actually saves the appearances by exceeding them':

> It recognizes that materialism and spiritualism are false alternatives, since if there is only finite matter there is not even that [. . .] by appealing to an eternal source for bodies, their art, language, sexual, and political union, one is not ethereally taking leave of their density. On the contrary, one is insisting that behind this density resides an even greater density.

Which Plato? Whose Platonism?

Deciding 'what Plato said' is not quite as clear as we might expect, and this is not uniquely true of Plato. In part that is because of the dialogue form, but it is also because of the act of interpretation necessary for understanding any text. Plato's thought also clearly evolved over the course of his life, so if we are to apply some of it, or take some of it as inspiration for our own thinking, we have to make a decision about which part to concentrate on. Bernard Williams, for instance, saw the story of the Cave as pessimistic: 'The world of desire, politics, and material bodies is essentially seen from above, from outside the cave, and we are left with a sense of it as denatured and unreal or as powerfully corrupting.'[29] However, he sees a much more positive relation between the world and the Forms spelt out elsewhere, and above all in the *Symposium*. There, 'the material world is seen with the light behind it, as it were, giving an image not of failure and dereliction but of promise'.[30]

---

29 Williams, *Plato*, pp. 39–40.
30 *Plato*, p. 42.

The even larger question is to ask what any of us thinks we are doing in aligning ourselves with a particular thinker, or in defending him or her. We have already seen the contrast between one group of thinkers, who read Plato and find him evacuating this world of value, and another who call for a '"more Platonic" Christianity' in order to give the world its due. To use a term from cultural theory, even if we are all reading the same texts of Plato, we can still come up with different 'readings'. One person might find one comment pivotal; another treats it as marginal and concentrates on another. One person thinks that arriving at a 'Platonic' position means saying no more than the most obvious thing that a text seems to say; another thinks that the truest Platonism will be to bounce off the text, perhaps working with that which is no more than implied, but now seems all-important. For my part, I am more interested in 'what can be thought with the help of Plato' than I am with sticking to 'what Plato thought'.

The same dynamic, and the same sets of options, applies to any other author or text, not excluding the Bible. Consider how some Christians build an entire eschatology, almost an entire theology, out of the idea of the 'rapture', while others find the idea obscure and of no great significance. Once the 'plain meaning' of certain texts was seen to support slavery; today the obvious logic of the whole opposes it.

Reading On

The complete works of Plato are available online in the Victorian translation by Benjamin Jowett, but it is better to work with a more recent translation. The principal dialogues have been published by Penguin and Oxford World's Classics, and the complete works are available in a single large volume from Hackett (1997), edited by John Cooper. Good dialogues with which to begin include the *Phaedo*, *Phaedrus* and *Symposium*. Morris Stockhammer's *Plato Dictionary* is another excellent way in (New York: Philosophical Library, 1963), presenting snippets arranged by subject.

Among secondary literature, Karl Jaspers wrote perceptively on Plato in *The Great Philosophers* (New York: Harcourt

Brace, 1962) and Catherine Pickstock's volume on the writer
(from OUP, forthcoming at the time of publication) will be terrific. In his novel *The Place of the Lion* (London: Gollancz, 1947),
the 'Inkling' Charles Williams imagined what would happen if the
Forms themselves were to descend into this world, including the
lion of the title. On the relation of the world to transcendence,
see Fergus Kerr, *Immortal Longings: Versions of Transcending
Humanity* (SPCK, 1997).

3

Aristotle

> You must know that a person cannot become perfectly prepared in phi-
> losophy other than by studying the two philosophers, Aristotle and Plato.[1]
>
> Albert the Great, *Commentary on Aristotle's Metaphysics*[1]

Alongside Plato, Aristotle is the other great source of philosophical ideas in the West. He stands at the end of a span of a mere
three generations (since we should include Socrates) that rank as a
moment of unsurpassed brilliance in the history of philosophy.

Aristotle's life falls in the middle of the fourth century BC
(384–322). He was taught by Plato. After Plato's death, he returned
to Northern Greece. There he is said to have taught Alexander
the Great. Aristotle later returned to Athens and set up a rival
academy to Plato's *Academy*, which he called the *Lyceum*. He is
sometimes described as 'the Stagarite' (after his place of birth) or,
in mediaeval writing, as simply 'the Philosopher'.

We have seen that Plato's work was marked by a flood of speculative energy and mystical fervour. Aristotle received this from
his teacher and channelled that flood into precisely demarcated
streams. If Plato was the founder of philosophy *in general*, then
it fell to Aristotle to start various disciplines *in particular*. His
interests were encyclopaedic. Aristotle was the greatest of polymaths. His work on logic laid the foundations for subsequent
thought about what it means to reason, serving as a textbook for
2,000 years. His *Metaphysics* carved out the subject. No work
on ethics is more important than his *Nicomachean Ethics*. Literary criticism as we know it starts with his *Poetics*. He is also the
first writer whose scientific discussions (of an enormous range)

---

1 Tractate 5, Chapter 15. Quoted by Aimé Forest, *La structure métaphysique du
concret selon Saint Thomas d'Aquin*, Paris: Vrin, 1956, p. 328. Translated by Héctor
Delbosco, amended.

demand to be taken seriously on a scientific basis, especially his treatises on animals and their composition, movement, birth and development. Many of the most significant philosophical concepts in current use were shaped by Aristotle, making him one of the most profound non-Christian influences on Christian thought.[2]

Aristotle's influence on theology and standing among theologians has not been uniform. The Church Fathers lived in the dying light of his first influence. They were less enthusiastic about Aristotle than Plato, who was the more obviously religious figure. In the West, only two works survived, both on logic (the *Categories* and *On Interpretation*), having been translated into Latin as the Roman Empire crumbled. Towards the beginning of the second millennium, Aristotle's writings returned, hitting the Western Church like a great wave. Umberto Eco recounts this, with a sinister overtone, in his novel *The Name of the Rose*. We will return to this below, in its historical sequence. The effect of the rediscovery of Aristotle on the Western Church is the best possible reminder that theological turmoil is not the sole preserve of our own time (or the nineteenth century, or the sixteenth, or any other). Of the Eastern Church we can say, as a broad-brush summary, that although Aristotle's texts were more widely available than in the West, his tendency towards metaphysical precision did not suit Orthodox theologians in the same way that it suited the more speculative theology of the West.[3]

---

2 Speaking personally, his name is important for me in the development of my attitude towards philosophy. I heard Nicky Gumbel quote Aristotle in a sermon at Holy Trinity Brompton back in the middle of the 1990s. A couple of days later, I was walking through Radcliffe Square in Oxford, thinking about this and, in the space of less than a minute, my approach to the world changed drastically. I entered the square antagonistic to 'secular thought'. Gumbel, however – a fellow evangelical – was willing to cite Aristotle when Aristotle had a good point. That broke something open for me. I left the Square wishing to 'test everything [and] hold fast to what is good' (1 Thess. 5.21).

3 For a comparison of the place of Aristotle, see David Bradshaw, *Aristotle East and West: Metaphysics and the Division of Christendom*, CUP, 2007.

Natural History and the *Physics*

Aristotle's father was a physician and, true to that influence, Aristotle was far more concerned to observe the natural world than Plato. Raphael got to the heart of the distinction with a fresco in the Vatican apartments, *The School of Athens*. He depicted Plato, mystical and interior, pointing upwards (towards the Forms); Aristotle, in contrast, practical and empirical, has his hand raised flat, level like the surface of the earth, which he scoured with such detailed observation. For a swathe of Christian history, when theologians worked with science they worked with the science of Aristotle. It is worth bearing this in mind when, for instance, Christian writers assume that women are inferior to men. This is Aristotle's influence.

That rather ruinous slip aside, in Aristotle's writings we encounter a never-dimmed sense that if we look carefully at the world it will reveal its truths. One of the great consequences of Aristotle's rediscovery by Christianity in the High Middle Ages was a reawakening to nature. The religion of the Incarnation had every theological reason to be fascinated by the world. In Aristotle, it found a philosophical inspiration to live up to this impulse.

The science laid out in Aristotle's *Physics* is particularly significant. For the most part it is a treatment of motion and change. Once again, change and stability lie at the heart of the philosophical endeavour. For Aristotle, motion – and change in general – was to be seen as *teleological*, which is to say, *for a purpose*. Whenever something moves or acts (and these are closely related), it is always in order to achieve a particular goal or end. Conversely, when something is at rest (neither moving nor acting) that is because it has achieved a goal; it will remain at rest until some other goal comes in view, when it will again move or act. This approach reigned until the late Middle Ages. Newton's mechanics was its final undoing. For Newton, nothing moves itself; it is always moved. Moreover, for Newton, movement itself is a sort of stasis: something will carry on moving in a straight line, at that speed, until it is acted upon again. (Aristotle assumed that if something carries on moving, it somehow continues to be pushed.)[4]

Aristotle's attachment to teleology is part of the larger picture of his view of causation. Aristotle proposed *four causes*.[5] They are an important part of the intellectual background to theology, especially in the Middle Ages. They are also one of Aristotle's most significant gifts to posterity. The 'four causes' are called material, formal, efficient and final. Ever since Aristotle, philosophers have explored them using the example of a statue.[6] The four causes are the four answers we can give to the question 'why is there a statue?' The statue is made out of bronze, which is the *material* cause of the statue. The material cause is 'that out of which' something has come to be. Asking in the twenty-first century 'why is there a statue?', few would give the bronze as one of the answers, but Aristotle is making an important point. We would have no statue without the material from which it is made. There is a practical earthiness to Aristotle here, which shows why he was taken up by Christian theologians concerned with the doctrine of creation. The statue is nothing without its material cause, and the world would be nothing had not God called its matter out of nothing. With the material cause, Aristotle gives materiality its due, and that struck a chord with Christians.

Moving on, we notice that the statue has a particular shape or form. This is the *formal cause* of the statue. Plato had asked 'how does this bed come to be a bed?' He answered that the carpenter consulted the universal 'Form of the bed'. The bed-ishness of the True Bed shines out in the material example before us. Aristotle did not believe in separate, self-subsisting forms – of beds or of anything else – but he believed in forms nonetheless. To anything

---

4 For a detailed consideration of the significance of motion for theology, from the perspective of both Aristotle and Newton, see Simon Oliver, *Philosophy, God and Motion*, Routledge, 2005.

5 *Physics* II.3; *Metaphysics* V.2.

6 Favoured examples turn up quite often. For instance, an unexpected example is usually a black swan; the small thing that makes a big difference is the flap of a butterfly's wing; a random example of a human being is often Socrates. These examples come to summarize a philosophical point in a single image. They also allow philosophers to demonstrate that they know the tradition.

there is a certain characterfulness: the bed-ishness of the bed, the humanity of the human being, the roseate character of the rose. Each of these words names a form. The form is 'that-which-it-is': bed, human, rose.

When we cause, we bring a form into something, into some matter or situation. 'Matter' and 'form' should be interpreted broadly: matter is what receives, in any way; form is what enters. A thing's form shapes it through and through. It is the thing's innermost reality. With the statue, 'form' does not go much further than its shape, but in a living thing it also refers to the complex interrelation of processes within the creature: in other words, to its life.

A material thing is somehow both material and also more than material. There is more to a jug than the matter of the jug: there is also what the matter adds up to, what emerges out of the matter. We might talk about a formal aspect and a material aspect to each material thing: a 'what' and an 'out of what'. To say that a jug has the form of a jug, which makes its matter have the nature of a jug, might seem rather circular. However, Aristotle has something indispensable in view, particularly in relation to living things. A swan is not just so much matter arranged in this particular way, not least because the particular matter comes and goes over the course of the swan's life, while the swan – through its form – remains. Just as significant is when the form changes but the matter remains. If I drop a jug, the matter remains but the form changes. The matter changes from having the form of a jug to having the form of shards of pottery. The matter remains, but that is of no consolation to the owner of a fine Art Deco jug. Aristotle's *form* names what we instinctively see as most significant about the jug-shattering incident.

In contrast, modern biology often has a reductionist obsession with parts over wholes, and the smaller the part the better, until biology becomes the science of the gene: the science of life, as Mary Midgley points out, is reduced to studying something too small to live.[7] The form of the thing is precisely what we miss: we cannot see the swan for its genes. We ignore the level at which the parts

---

7 Mary Midgley, *The Solitary Self: Darwin and the Selfish Gene*, Durham: Acumen, 2010, pp. 19–21.

add up to something. In contrast, Aristotle thought that the swan possessed an all-important swan-ishness, which orders or informs (literally in-*forms*) the matter it possesses at any particular time.

Formal and material causes are best understood together, and taken together they define an approach called hylomorphism. This is the proposal that to each physical thing there are two dimensions: form and matter, or in Greek, *hūlē* and *morphē*. These two dimensions are not separable; they are two aspects of a unity rather than two detachable things. Form and matter can be pithily summarized as being two 'coconstituting substantial principles'.[8]

One reason Aristotle wanted to make a distinction between form and matter was to explain how we know material things. In each case, there is *what* we know when we know a physical object, namely the form (the apple-ishness of an apple, for instance), and there is what is left behind when we know, which is the matter, since we only ever know an apple mentally. The apple is in my mind immaterially but, fortunately, not in my brain materially.

Whenever something changes, something has acted to bring about the new form. For this reason, we should not only think of the formal cause of the statue as being in the statue. The form was first of all in the mind of the sculptor. She imposed that form on the bronze, impressing something that was in her mind into the bronze. This process of making stands as something like the opposite of the process of knowing, where the form enters the mind detached from its materiality.[9]

A form is constantly poised to express itself as a formal cause. The form of the statue would be the formal cause of its imprint in a photograph, just as the idea of the statue in the mind of the sculptor expressed itself as a formal cause, shaping the bronze. The most significant formal cause for us as human beings is the human form, which we call the soul. In acting, we express ourselves; everything that we do in or to the world has, in a sense, to be in us first. This might remind us of the saying of Christ:

---

8 W. A. Wallace, *New Catholic Encyclopedia*, vol. 7, Gale, 2000, p. 237.

9 On the other hand, the sculptor might rightly say that making is a certain practical way of knowing.

Beware of false prophets, who come to you in sheep's clothing but inwardly are ravenous wolves. You will know them by their fruits. Are grapes gathered from thorns, or figs from thistles? In the same way, every good tree bears good fruit, but the bad tree bears bad fruit. A good tree cannot bear bad fruit, nor can a bad tree bear good fruit. (Matt. 7.15–18)

We can move on to the other two causes. The *efficient cause* is whoever or whatever is responsible for the change that brought the statue into existence, such that *this* form is *now* in *this* matter. In our example, the efficient cause is the sculptor. The efficient cause is familiar to this day. Indeed, it is the only one of Aristotle's four causes left in common use. When we ask 'why is this like that?', we usually name the agent in reply, which is to say the efficient cause: *Jamie* smashed the jug; *Suzanne* cast the sculpture. It is possible for someone to be a cause in more than one way. The sculptor is the formal and efficient cause of the statue; parents have both of these relations to their children.

Jamie smashed the jug; *Suzanne* cast the sculpture. If asked for the cause, that is about as far as we could typically go today. Aristotle would find this answer impoverished, most of all because it omits the last of his four causes: the *final cause*. Jamie smashed the jug: why? Suzanne cast the sculpture: why? The final cause is the purpose for which the action is performed or the object is made. This places *teleology*, or acting for a purpose, at the heart of Aristotle's system. Jamie smashed the jug, because it reminded him of a lost love; Suzanne cast the sculpture, because it represents Christ, and she is going to give it to her local church, because last year she returned to the faith and is grateful. Without the final cause, our understanding is incomplete. 'How come you've lost weight?', you ask someone. 'Because I've been eating less' is not even half an answer. 'Because I was overweight, and I want to be healthier' is much better. Health was the final cause, the end for the sake of which I acted. Aristotle's sense of teleology chimes with much Christian thought. It takes people seriously as moral agents, who exercise choice with a sense of purpose. Ultimately, we would want to line up final causation with God, who is the fullest final cause, so that our goals are oriented to God as our best goal, just as we want see the potential for anything to be an efficient cause as coming from God as the first beginning, the efficient cause who allowed there to be other efficient causes.

Moving on, elsewhere in the *Physics* Aristotle laid the foundations for subsequent discussions of place, time and infinity. Place, for him, made sense only as the location of some object, and not on its own terms as potentially empty *space*. The distinction remains: 'space' is neutral in a way that 'place' is not. The significance of place as a theological topic has been taken up in recent years.[10] Today we might say that space belongs to physics. At least since Descartes, physics has been worked out in the endless neutrality of three spatial dimensions. Place, however, is metaphysical; it has local colour. Theology holds to the importance of location and to the allied sense that distance might have resonances beyond simple spatial extension.

Time also fascinated Aristotle, as it has many philosophers since. His position over time resembles his position over space. Time is not abstract; it only makes sense in terms of something moving or developing. Time is therefore not simply *measured* by things changing, it is bound up with that change. Over infinitude, Aristotle made a perennially useful distinction between an *actual* and a *potential* infinitude. An infinite number of objects, together all at once, would be an actual infinite. They are only a potential infinite if they come one after another, not together. Aristotle had no trouble with potential infinitude. He believed that the world was eternal and that species were unchanging, implying a potentially infinite number of sparrows, and of everything else. Similarly, a human mind is open-ended as to the number of thoughts it can think. However, the actual infinite was an object of horror for Aristotle. It is the nature of things to have limits, so an actual infinitude would be imperfect, bursting the boundaries that make something good and particular. When Christian theologians later

---

10 John Inge, *A Christian Theology of Place*, Aldershot: Ashgate, 2003; David Brown, *God and Enchantment of Place: Reclaiming Human Experience*, OUP, 2006.

wished to describe God as infinite, many realized that they had to rehabilitate the notion of the actual infinitude, for instance by aligning it with simplicity rather than multiplicity.

Metaphysics

The word 'metaphysics' has a mundane origin: it means after physics. Once you have studied physics, which is how material things behave in physical ways, there is more to be said. Physics is mainly concerned with movement, but beyond movement lie deeper, more inscrutable, all-embracing questions. Beneath the observation that beings move is the question of how to understand being itself. These questions come *meta-*, which is to say 'after', *physics*.

The question of how one discipline relates to another was important for the ancient mind, as it was for the mediaeval mind. In part, this came down to asking what you have to understand before you can understand something else. Beyond this, some fields of enquiry, even if they were complete, would go on to beg further questions. Physics leaves us asking metaphysical questions just as, after we have discussed how an individual human being lives well (ethics), we ask further questions about how we live well together in a society (which Aristotle called 'politics').

Metaphysics is the study of *being*. This is philosophy at its most basic, and most determinative. *Everyone* has a sense of metaphysics, however implicit that might be. Christian theologians picked up their metaphysics like magpies and, more than any other aspect of philosophy, their understanding of being was to be transformed into new shapes by its deployment in Christology and Trinitarian theology.

We will consider four aspects of Aristotle's metaphysics. We have encountered the first, form and matter. Form is what changes; matter is what stays the same. Unlike Plato, as we have seen, Aristotle did not believe in the *realm* of the Forms. Form, for Aristotle, was 'immanent', not 'transcendent'. Each thing has a form (its *immanent* form), but it receives that form only from other things within the world, not from beyond the world: the potter makes the jug; the rabbit begets the rabbit. Raphael painted Aristotle with his hand extended flat, like the surface of the earth. Aristotle's metaphysics is flat. Forms exist within the material world and need no explanation from any transcendent source. Neither does the world as a whole, which is eternal, need any explanation. It *just is*. In this, his metaphysics is not very religious.

The nearest Aristotle gets to God is his 'prime mover', but this is far from God as a Christian understands God, as we will see. From Aristotle's perspective, the sort of questions that Christian theologians ask – Why are there rabbits? Why is there anything at all? – are naive questions, the musings of the untutored. Various atheist philosophers have taken up this position in recent centuries. In a famous radio exchange in 1948, Frederick Copleston had insisted that there must be a reason why there is anything rather than nothing. Bertrand Russell replied that there is no reason; the universe is just a brute fact.[11] Russell was being Aristotelian. From the perspective of Christian philosophy, his refusal to ask the ultimate 'why' question (and Aristotle's refusal) is a failure of imagination and of a proper sense of curiosity and wonder. This judgement is important for Christian apologetics today.

Closely related to form and matter are *action and potential*. *What* something is can be described as a sort of act, indeed as its innermost act. This innermost act plays out what it has in its form to be. Alongside that action, however, remains an element of potentiality: it is *this* but it could also be *that*. Potentiality comes from matter, because even while being informed in this particular way (as a jug) the matter could be informed in another particular way (as shards of pottery). This makes form the principle of particularity and matter the principle of generality.

An acorn can become an oak tree, and yet it is a seed and not a tree. An acorn is a seed in actuality (or 'in act' – it is actively a seed) but a tree in potentiality (in that it has potential to be a tree). What something is now (its actuality) depends on its form; that it can develop to be something else depends on its matter (which is the principle of potentiality). All the same, what it can potentially

---

11 The transcript is widely available online.

turn out to be rests back on the form: the acorn can become an oak tree, not an elm tree. This provides very powerful language with which to speak of God: God is pure act or, as we might see it written in Latin, *actus pūrus*. There is no potential in God, no irresolution, no lack compared to what God 'could be'. For one thing, this is because something moves from potential to act because it is prodded by something else, and nothing exists that can prod God. God cannot be acted upon, which is part of what it means for him to be Lord. God is always, and eternally, fully what he is. Unlike us, God is not a work in progress. Developed in the right way, this idea helps us to understand God's unchangeability not as a lack but as a fullness or plenitude of action.

Aristotle's metaphysics proceeds in pairs: form and matter, act and potential. We turn now to another pair, substance and accidents. But first we should pause and ask where these pairings come from. Aristotle would say that they come from the world: this is the way the world is; this is the way it hangs together. Later philosophers have sometimes made a different claim about their categories, saying that they are not discovered but imposed. That is a far more pragmatic account, according to which philosophical language simply provides a helpful framework for explaining how we might do or make things, and nothing more; little of this has a basis in 'the truth of things' (which is a category they are likely to approach with suspicion). Aristotle, however, was a 'realist' about his philosophy. He thought that his concepts lined up with reality, and indeed that they came from observing reality. Here we can deploy a phrase of particular brilliance from Plato: the realist thinks that her concepts 'carve the world at its joints': that our minds separate the world along real fault lines, like a chef inserting the knife in the chicken at just the right place, rather than hacking away at a bone in the middle.[12]

The distinction between substance and accidents seeks to insert the mental knife between *what* something is (its substance) and *how* something happens to be (its accidents). This distinction applies to everything that exits, which is one good reason why we

___
12 *Phaedrus* 265D–E.

ARISTOTLE

should not speak of God as *a thing among things*, since there is
nothing to God that he *just happens* to be. God has no accidents.

As an illustration, consider that at the age of 75 someone is
significantly different from the person that she was at the age of
50 or 25. Very many things will have changed, and yet we say that
she is the same person. Moreover, she will rise at the general resurrection not, presumably, quite as she was at any particular age,
but certainly as the person who somehow existed across all of that
time and as the subject of all of those changes. The resurrection,
as with many other aspects of theology, calls upon us to explain
what is primary and what is secondary about a person, and how
those dimensions relate. As another example we could turn to the
idea that the Incarnation has a saving effect simply as the Incarnation, simply as God's wholehearted identification with human
beings (for all we might want to say more: about the crucifixion,
for instance). But, we might reply, if Jesus was a man, does that
mean that he identifies only with men and not women, or only
with Jews, being a Jew, or only with carpenters? In response to
questions such as these it is useful to have the categories of substance and accidents to hand. His identification is through what
he is substantially, a human being, not what he was accidentally.

The *Oxford Concise English Dictionary* defines substance as
'the essential material, esp. solid, forming a thing' and 'a particular kind of material having uniform properties (*this substance is
salt*)'.[13] In philosophy it is 'the essential nature underlying phenomena, which is subject to changes and accidents'. If it helps to
remember meanings by reference to etymologies, the word comes
from *sub-* (meaning 'under') and *stare*, to stand. Substance is
that overarching quality about a thing, *under* which other more
mutable aspects *stand*. Once again, we find philosophy trying to
understand what it means for something to change, and to stay
the same, and how they relate.

The dictionary is less helpful when it comes to the other word,
'accident'. Its meaning in common parlance, 'an event without
an apparent cause, or is unexpected [. . .] occurrence of things by

---

13 Oxford: Clarendon Press, 1995.

43

chance', is not what we mean here. The primary point is that while substances have a certain solidity, accidents do not exist by themselves. They are what *stands under* substance, or what leans against, or even 'falls under', substance, which seems to be what the etymology of accident means ('fall towards' and therefore 'fall under'). We encounter a (substantial) human being standing before us, but we do not encounter oboe playing on its own. Playing the oboe, and the quality of being able to play the oboe, is an *accident*, which means that we only ever find it inhering in a substance, namely that of a human being. Almost two millennia later, Thomas Aquinas was to give us a helpful definition: 'The essence of an accident is to inhere.'[14]

Aristotle described nine categories of accident and his list was widely accepted by theologians in the Middle Ages. These categories are quality, quantity, relation, place, time, position, state (or possession), action and passion (or receptivity). They are all the simple things, he thought, that can be said of something. Add substance, and we have Aristotle's ten *categories* of being:

- Substance: being *this* thing, the nature of what something is – e.g. a human being, a horse, Socrates
- Quantity: how much – e.g. one and a half metres
- Quality: what sort – e.g. black, musical
- Relation: related to what – e.g. double, half, smaller
- Place: where – e.g. in London, in the cathedral
- Time: when – e.g. today, last week
- Position: being situated – e.g. stands, sits
- State: having or possessing – e.g. is clothed
- Action: doing – e.g. cuts, burns
- Passion: undergoing – e.g. is hit, is promoted.

Robert O'Donnell provides an example which he analysed according to the categories: 'Abraham Lincoln was a tall white lawyer who often wore a top hat and who, as President of the United States, freed the slaves, and was, while sitting in a box at Ford's Theatre,

---

14 *ST* I.28.2.

murdered by John Wilkes Booth in 1865.'[15] The substance is Abraham Lincoln; the quantity is tall; the quality is white; the relation is to his murderer; the action is freeing the slaves; the passion is being murdered; the time is 1865; the place is Ford's Theatre; the position is sitting; the state is wearing a top hat.

Our final example of Aristotle's helpful distinctions has not two elements but three. Aristotle noted that objects can be grouped into kinds. His terminology was of genus, species and individual. These words have entered scientific usage in relation to living things and, indeed, Aristotle was mainly thinking about living things across his philosophy. In contrast, philosophers today, guided by contemporary science, tend to think of living things as an exception or minor category; if they are important to us, that reflects the bias inherent in being living things ourselves. The Christian philosopher might rather take Aristotle's view. Only a tiny fraction of the matter in the universe belongs to a living thing but, even if the only life is on Earth, we can say that the universe is alive, since there is life in this universe. Life is the crowning feature of the universe, and indeed the reason why there is a universe at all.

Genus, species and individual have applicability beyond analysis of living things, but we might start there. Every individual cabbage belongs to the species *cabbage*. Species can then be grouped into a genus. In the case of cabbages, they belong to the genus *brassica*. Species and genus relate to substance, rather than to accidents. It is by being substantially *a cabbage*, and not as green or bitter tasting, that an object belongs to the species cabbage and genus brassica.

A distinction between individual, species and genus is useful because it provides us with language to describe how things can be grouped together at more than one level. We can group cabbages together, we can group cauliflowers together, and, at a higher level, we can group cabbages with cauliflowers, since they are both brassicas, as is broccoli and the Brussels sprout. We can ask various questions in these terms: for instance, whether Christian priests

---

15 Robert A. O'Donnell, *Hooked on Philosophy*, New York: Alba House, 1995, p. 21.

are really *priests*. Does the species 'episcopally ordained Christian minister' fall within the same genus as other examples that might be thought of as priests?

God

The nearest that Aristotle comes to talking about God is the 'prime' (or 'first') mover. This being is the ultimate cause of movement and change in the universe, but it is itself entirely unconcerned with what moves or exists. In the *Physics*, the emphasis is on the movement of the heavens, which for Aristotle communicate motion and change from the prime mover to the earth (or 'sub-luminary' sphere, since it is what lies beneath the innermost orbit in his system, that of the moon).[16] Christian thinkers, accepting this model, might not have approved of astrology, but they certainly thought that the planets had an influence on natural life. 'Influenza', as its name suggests, was thought to be caused by the influence of heavenly bodies. 'Sideration' was recorded as a cause of death in the Middle Ages (from *sidus*, Latin for 'star'), along with 'planet'. In acting through the heavens, the prime mover exerts efficient causation. In the *Metaphysics*, however, Aristotle portrayed the first mover as acting through final causation.[17] It functions as a lure, and all creation moves out of desire for it. This has real Christian potential.

Theologians have made a great deal of God-as-first-efficient cause, particularly as part of arguments for the existence of God: that there could be no motion without an unmoved mover or causation without an uncaused cause. The idea of God as final cause, or goal of all longing, is just as promising, although this aspect has often been passed over. It is a good example of the way in which Aristotle is not always quite as far from the religious mysticism of Plato as is sometimes assumed. Among the greatest of theologians to have worked out a theology on the basis of desire and final causation was the Syrian, Pseudo-Dionysius. Although

16 *Physics* VIII.
17 *Metaphysics* XII.6.

very much a Platonist, he also stands on the same territory as Aristotle at his most mystical:

> After the Good all things yearn: those that have mind and reason seeking it by knowledge, those that have perception seeking it by perception, those that have no perception seeking it by the natural movement of their vital instinct, and those that are without life and have but basic existence seeking it by their aptitude for that bare participation through which this basic existence is theirs.[18]

All the same, Aristotle's god is not close to God as understood in Christian theology. It is not, for instance, the creator of the universe. For Aristotle, the world, like the prime mover, always existed. In that sense, and very much unlike God for Christian theology, the prime mover is simply another *part of the furniture of the universe*. This prime mover explains why things move but not why things exist in the first place. In another sense, however, Aristotle's god is *cut off from the world* in a way that Christian theologians would never suppose. The prime mover is described as thought thinking itself: 'It must be of itself that the divine thought thinks (since it is the most excellent of things), and its thinking is a thinking on thinking.'[19] Christians have no problem understanding God in terms of thought, since the Son is the *Logos*. However, since God *has* created, God is not lost in his own self-contemplation, oblivious of the world.

Aristotle provided resources to be deployed but Christians knew that they would have to go far beyond him in talking about God and creation. To God as efficient and final cause, found in Aristotle, they added God as the formal cause of all things, since the essence of everything stands as a participation in God. Although God is not the material cause of creation, the idea of *creation out of nothing* makes the revolutionary claim that God is the cause of matter.

---

18 *On the Divine Names* IV, trans. C. E. Rolt, SPCK, 1920, with modifications.
19 *Metaphysics* IX.

Logic

Aristotle thought a great deal about thinking. A group of his works, taken together, propose a complete system for reasoning. Called the *Organon*, it comprises the *Categories*, *Prior Analytics*, the *Posterior Analytics* and *On Interpretation*. Aristotle's logic represents an important break with Plato. The older thinker wrote in literary Greek, affecting the style of everyday speech. In contrast, Aristotle was concerned to see how speech could be disciplined far beyond anything like ordinary usage, to achieve the highest degree of precision. His method is often that of the syllogism (from *syllogismos*, meaning 'conclusion' or 'inference'), which involves distinguishing the structure of the argument from the content. Perhaps the most famous example is the following:

> All human beings are mortal.
> Socrates is a human being.
> Therefore, Socrates is mortal.

A syllogism rests upon the stable 'middle term', in this case 'human being', which is common to the first and second lines but drops out in the third, having done its connecting work. The first line is called the *major premise*, the second is the *minor premise* and the third is the *conclusion*. The syllogism shows Aristotle at his most *deductive*: proceeding on the basis of what is taken to be sure. His natural history shows some influence of another method, inductive reasoning, which is based on repeated observations.

Plato's account assumed that we can never quite say what we want. That is why we need to keep talking to one another. Aristotle's system, on the other hand, aims for absolute clarity. If we argue from first principles by ruthless logic then the final result will be as true as our first principles were. This can lead to a certain formalism: we can say that if *a* and *b* are true then *c* follows, independent of knowing whether *a* or *b* are in fact true.

The middle term has to be 'stable'. In our example, it was 'human being'. However, this syllogism requires a stability that creatures may, perhaps, not have. What would happen if a person appeared who was not mortal? Might it be that humanity is not sufficiently well grasped to fit into a syllogism, or mortality for that matter?[20] In a sense, we know what 'mortal' means. In the usual sense, Socrates was mortal, and died. In another sense, it is worth noting that we are discussing Socrates in the twenty-first century. When it comes to enduring reputation, Socrates was not quite as 'mortal' as other people who lived in Greece in the fourth century BC. In that sense, and maybe others, Socrates lives on. Our syllogism may be dissolving.

Most significant of all, we should ask whether God can be discussed in this way. Syllogisms proceed by a general structure into which one then inserts objects: *a* implies *b*; *b* implies *c*; therefore *a* implies *c*. We should insist, however, that God is not a thing like other things and that God is not an example of any general category in any way. In his *Philosophical Fragments*, Søren Kierkegaard wrote that we cannot discuss God by such a method. Syllogisms work on the basis of clarity, but God is supremely 'unknown'. A response might be to say that the God who would otherwise have been unknown has been revealed to us. Nonetheless, what we know is but 'the outskirts of his ways' (Job 26.14). God cannot be squashed into a syllogism.

Despite that criticism, the syllogism can be helpful for teasing out what is wrong when we sense a fault of logic. In particular, it can help us spot a missing step or unacknowledged assumption. As an example, I remember a sermon in a Cambridge college chapel in which the preacher told us that 'God does not need the prayers of the saints, therefore the saints are not intercessors'. I fault the truth of his conclusion, as it happens, but that is only half of the problem. I also fault his logic. Something is missing. We cannot go from 'not necessary' to 'does not happen' without another step. The preacher gave the major premise: God does not need the prayers of the saints. That is true: he does not need the prayers of anyone. The preacher did not give us the implicit minor premise, which alone would yield his conclusion, that God only

---

20 Writing on the idea that it is mistaken to try to prove the existence of God, Søren Kierkegaard called it a 'daring' to suppose even to know what it means to be human (*Philosophical Fragments* 3).

orders the world so as to fulfil in some minimal sense what is strictly necessary. Supply the minor premise, the conclusion follows, and it makes no sense to speak of the saints as intercessors. On that logic, however, it would make no sense to talk of *anyone* as an intercessor. A more elaborate minor premise might yield his conclusion without undoing intercession *tout court*, but it was not provided.

Perception and Psychology

Among the most influential of Aristotle's works is his *De Anima* or 'On the Soul'. From this work theologians obtained a new and valuable way to describe the soul, namely as 'the form of the body'.[21] As the form of the teapot is to the teapot, so is the soul to a living thing. For Aristotle, every living thing has a soul for its form. Soul in Latin is *anima* and to be living is to be moving, or *animated*; it is to have a form characterized by animation. The human being is distinguished among living things by having a *rational* soul (and, for theologians, by having a soul capable of immortality). This follows because a form is what makes something what it is: the soul of the human being must relate to what is distinctive about a human being.

The move of identifying the soul with form has paid huge dividends. For one thing, it closely identifies the soul with life, and sees this life as being in the whole of the creature: the form is what makes the parts what they are and what makes them add up to the whole. It takes materiality seriously, since the form is the form of a material being, while also stressing that what is so extraordinary about a living being is what emerges within that matter, namely life. In Plato, or at least in a significant strand of Plato's thought which has been influential on Christian theology, the soul is a stranger to the body. Aristotle's wisdom was to dispute this. The soul is an aspect of the whole. We are material beings whose life is more than simply material.

---

21 II.1.

Ethics

Aristotle worked out his ethics in terms of the sort of beings we are and what we should be on the basis of that: our goal is to fulfil our nature. These are vital questions, making the *Nicomachean Ethics* a good place to start among Aristotle's works.

For Aristotle, human fulfilment has something of the sense in which we use the word today. It includes, for instance, 'happiness' or *eudemonia*. In another sense, however, he uses 'fulfilment' and 'happiness' in unfamiliar ways. Fulfilment consists in living with 'nobility and greatness of soul', in being 'truly good and wise'.[22] Happiness rests on knowing that one has lived well rather than in anything provided by external circumstances, since they are beyond the control of even the great and good. Happiness, for Aristotle, is extraordinarily objective. The glutton may have seemed blissfully content, but if he was deflected from human excellence he was, objectively, far from happy. King Priam might have his entire empire destroyed but, if he lived well, he was happy.

Aristotle put the emphasis in morality on living rationally, since reason is the distinctive human excellence. The Greek for 'excellence' is *aretē*. It is usually rendered in Latin as *virtus* and the strain of ethics concerned with excellence, and being what a human being should be, is therefore called 'virtue ethics'. This approach has enjoyed a revival in recent decades, due in part to the work of Alasdair MacIntyre and his book *After Virtue*, which changed the direction of philosophy and ethics for many Christians in the late twentieth century.[23]

Virtus is close to the word for 'strength' and we might usefully talk about the virtues as 'strengths of character'. Aristotle has been particularly significant for Christian moral thought because his theory has a strong practical dimension. The virtues are habits, which is to say that they are things we grow into, not least through practice. Virtues, as habits, come to us as a sort of second nature. Aristotle's work set four virtues in first place: prudence,

---

22 *Nicomachean Ethics* X.
23 London: Duckworth, 2007.

justice, temperance and courage. These are the 'cardinal' virtues; cardinal meaning 'principal' or 'essential'. Ultimately, the origin is in *cardō*, meaning 'hinge'. Prudence is skill in deliberation; justice sets the standard to be sought; temperance strengthens us against distractions from living well; courage steels us to overcome obstacles to doing what is right. To the four cardinal virtues, Christian theologians added Paul's trio from 1 Corinthians 13, the 'theological' virtues of faith, hope and love, giving a roll call of seven principal Christian virtues.

Reading On

Terence Irwin and Gail Fine assembled and translated a good introductory anthology: *Aristotle: Introductory Readings* (Hackett, 1996). Richard McKeon's selection *Basic Works of Aristotle* (New York: Modern Library, 2001) is longer and includes some complete works. Thomas Kiernan's *Aristotle Dictionary* provides a selection of short excerpts by topic (London: Owen, 1962). Both Penguin and Oxford World's Classics have excellent translations of principal individual works and the complete works are available in two volumes from Princeton University Press (1984), translated by Jonathan Barnes.

Alongside the *Cambridge Companion to Aristotle* (1995), edited by Jonathan Barnes, stands a *Companion to Aristotle* (Wiley-Blackwell, 2009), edited by Giorgios Anagnostopoulos. On the relationship of Aristotle to Plato, see Lloyd Gerson's wonderfully provocative *Aristotle and Other Platonists* (Ithaca: Cornell University Press, 2006). In *Four Cardinal Virtues* (South Bend: University of Notre Dame Press, 1966), Josef Pieper presents Aristotle's ethical vision as adopted and transformed by Thomas Aquinas.

4

The Bible and Philosophy

Philosophy and the Old Testament

The New Testament was written in Greek, with Greek philosophy in the air. The New Testament stands in relationship to that tradition, sometimes criticizing it, sometimes endorsing. We will come on to that later in this chapter. First, however, we might ask about the relationship between philosophy and the Old Testament. Stylistically, only the later books, which some Christian traditions place outside the Old Testament and in the Apocrypha, contain passages that resemble 'philosophical' literature in a Greek mould. The books of Wisdom and Sirach (also known as Ecclesiasticus) are good examples. Consider this passage: 'by his [God's] word all things hold together. We could say more but could never say enough; let the final word be: "He is the all"' (Sirach 43.26–7).

Both the invocation of the word of God (*Logos*) and the phrase 'He is the all [or All]' bear a close resemblance to Greek Stoic philosophy, as does the idea that the world is pervaded by God's spirit (Wisd. 1.7) or that its order reveals its creator (Wisd. 13.5). There is much in common with Platonic thought when we read in Sirach that God 'created' the world from 'formless matter' (Wisd. 11.17).[1]

When the later Jewish philosopher Philo took up Stoic and Platonic ideas, he was simply walking in the footsteps of Sirach.

for all other things are intrinsically and by their own nature loose; and if there is any where any thing consolidated, that has been

---

1 These examples come from Anthony Meredith, *Christian Philosophy in the Early Church*, T&T Clark, 2012, pp. 63–4.

bound by the word of God, for this word is glue and a chain, filling all things with its essence. And the word, which connects together and fastens every thing, is peculiarly full itself of itself, having no need whatever of any thing beyond.[2]

Such passages in the Old Testament, however, are the exception, and nothing in the rest of the Old Testament reads quite like them. This is not surprising. Whatever positions various scholars might take over dating the Old Testament, it is undeniably an ancient book, and written in the genres of its time. Hebrew literature from the eighth century BC does not read like Hellenic philosophy, but then neither does *Greek* literature from the eighth century.

In his excellent recent book, Yoram Hazony paints a bleak and accurate picture of just how little the Old Testament has been considered worthy of philosophical attention.[3] He describes this as a Christian tendency, but that is less accurate. On the same basis that Old Testament writings were, and are, written off as 'not philosophical', Christian writings have also been dismissed. The Old Testament may have come off badly from the Enlightenment preference for the ancient Greeks,[4] but the New Testament did not fare particularly well either.

What, then, might we be looking for in the Old Testament that we might call 'philosophy'? It will not be anything comparable to later 'philosophy' in style, nor necessarily in the answers it gives. More likely, the link will be in what it seeks to accomplish and in the topics it seeks to address. The individual books of the Old Testament (and the Old Testament as a whole, under God's providence) seek a framework within which to understand the world. That is a philosophical task, and the Old Testament authors can ask it as legitimately as can the authors of 'philosophy', as it is usually called, or the authors of the New Testament for that matter.

2 Philo, *Who is the Heir of Divine Things?*, Chapter 38, §188. This and other quotations from Philo are from *The Works of Philo*, trans. C. D. Yonge, Peabody: Hendrickson, 1993.

3 Yoram Hazony, *The Philosophy of Hebrew Scripture*, CUP, 2012, p. 17.

4 Hazony, *Philosophy*, p. 14.

THE BIBLE AND PHILOSOPHY

Writing in 1946, Erich Auerbach argued that the Bible, more than any other book, reaches out to drag the reader into its world.[5] He principally had the Old Testament in view. Whereas we read other books, the Bible reads us; whereas we integrate other books into our story, the Bible situates us in its own.[6] Mention of story is crucial here. The Bible may sometimes provide us with abstract categories, more so in the New Testament than in the Old, but principally it proceeds by means of story.

The Bible, following Auerbach's point, has grabbed hold not only of individual readers but of whole cultures. On account of that, much of the philosophical subtlety of the Scriptures risks going unnoticed, because we take it for granted. To take an example, we think of history as linear. The biblical vision is also of time as linear, so that does not strike us as particularly significant, or philosophical. In fact, it is both. In the world's great schemes of thought, thinking of history as having a beginning and an end has been quite rare. More often, time has been conceived as endless or cyclical. If *we* think of history as linear, with a beginning and end, it is because the Hebrew perspective has changed our philosophical conception of time and history. As an idea, it now goes without saying. We do not notice it, but it is revolutionary.

'Nothing in the principal Hebrew texts', writes Hazony,

suggests that the prophets or scholars of ancient Israel were familiar with [. . .] an opposition between God's word and the pronouncements of human reason when it is working as it should [. . . To] a remarkable degree, the God of Israel and those who wrote about him seem to have been concerned to address subjects close to the heart of what later tradition calls works of reason.[7]

---

5 Erich Auerbach, *Mimesis: The Representation of Reality in Western Literature*, Princeton University Press, 1953.

6 We might also think of the provocative title of Walter Brueggemann's book, *Redescribing Reality: What We Do when We Read the Bible*, SCM Press, 2009.

7 Hazony, *Philosophy*, p. 2.

Hazony's book *The Philosophy of Hebrew Scripture* is the most significant study of the Old Testament as philosophy for decades, possibly longer. He argues that the writers of the Hebrew Scriptures were involved in something directly comparable to philosophy, in that they were engaged in the work of *reason*: they explored ethics and politics, for instance, and the nature of reality and our place in it. These are all good philosophical topics. To this Hazony adds epistemology (the theory of knowledge), especially in the book of Jeremiah, and an implicit metaphysics (the study of being and its structures), examined in terms of the relation of 'truth' and 'being'. That metaphysical vision, Hazony thinks, is of things existing in relation rather than as isolated individuals. As for the 'philosophy of religion', the emphasis is on the nature of faith and, within that, on the trustworthiness of God. This is, in fact, what Aquinas and Luther also both stressed, and it is increasingly the consensus over what faith meant for Paul.[8]

Among the hurdles to reading the Old Testament as philosophy, as we have seen, is the preponderance of story and narrative forms. There is also poetry and wide use of metaphor. The Law of Moses, for instance, is not given independent of a historical story. Indeed, as Hazony has it, the law is 'dependent on these narratives for its force and significance'.[9] But then, the proposal that texts in general derive their authority for the stories that are told about them would come as no surprise to some late twentieth-century philosophers. For those, however, who like their philosophy to look like mathematics (the 'analytic' school), the Old Testament cannot be particularly philosophical because narrative and metaphor are not thought to be proper means of expression for reason or, as Hazony puts it, 'arguments of a general nature'.[10] It will come as no surprise that it has been philosophers of the other dominant philosophical tradition (called 'Continental'), such as Levinas and Ricœur, rather than philosophers of an analytic tradition, who have most typically drawn on the Old Testament in recent decades.

---

8 Faith is trust in God, not belief that God exits or in a particular list of truth (Hazony, *Philosophy*, pp. 240–2).

9 Hazony, *Philosophy*, p. 254.

10 Hazony, *Philosophy*, Chapter 3.

Throughout this book we will run into the question of the limits of reason, not least in respect of God. Few questions in philosophical theology are more important for the theologian, not only for the discipline itself but also for the piety of individual Christians and their apologetic witness to the faith. Following Hazony, we can find a rich seam of discussion on this topic in the Old Testament. Even for figures favoured by God, for individuals 'gifted with relative clarity of vision' towards divine things, God is presented as being elusive: he is silence for Elijah; he is veiled with smoke for Isaiah.[11] Christianity is no stranger to this insight. God's transcendence – the sense that he cannot be contained in human reason – is central to much Christian philosophical theology. This is the 'negative' or 'apophatic' way, celebrated down the centuries. The central image has often been of Moses lost in the cloud on the summit of Sinai, as for instance in Gregory of Nyssa's *The Life of Moses*. Insisting on divine ineffability is no theological detraction of philosophy. Even Aristotle, who generally celebrates the expansiveness of rationality, wrote that the most significant truths are the least knowable, because of a suffusion of light, not its absence.[12] They remain, however, the most significant.

This leads us to 'epistemology', the philosophy of knowledge, and what it means for the Bible to teach, and to teach clearly. Some Christians are committed to the idea of the perspicacity of Scripture: that it says everything clearly. There is something important in this, namely confidence that the Scriptures contain 'all things necessary to salvation' and that they communicate this to us in a way that offers salvation freely and generously.[13] In another sense,

---

11 Hazony, *Philosophy*, p. 227.

12 'Just as bats' eyes are towards daylight, so in our soul is the mind towards those things that are clearest of all', *Metaphysics* 993b, trans. Hugh Lawson-Tancred, Penguin, 1998.

13 However, the principal way in which God makes the Scriptures clear, is through the accompaniment of the Church as pastor and teacher. In a popular parable, a man sits on the top of his house during a flood and on three occasions turns down the offer of a lift to safety, since 'God will save me'. After he drowns, he reproaches God for not coming to his aid. To this, God replies, 'I did: with a rowing boat, with a police boat and with a helicopter.' The person who seeks to understand the scriptural message outside the history of its interpretation in the Church is similarly looking a gift horse in the mouth.

however, perspicacity is a peculiar category to apply to the Scriptures. Much of the Bible is written in poetry, and what might it mean for poetry to be 'perspicacious'? Much of it is also written as a narrative, full of human foibles. Most of the time it is clear whether a particular character offers a good example or bad, but on other occasions it is less clear cut.

Attachment to the idea of perspicacity may rest on an unacknowledged sense that reason is about true propositions, and therefore that revelation involves God handing over a collection of such true propositions. Hazony is right to dispute that this is a biblical account of revelation or even of reason. The Bible is true, but most of the time truth is not communicated in cut and dried propositions, as a series of uncomplicated true statements: in the Bible or anywhere else. If it were, we could condense the message of the Bible to so many points and leave the text of Scripture behind. We cannot, however, and must not, do that. As Auerbach had written, the Bible resists being dragged into our world (and being minced and turned into the sausages of our summaries, we might add). The Bible drags us into its world. As Hazony puts it, the Old Testament is *deliberately* resistant to summary (or 'catechism' as he calls it).[14] The Christian might reply by saying that the Church wants both – catechism and Bible reading – but that it has always ensured that Bible reading takes pride of place.

For the Old Testament, God is beyond sewing up – ineffable, transcendent, elusive – but that is no endorsement of irrationality. Although God's ways are 'beyond our ways', that is no celebration of absurdity. Rather, God, and the revelation of God, and thinking about God, are associated with understanding and insight.[15] Faithfulness to God involves using *lev* (in Hebrew), which Hazony argues should be translated as 'mind' (and not as 'heart', as it is frequently). Figures in the Old Testament are praised when their *lev* is open.[16]

---

14 Hazony, *Philosophy*, p. 226. He concedes the *Shema Israel* ('Hear O Israel' Deut. 6.4), but notes how short it is.

15 Hazony points to Deut. 4.6–8, 30.15; Ps. 19.8; Isa. 2.2–3, 51.4; Micah 4.1–5 (*Philosophy*, pp. 235–6).

16 Hazony, *Philosophy*, p. 250.

Hazony's invites us to read the Old Testament as a work of reasoned exploration. This, in its way, is a brilliant insight, even if it is not the whole picture. He gives the example of Jeremiah, who is praised by God for having 'excelled in seeing' (Jer. 1.12).[17] This implies that Jeremiah's role, *precisely as inspired prophet*, was not 'simply to look at ready-made images that God placed before him', since in that case, 'it would be God who had excelled in presenting', not Jeremiah in seeing.[18] However it was that God inspired Jeremiah, it did not involve taking away Jeremiah's role in seeing (after all, that power of sight was itself a gift from God, since every good faculty is such a gift). Moreover, Hazony holds that the Law of Moses was given with no intention 'of contravening human reason – any more than the law of any nation is taught with the intention of contravening human reason'.[19] The entire 'natural law' tradition in Christianity, which proceeds on the basis that the revealed law is consonant with the order we find in creation, endorses this.

Hazony is right to say that the Old Testament is a work of reason, and we can agree we would 'destroy' the Hebrew Scriptures if we read them as 'revelation' *in such a way* as to stop them being a work of 'reason'.[20] However, for all Hazony thinks that a 'reason–revelation distinction' is 'alien' to the Old Testament, he often assumes that we are 'forced to choose' between them: the question is 'whether the Hebrew Scriptures can profitably be read as works of reason, *rather than* revelation'.[21] Faced with that choice, Hazony thinks that we must choose to see the Old Testament as reason. We would do better to follow Hazony's basic assumption more closely and insist that reason and revelation are not in tension. Ultimately, the problem lies with what Hazony sees as the 'Christian' vision of reason: namely that 'reason involves deducing perfectly certain propositions from other propositions taken

---

17 Hazony, *Philosophy*, pp. 262–3.
18 Hazony, *Philosophy*, pp. 261–2.
19 Hazony, *Philosophy*, p. 253.
20 Hazony, *Philosophy*, p. 8.
21 Hazony, *Philosophy*, pp. 259, 260, emphasis added.

to be self-evident, or derived from immediate sensation'.[22] This resembles a profoundly *un-Christian* ('positivist') stance towards reason, rather than anything Christian. More representative of the Christian approach at its best would be to say that the Bible is both revelation and a work of reason: parallel to the incarnate God to whom it bears witness, it is human without being less divine, divine without being less human; it is a quest and a revelation, an end and a beginning.

The New Testament

Scholars of the New Testament do not typically place much emphasis on the philosophical backstory of the time of its composition. That might be because they were brought up on the titans of Greek thought, such as Plato and Aristotle, whose influence on the New Testament is all but undetectable. The New Testament, let us admit, was written during a philosophical lull; the first century was not a high point of philosophical innovation. The days of Plato and Aristotle were well past; compelling Neoplatonism had yet to take off. The New Testament background is of fragmented schools and tendencies: Stoics, Cynics, Epicureans, Skeptics. Some of the best philosophical writers of the time, such as Cicero, combined influences from more than one school and the boundaries are therefore not always easy to draw. Moreover, the tasks that philosophers set themselves during this period were often reasonably modest, with a strong interest in many cases in what one could not know, and on practical matters, such as the nature of a good life and of good government.

Abraham Malherbe provides a pithy summary: ancient philosophy is not 'generally regarded as having had an influence on the writers of the New Testament'.[23] He cites three giants of scholarship. Among them, Henry Chadwick considered only two passages in the New Testament bear comparison with the sort

---

22 Hazony, *Philosophy*, p. 260.

23 Abraham Malherbe, *Paul and the Popular Philosophers*, Minneapolis: Augsburg Fortress, 1989, p. 1.

of philosophical exposition we find later in the Fathers: the Prologue to John's Gospel and Paul's speech at the Areopagus in Acts 17.16–34.[24] We have already discussed the backstory to the use of *Logos*. In the second case, the speech at the Areopagus ('Mars Hill'), Paul quotes Aratus, a Stoic: 'In him we live and move and have our being' and 'we too are his offspring' (Acts 17.28).

The omission of the Letter to the Hebrews from Chadwick's list is a little odd.[25] Its language of earthly copies of heavenly archetypes works with ideas with a Platonic pedigree. Then there is the passage in Romans about the witness of creation and its order (Rom. 1.19–21), which seems to draw on Stoic ideas[26] and, in this, echoes the book of Wisdom (compare Wisd. 13.5). Malherbe suggests a similarity between Paul's language of Christ as the head of the Church, as his body, and a passage in Seneca (*Epistle* 95.52), where God is described as relating to the world as parts of a body are related to its head.[27] Moreover, wherever Paul, or his school, talk about wisdom in the Epistles (often in the form of Christ-as-wisdom) he would be recognized as making a claim about Christ as the true source of enlightenment, parallel to what other philosophers, with their wisdom, were also claiming to offer (for instance, Rom. 11; 1 Cor. 1–3; Eph. 1, 3; Col. 1–3).

In assessing the relation of the Greek philosophy and the New Testament, we should strike a balance. The assumptions of the average Christian are correct: it is far more important to inform a Christian vision of the world from the Bible than it is to turn to ancient philosophical ideas in order to understand the Bible. However, we can accept that point without turning our back on placing the New Testament in its first-century intellectual context. We can aid our understanding of the Bible if we try to appreciate the resonance that a word or idea would have had for the New Testament authors and readers, and some of that resonance will

---

24 Henry Chadwick, *Early Christian Thought and the Classical Tradition: Studies in Justin, Clement and Origen*, OUP, 1966, pp. 3–4.

25 See J. W. Thompton, *The Beginnings of Christian Philosophy: The Epistle to the Hebrews*, Catholic Biblical Quarterly Monographs 13, 1982.

26 Malherbe gives Seneca's *Epistle* 65.19 as an example.

27 Malherbe, *Paul*, p. 45.

be 'philosophical'. The Bible is God's revelation to us in human words and words are a philosophical matter. Every time we go to our lexicon to find out what a word means, we are engaging with the philosophical assumptions of the authors of the Bible and the culture of its first readers (and of lexicon writers). When we read at the beginning of Hebrew (1.3) that Christ is the exact representation of God's *hypostasis*, what does that mean? It is a philosophical concept: it means being or nature. Similarly, there will always be philosophical freight in the notions concerning time, personhood, action, and so on.

Just as important is to recognize that the Bible is a text, or a collection of texts, and little is more philosophically charged than a text. A discussion, then, of philosophy and the Bible should also draw in ideas from literary theory, which we will consider in Chapter 15. The judicious application of literary theory is one of the most significant fruits of the twentieth century, when it comes to the study of the Bible.

Moral Philosophy

The New Testament might only rarely draw on the high metaphysical repertoire of ancient philosophy, with its grand ideas about the structure of reality. Metaphysics, however, was not the only branch of philosophy receiving attention. The emphasis of the philosophical schools at the time, and of contemporary philosophical writing, was also very much on *moral* philosophy. 'Moral' here does not necessarily mean a *moralistic* list of what was permissible and what was forbidden. 'Moral' meant the pursuit of a good and excellent life. On this territory we are closer to the terrain of much of the New Testament, and especially the Epistles, than if we search for veiled references to metaphysics.[28] Philosophical kinship rests on more than direct quotation, but even a simple trawl of quotations in the Epistles shows the resonances in 'moral philosophy'. In 1 Corinthians, Paul quotes the

---

28 As Malherbe points out.

Thais of Menander: 'Bad company ruins good morals' (1 Cor. 15.33). In Titus we find a citation from Epimenides (from *On the Oracles*) with a devastating moral assessment of the Cretans: 'Cretans are always liars, vicious brutes, lazy gluttons' (Titus 1.12).[29] The passage about the law being written on the heart in Romans (Rom. 2.15) shows close affinity with Seneca (*Epistles* 16 and 54) and Epictetus (*Discourses* 1.4.18).[30]

The world of ancient moral philosophy is as significant for our study of *how* the apostles wrote (and primarily we have Paul in view) as it is for a study of *what* they wrote. The Epistles show close parallels with contemporary philosophy over what Malherbe calls Paul's 'arguments and forms of address'.[31] This is not surprising. Writing today, we use the forms of argument and styles of writing of our time. Our appreciation of Paul as a teacher, preacher and letter writer can only be enlarged if we set him in the context of how people taught, preached and wrote in the first century. Paul scholarship is currently in a particularly vigorous and exciting period, and part of this comes from comparisons between Paul and his contemporaries over how they constructed arguments and sought to persuade their hearers or readers. Some of Paul's liveliest writing, for instance, takes the form of a list. This approach was common among Cynic philosophers (a school we have not considered) and is known as the 'diatribe'. Excellent examples are Romans 3.1–4 and 1 Corinthians 6.2–19.

Beyond ideas and forms of writing, there is also the question of forms of life. Ancient philosophy was as much about ways to live, as we have seen, as it was about ideas. Here, again, there are parallels with Paul, and differences. Like the philosophers of his time, and before, Paul lived a certain way and encouraged others to imitate him: 'be imitators of me', he writes twice, adding the second time 'as I am [an imitator] of Christ' (1 Cor. 4.16; 11.1).

---

29 Since Epimenides was himself a Cretan, this is one of the earliest statements of a self-denying paradox.

30 Meredith, *Philosophy*, pp. 44–5.

31 Malherbe, *Paul*, p. 2.

The 'Hebrew–Greek Distinction'

Read about the relation of theology to philosophy and before long you encounter the commonplace that the purity of Hebrew theology (conveniently considered to extend as far as the New Testament) was corrupted by philosophy in the early Church. (At other times, these very writers will express admiration for the early Church, as preserving the airy simplicity of the 'biblical church'.) O. C. Quick (a prominent figure on the mid-twentieth-century theological scene in the UK), for instance, understood the history of Christian thought as a battle between Hebrew and Hellenic approaches. He hoped that Hebrew, scriptural purity would win, which would require us to throw out Greek philosophical categories.[32]

This idea is taken beyond the bounds of parody in Barna's and Viola's recent book *Pagan Christianity*, where they argue that the Christian message was all but ruined by Greek influences: ruined, indeed, almost as soon as the ink was dry on the New Testament.[33] Christian *thought* was only one of the casualties. An otherwise pure Christian way of life was saddled with other such pagan perversions as church buildings, liturgy, clergy, and tithing and clergy salaries. The book is too ridden with factual errors to be taken particularly seriously, but it stands as a forceful, recent and popular example of the presupposition of a corruption of the Christian by the Hellenic.[34]

Over the past decades, such an antithesis between Greek philosophy and Hebrew religion has become harder and harder to maintain. Robert Wilken, a historian of early Christian thought, has put it like this:

The notion that the development of early Christian thought represents a hellenization of Christianity has outlived its usefulness.

---

32 O. C. Quick, *Doctrines of the Creed*, London: Nisbet, 1938, p. 152.

33 Carol Stream: BarnaBooks, 2008.

34 In a particularly telling passage, they criticize the philosophical presuppositions of gothic architecture (a style they erroneously attribute to 'the Goths') while assuming that the late capitalist architecture of their own meeting places is metaphysically and ethically neutral.

The time has come to bid a fond farewell to the ideas of Adolf von Harnack [. . .] whose thinking has influenced the interpretation of early Christian thought for more than a century [. . .] a more apt expression would be the Christianization of Hellenism, though that phrase does not capture the originality of Christian thought nor the debt owed to Jewish ways of thinking and to the Jewish Bible. Neither does it acknowledge the good and right qualities of Hellenic thinking that Christians recognized as valuable, for example, moral life understood in terms of the virtues.[35]

Wilken concludes that 'one observes again and again that Christian thinking, while working within patterns of thought and conceptions rooted in Greco-Roman culture, transformed them so profoundly that in the end something quite new came into being'.[36]

Historically, in any case, the New Testament is not simply 'Hebraic' *in contrast* to being 'Hellenistic'. For one thing, the Hebrew tradition was itself substantially in constructive dialogue with Greek thought by this period. Like any other mature tradition, never mind one under the strongest providential hand, Judaism entered into dialogue with what was around it and 'tested all things, and held fast to the good' (to use Paul's formulation in 1 Thess. 5.21).[37]

The drama of the New Testament is set geographically in territory where the more Jewish and the more Greek were often cheek by jowl. Part of the ministry of Christ took place in the Decapolis, the Greek-speaking part of Palestine. One of his disciples, Philip, has a Greek name.[38] Tellingly, it is to Philip that certain 'Greeks' come saying 'we wish to see Jesus' (John 12.20–2). The whole ministry of Paul, as Meredith notes, was 'to bring my name [Christ's] before Gentiles and Kings' (Acts 9.15).[39]

35 Robert Wilken, *The Spirit of Early Christian Thought: Seeking the Face of God*, New Haven: Yale University Press, 2003, pp. xvi–xvii.

36 Wilkin, *Spirit*. p. xvii.

37 See Martin Hengel, *The Hellenization of Judea in the First Century after Christ*, SCM Press, 1989.

38 As Meredith points out, *Philosophy*, p. 17.

39 Meredith, *Philosophy*, p. 2.

Not only did Jewish thinkers take note of their Greek neighbours but, to a small but highly significant degree, Greek thought (supposedly at the opposite pole to Hebrew religion) was itself shaped by Judaism. The revelation of God to Moses as YHWH was particularly admired. This name was rendered in the Greek translation of the Old Testament as *I AM WHO I AM*. This chimed with Greek thought about God as the origin of being. We find an esoteric but strangely parallel example in Greek meditation on the meaning of a letter *E* that was said to have appeared miraculously at the shrine to Apollo in Delphi. Ammonius interpreted this as 'you are' (addressed to Apollo),[40] attributing to Apollo that self-subsistent and originatory being that Christian philosophers found in the revelation of the divine name to Moses: 'I AM WHO I AM'. Eusebius, for instance, seized upon this parallel in his book of apologetic explorations, *Preparation for the Gospel* (in Book 12).

To anticipate a later story, we usually hear a tale of Christian theologians learning from Neoplatonists such as Plotinus, or being led astray by them. Certainly, Augustine was only able to do what he did theologically because of ideas he learned from reading Plotinus and others close to him.[41] More and more, however, scholars recognize that the traffic and debt was not all one way. We can reasonably suppose that Plotinus knew about Christian theological philosophy since it seems likely that he was himself once a Christian. He is also said to have known Numidius, who knew some of the Old Testament and quoted it with extreme reverence.

To take a particular example, Plotinus is traditionally credited as the first figure to see infinitude as a positive characteristic. Roberto Radice, however, has pointed out that Philo did this long before Plotinus, on the good theological basis that God is presented in the Old Testament as transcendent and as the plenitude of being, at least if we follow the Greek translation of Exodus 3.14.[42] Nor is it unlikely that this idea passed to Plotinus *from Philo*, not if we

---

40 See Meredith, *Philosophy*, p. 34.

41 See Phillip Carey, *Inner Grace: Augustine in the Traditions of Plato and Paul*, OUP, 2008.

42 'Philo's Theology and Theory of Creation', in *The Cambridge Companion to Philo*, ed. Adam Kamesar, CUP, 2009, pp. 124–45, especially pp. 130–1.

overturn the past orthodoxy and imagine, for reasons just given, that Plotinus knew Christian and Jewish sources.[43] Having mentioned the figure of Philo, it is to him that we now turn.

Philo

The prime example of Jewish attention to Greek philosophy around the time of the writing of the New Testament is Philo of Alexandria. It is likely that he wrote in the decades leading up to AD 50 and that most of his large collection of writings has come down to us intact. It makes for accessible and stimulating reading.

Much of Philo's work is concerned with the interpretation of the Bible (which is to say, the Old Testament) in a way that drew upon the breadth of contemporary philosophy. His work demonstrates how much the various streams of philosophical tradition were mingling; he melded Stoic and Platonic ideas in a way that was typical of the period. Stoicism had started out with a fairly limited, practical range of interests, but by the first century it had become more speculative and religious, especially by drawing on Platonic ideas.

Philo holds a vital place among the Jews and Christians who formulated the distinctive notion of creation out of nothing, in sharp distinction to the various philosophical traditions of the time. Philo paid particular attention to this question in his treatise *On the Creation of the World*. In Chapter 10 he considers what place there could be in a Judaic philosophical vision for Plato's Forms. His answer picks up the language that will be used in the opening of John's Gospel and anticipates parallel answers in later Christian theology. Philo adopted the Stoic idea of the *Logos* (word or reason), which we first encountered in Heraclitus: 'The incorporeal world [the Forms]', Philo wrote, 'was already completed, having its seat in the Divine Reason [*Logos*]; and the world, perceptible by the external senses, was made on the model of it'.[44] We will find this interpretation of the divine ideas taken up by Plotinus, and later by Augustine and Maximus the Confessor.

43 See Radice, 'Theory of Creation', pp. 142–4.
44 X, §36.

This looks very philosophical for a Jewish writer, at least if we accept the (deeply problematic) dualism 'pure Hebraic religion' and 'corrupting Hellenistic philosophy'. However, far from going against his theological tradition in writing like this, it was Philo's biblical heritage that made these ideas attractive to him. In Genesis, God makes the world through his word: 'In the beginning . . . God *said* . . .' and we find a similar idea in Psalm 33: 'By the word of the LORD the heavens were made, and all their host by the breath of his mouth' (v. 6).

According to Philo, the *Logos* proceeds from God yet it is also called God. This reflects a trend in Jewish thought called 'hypostatization' (the Greek word, we should note, that was used for the Persons of the Trinity). This trend ascribed existence to an aspect or agency of God, such that it is at once both united to God and in some sense also distinct. As Anthony Thiselton puts it, 'Jewish thought between the two Testaments tended to hypostatize the word of God as a quasi-independent divine attribute which, alongside wisdom, preexisted the world.'[45] The idea is already at least half present in the book of Proverbs, with the figure of divine wisdom (*Sophia* in Greek)[46] and in Isaiah 55.11:

> so shall my word be that goes out from my mouth;
> it shall not return to me empty,
> but it shall accomplish that which I purpose,
> and succeed in the thing for which I sent it.[47]

In Philo, as throughout the Jewish mystical literature of the time around and just before the birth of Christ, God's word is sometimes seen as separate from God (as his 'Son' or an archangel) and

---

45 'Word of God', in *Dictionary of Biblical Tradition in English Literature*, ed. David Jeffrey, Eerdmans, 1992, pp. 848–50, p. 849.

46 Consider Prov. 8.22–6, 30; Wisd. 7.25–7; 8.1. The first of the great antiphons sung in the Western Church in the days immediately before Christmas identifies this wisdom with Christ: 'O Wisdom, coming forth from the mouth of the Most High, reaching mightily from one end to the other, and sweetly ordering all things: Come and teach us the way of prudence.'

47 Also see Wisd. 18.15–16.

sometimes as identical to God. The consensus among scholars is a stress on identity over distinction. The *Logos* is God-as-revealed, God turned towards the world.[48]

Philo did not make a distinction between the word and wisdom of God, but postulates something like a combination of the two as a mediating figure. We find this for instance in *Who is the Heir of Divine Things?*:

And the Father who created the universe has given to his arch-angelic and most ancient Word a pre-eminent gift, to stand on the confines of both, and separated that which had been created from the Creator. And this same Word is continually a suppliant to the immortal God on behalf of the mortal race, which is exposed to affliction and misery; and is also the ambassador, sent by the Ruler of all, to the subject race.[49]

Meredith makes a convincing point that just such a mediating principle in God, who was in a sense *in* God but in another sense *between* God and the world in God, was important for Philo, because he stressed the incomprehensibility of God (following a lineage that can be traced back to Plato and the passage we considered above from *Timaeus* 28c). Once again we find a theologian drawing upon philosophical sources to stress something at the same time profoundly biblical, in this case the transcendence of God, which is underlined in every prohibition of idolatry.

Where Philo does distinguish two hypostases, as he often does, they are the 'creative power' (associated with the Word) and the 'royal' or 'ruling' power. We therefore find Philo, a devout Jew, interpreting the appearance of three angels to Abraham in Genesis 18 in terms that are familiar from Christian *Trinitarian* interpretations:

48 Peter R. Carrell, *Jesus and the Angels: Angelology and the Christology of the Apocalypse of John*, CUP, 1997.
49 *Heir*, 42 (§205).

the one in the middle is the Father of the universe, who in the sacred scriptures is called by his proper name, *I am that I am*; and the beings on each side are those most ancient powers which are always close to the living God, one of which is called his creative power, and the other his royal power. And the creative power is God, for it is by this that he made and arranged the universe; and the royal power is the Lord, for it is fitting that the Creator should lord it over and govern the creature.[50]

The Stoics

The name Stoic comes from 'stoa', the porch under which the founders of this school delivered their teaching. They were not the first group to be named after an architectural feature. Aristotle and his followers are called the 'peripatetic' philosophers after *peripatoi*, the colonnades of their college in Athens where they congregated.

The Stoics differ markedly from Aristotle, and Plato before him, for the relatively modest scope of their interests. Not for them sweeping metaphysical questions about the nature of being or the structure of knowledge (or, not at first: these questions have their own fascination, and they crept back in as the Stoic tradition matured). 'Their primary interest', as Meredith puts it, 'was intensely practical.' It was the task to help people 'live modest and useful lives'.[51] Continuing a theme we have encountered before, they saw philosophy as a 'way of life', an exercise or practice, by which we grow in knowledge, virtue and self-possession.

There was more to Stoicism than the disposition towards resilience and self-reliance which goes by the name 'Stoic' today, but that was certainly part of their teaching and outlook, especially in the strand associated with Epictetus. His advice was to define carefully what you think counts as important. If happiness consists in virtue alone, and is not in any way related to one's situation

---

50 *On Abraham* 23 (§121).
51 Meredith, *Philosophy*, p. 27.

or material status, then nothing about that situation or material status can make one unhappy. This is, however, quite a big *if*. From a Christian perspective it seems to underplay the significance to human life of community and the body. We can also ask 'what counts?' in terms of what benefits someone, and that was another favourite Stoic approach. The answer is that any number of things benefit me in some situations but not in others (such as money). Since these are not unqualified goods they ultimately count as *indifferent* (a favourite Stoic phrase). They need not be ignored under all circumstances, or even under most circumstances. Cicero picked up a beautiful quotation of Terence here: 'nothing human is alien to me'.[52] All the same, nothing external can figure as central to a Stoic account of human life.

Paul can be reminiscent of the Stoics at times, for instance when he writes that he has learned to live both with need and with plenty (Phil. 4.12). In a sense, there is also something Stoic, at least in form, to the idea that 'neither circumcision nor uncircumcision is anything' (Gal. 6.15), although the Stoics would not have made much sense of what Paul goes on to say: 'but a new creation is everything!'

In contrast to Plato, and even to Aristotle, the early Stoics were little concerned with spiritual matters of transcendence. By the time we get to the contemporaries of the apostles and the early Fathers, Stoicism has become decidedly more theological. Seneca is an example and Cicero also had theological interests.[53] Marcus Aurelius, the best amateur philosopher among the Roman emperors, was largely Stoic. Later Christian thinkers often looked upon him kindly, for his intellectual sophistication, despite the fact that he persecuted their forebears (although not with the violence or rigour of some other emperors).

Seneca showed interest in all the main branches of philosophy but, by and large, he was primarily concerned with ethics. His emphasis was balance, self-control and a life lived in harmony with human nature. His philosophy has a certain practical wisdom

52 *On Duties* I.30.
53 Meredith, *Philosophy*, pp. 29–30.

and it was often addressed to a particular reader, in the form of a letter. Reading him can be like overhearing the wise council of a learned friend, so much so that Martha Nussbaum took him as a good example of 'philosophy as therapy'. To call it 'therapy', however, according to the contemporary meaning of that word, fails to capture quite how *religious* even the Stoics were. Like Aurelius, Seneca was received respectfully by Christians. Dante placed him in limbo, the first circle of hell, where there is no pain (even if there is neither any delight). Erasmus published a volume of his works and John Calvin wrote a commentary. A very early Christian author faked an exchange of letters between Seneca and the apostle Paul.

The Stoics are important for their concept of the *Logos*, which we have found originating in Heraclitus and put to work by Philo and Christian writers. The Stoic account of the *Logos* belongs as part of a dualism that we have seen running from Plato onwards, between form and matter, between the shape-giving and the shape-receiving, informing and informed. The Stoics distinguished between two eternal principles of the universe, matter and *Logos*. Their *Logos* (or, sometimes, fire) is the principle of order and reason. It drives the endless cycle of time forwards, giving things their form and purpose. We can see how this word, *Logos* (which means word, or reason), would lend itself to John for describing the eternal Son, who gives life and order to all things (John 1.3–4). Set against the Stoic background, however, the difference between their *Logos* and the Christian *Logos* is also very clear. For the Stoics, *Logos* is an eternal principle of an always-existing world, just as much as matter is. It is part of the scheme, or furniture, of the universe. There was no 'In the beginning was the Word' for them, not in John's sense of placing the Word prior to the beginning of creation.

Reading On

On the Old Testament, Yoram Hazony's *The Philosophy of Hebrew Scripture* has been discussed (CUP, 2012). On the New Testament, see Abraham Malherbe, *Paul and the Popular Philosophers* (Minneapolis: Augsburg Fortress, 1989), T. Engberg-Pedersen, *Paul and the Stoics* (Louisville: Westminster John Knox, 2000) and the beginning of Anthony Meredith's *Christian Philosophy in the Early Church* (T&T Clark, 2012).

The works of Philo were translated in the mid-nineteenth century by C. D. Yonge. This translation is available online and cheaply in print as *The Works of Philo* (Peabody, MA: Hendrickson, 1992). A more recent translation of the complete works accompanies the Greek text in the Loeb Classics edition (translated by F. H. Colson et al., Cambridge: Harvard University Press, 10 volumes and 2 supplements, 1929–62). A volume in the Classics of Western Spirituality series is devoted to him: *The Contemplative Life, the Giants, and Selections*, translated by David Winston (Paulist Press, 1981). Among the secondary literature, a good place to begin is Adam Kamesar's *The Cambridge Companion to Philo* (CUP, 2009).

The background to first-century understandings of Christ as the Word, a hypostasis of God, has been covered in two recent books: Larry Hurtado, *Lord Jesus Christ: Devotion to Jesus in Earliest Christianity* (Eerdmans, 2003) and Simon Gathercole, *The Pre-existent Son: Recovering the Christologies of Matthew, Mark and Luke* (Eerdmans, 2006).

Brad Inwood and Lloyd P. Gerson collect works by Stoic philosophers in *The Stoics Reader: Selected Writings and Testimonia* (Hackett, 2008). The *Meditations* of Marcus Aurelius are a good place to start (translated by Robin Hard, OUP, 2011). So are the letters of Seneca, translated by Robin Campbell as *Letters from a Stoic* (Penguin, 1969).

5

Philosophy and the Earlier Fathers

The Apologists

The second century AD, into the third, belongs to the Christian Apologists. These theologians faced a number of pressing challenges. One was to consider the form and structure of the Church, given that it now seemed that Christ was not necessarily going to return immediately. Ignatius of Antioch (c. AD 35–c. 108) and Irenaeus of Lyons (AD 130–202) are among the founding ecclesiologists of the Church. Another task was to explore what theological conclusions could legitimately be drawn from the biblical texts. The question of who Christ was – Christology – loomed large. Clarity was often achieved by weighing options, several of which were seen to be wrong turns, which is to say heresies. A further challenge, significant for our purposes, was the task of proclaiming and defending the Christian gospel in a world of Roman thought and culture. This task put those second-century Christians at the forefront of relating theology to philosophy, and for that they are given the name *apologists*. The word comes from the Greek *apologia*, meaning not 'apology' but 'defence' or 'account', following 1 Peter 3.15: 'Always be ready to make your defence [*apologian*] to anyone who demands from you an account of the hope that is in you.'

Already, in this period of the very early Church, we find the full range of attitudes towards philosophy, ranging from Tertullian (AD 160–220) to Justin Martyr (AD 100–65). Tertullian wrote that Greek philosophers are the source of all heresy[1] and

---

1 *Prescription against Heresies* 7.

famously asked 'what does Athens [philosophy] have to do with Jerusalem [faith]?'[2] Justin, however, trained in philosophy before his conversion, and he continued to wear the clothing of a philosopher in order to demonstrate that Christianity was the true philosophy.

Tertullian is a remarkable figure, by turns enormously creative and enormously conservative, brilliant and wayward. Later tradition is in debt to him on several points but was also to find him in danger of heresy on others. The early Fathers were uniquely creative, almost by definition: all Christian theology remained to be worked out. Even by the standard of his peers, however, Tertullian was remarkably innovative. He came up with the word 'Trinity' (*Trinitas*) and seems to have been the first person to have pressed the words *substantia* (substance) and *persona* (person) into the service of theology. These are the words on which much of the later controversies about the union of humanity and divinity in Christ would hinge.[3]

Reading Tertullian can feel like time travel, as if we have somehow jumped ahead in theological history. In the same work, he turns to Christology and writes that there is to Christ 'a double quality, not confused but combined [. . .] one person, God and human being' (§27), anticipating the language and even the argument of Leo (*c.* AD 400–61) and the Council of Chalcedon (AD 451).

Tertullian's polemic against philosophy can be so severe as to sound anti-intellectual and appear to make him the first of the fideists: those who see faith as operating independent of reason.[4] He writes, 'there is nothing in heathen writers which a Christian approves'.[5] However, this is not the whole picture. As we have already seen, Tertullian coined so much of our most significant theological language. This makes him a profound philosopher himself: thinking carefully about how to say what one wants to say

---

2 *Against Heresies* 7.
3 *Against Praxeas* 2.
4 See Anthony Meredith, *Christian Philosophy in the Early Church*, T&T Clark, 2012, p. 59.
5 *The Soul's Testimony* 1.4, quoted by Yoram Hazony, *The Philosophy of Hebrew Scripture*, CUP, 2012, p. 223.

is the philosophical task. For all his vitriol against Greek thought, he could on occasion show considerable respect for pagan thinkers, especially the Stoics. At one point, for instance, he referred to Seneca as 'Our Seneca'.[6]

Turning back to Justin Martyr, he sought ways to explain Christianity to an often hostile pagan audience by looking for parallels between Christianity and Greek philosophy. In doing so he and other Apologists left us many important formulations and insights. His method itself often sets an excellent example for Christian theologians in later centuries who wish to engage with the culture and thought of their age. Justin found creative ways to express the faith, which a pagan might find sympathetic or eye-catching. This did not, however, make Justin a syncretist. Part of his programme was to show how the Christian revelation was superior to both pagan myths and pagan philosophy.

Equally, Justin was unafraid to point out where the philosophers had got it wrong. His generous statement that the best of the pagan philosophers were 'Christians before Christ'[7] belongs alongside his claim that they only knew anything of the truth because of Christ, such that whatever is true in their works 'belongs to us as Christians'.[8] His method was to employ the familiar motif of the *Logos* and, more particularly, their sense of the *Logos Spermatikos*: the seed-like word.[9] God has sown his word in the world like a sort of seed. This allows the truth to be known; indeed, it is the only way in which truth can be known. Justin then links this use of *Logos* with that in John's Gospel: the truth that can, and had, been known in fragments hitherto has now arrived in all its fullness, incarnate in Christ. To this day, this remains a forceful approach in Christian interaction with intellectual systems of all sorts.

---

6 *On the Soul* 20. Quoted by Meredith, *Philosophy*, p. 60.
7 *First Apology* 46.
8 *Second Apology* 13.
9 *Second Apology* 8.13.

The Early Alexandrian Fathers

The early Apologists were largely from the Near East (although Tertullian was from Carthage, on the coast of North Africa). A generation later, Christian thought flowered particularly in northern Egypt, especially in Alexandria. It flourished there, in part, because philosophical thinking in general flourished there. In the history of Alexandria, we have a microcosm of the varying fortune of philosophy in Christian circles. We will consider the Neoplatonists in detail below: Alexandria was their epicentre, and the home of some of their most significant teachers and schools. People with Neoplatonist sympathies turned to Christianity, because they found in it a fulfilment of their instincts, mystical as well as intellectual. A Christian school grew up, nurtured in part by the traditions these converts brought with them. Finally, when Christians had grown confident – arrogant, even – they burned the Library of Alexandria to the ground, and destroyed the greatest collection of ancient philosophical manuscripts ever assembled.

Before that cataclysm came a period of learning. We have already read Clement of Alexandria ask 'what is Plato, but Moses speaking in Attic Greek?',[10] and it was Plato in particular who fascinated and inspired the Christian thinkers of Alexandria. Among them, Clement was a forceful advocate of Christianity as 'true philosophy'. We find a good introduction is his thought in *Exhortation to the Greeks*. He was an attractive writer; other texts to explore include his *Stromata* or 'Miscellanies', and *Paedagogus* or 'The Instructor'.

The same mixture of celebration and judgement is to be found in the Alexandrian writers as in the Apologists. Plato is quoted frequently, as are other philosophers. There is a humane willingness to acknowledge truth wherever it is to be found, along with a resolute sense that the fullness of truth is found only in Christ. The greatness of ancient thought is seen precisely as a preparation for Christ, and without Christ it has enormous deficiencies. Origen,

---

10 *Stromata* I, 22.

for instance, wrote that the best of the Platonic tradition might take you to the Father and the Son, but that only Christians know of the Spirit.[11] Origen worked in the best tradition of the *Logos Spermatikos*: that the Word underlays the intelligibility of all that is true. With such an idea, Christian thinking can be both confident and generous, and indeed generous precisely because it is confident. There is nothing measly here, nothing of Christians putting the truth in protective cases because it is fragile. All truth, they are saying, is God's truth, so we should seek to apprehend it wherever it might be apprehended. This is the strength of this *Logos*-centred approach. Its weakness is a danger of abstraction. The 'Son' here is the *eternal* Word. The philosophers are credited with having lighted upon intimations of the Word ever in the bosom of the Father (John 1.18). However, as John also writes (John 1.3), that Word 'was in the world'. Of this, those philosophers only knew of his likeness in created things, not of his incarnation. Augustine made exactly this point 180 years after Origen's statement about the Holy Spirit: from the Platonists we might know that the Word eternally proceeds from the Father, but no philosopher could ever imagine that the Word would be made flesh.[12]

We might ask why Plato's star rose so far above Aristotle's in the early Church. It seems likely that Aristotle came to enjoy a bad reputation among mainstream Christian thinkers because his logic had been deployed by heretics such as Arius. Aristotle did not, however, come off as poorly as this might suggest. Some significant elements of his thought were synthesized within the larger matrix of Neoplatonism and Middle Platonism, its precursor, so he continued to have an influence, even if his name was rarely mentioned.

The early Fathers accepted that the pagan quest for truth, and a life well lived, was a noble one. Conversion did not mean giving up on the quest for truth and goodness. In turning to Christ, the pagan would advance in this journey. There was also much that one must reject in conversion and part of this will be turning one's

---

11 *De Principiis* I.11

12 *Confessions* VII.9.14. It may be that Augustine exaggerates what he learned from the Platonists. He favours them because they rescued him from Manicheanism.

back on erroneous ideas. They are rejected, however, precisely for being false. Meredith has called this the quest to break the Greek inheritance in half. There is a religious dimension, which was to be rejected, and there is a philosophical dimension, which was generally more clearly on the right track, even if it also needed careful emendation in the light of the Christian faith. We can see the significance of this move in the reaction it provoked among perceptive pagans. One of the earliest works of anti-Christian polemic about which we know much is *The True Account* by Celsus (although only by piecing it together from Origen's rebuttal, *Contra Celsum*). In Meredith's words: 'It rejected the attempt made by Justin and others of the Apologists to break up Hellenism into two separate elements: philosophy and religion, and then claim the first member for the gospel.'[13] Celsus could see that Christian success on that front posed great danger for paganism. At the other end of the pagan counterblast to Christianity, at paganism's last gasp, we find the Emperor Julian the Apostate. In Julian's decision to ban Christians from all positions of education we find the same dynamic at work as with Celsus: it would not do to claim, as Christian intellectuals did, that they were true teachers and true philosophers, because for Julian the only way to be wise was to be pagan in a thoroughly religious way.[14]

A Hellenistic Takeover?

Our survey has reached the period of the great councils of the Church, and the development of the creeds. We have already encountered the claim that these discussions amounted to the corruption of Christian thought by Greek philosophy. The principal target for criticism is the way in which the two pillars of Christian doctrine were being worked out: Christology and the doctrine of the Trinity. In the UK, for instance, Maurice Wiles (1923–2005) claimed that the classic formulations of belief about God and Christ were far from definitive. Indeed, he considered

13 Meredith, *Philosophy*, p. 71.
14 Meredith, *Philosophy*, p. 150.

them to be hardly intelligible today. Just as the light of historical criticism of the Bible had not hurt our eyes, he contended in his inaugural lecture at the University of London, so now we need to shine just such a light on Christian doctrine.[15] He put this idea to work most famously in his contribution to the collection *The Myth of God Incarnate* (edited by John Hick), where he argued that belief in the divinity of Christ is relatively insignificant as far as Christian foundations go.[16] Wiles was the chair of the Church of England's Doctrine Commission when it produced its report *Christian Believing* in 1976. This is widely considered to be the low point among Church of England reports: the assorted theologians seemed unable to agree on what theology even looks like, never mind what it might say. Had the report carried the field, it is unlikely that we would be reciting the creed today (although if that position had prevailed, there may not be people in our churches today to not recite it).

In relation to these accusations, it is worth turning to some specific points in the early history of the development of doctrine to see whether they really do represent the capitulation of theology to philosophy. A first cluster of examples comes from Christology and Trinitarian theology, and the crucial word *hypostasis*. The Council of Chalcedon defined Christ as one person in two natures. The word for person is *hypostasis*. Similarly, to confess God as Trinity is to say that God is three Persons (*hypostasis* again) in one being (*ousia*). Neither formulation appears in the New Testament, nor is the word *hypostasis* important there. A standard criticism is, therefore, that Christian ideas were damaged by subordination to non-Christian ideas. Wiles would add that if *hypostasis* is only a Greek imposition then it is of no necessary significance in our own time.

The word is not important in the New Testament, but it is used in one important Christological statement, in Hebrews 1.3: Christ is

15 Malcolm Yarnell, *The Formation of Christian Doctrine*, Nashville: Broadman and Holman, 2007, p. 45. See Maurice Wiles, *The Making of Christian Doctrine: A Study in the Principles of Early Doctrinal Development*, CUP, 1967.

16 Maurice Wiles, 'Christianity Without Incarnation?', in *The Myth of God Incarnate*, ed. John Hick, SCM Press, 1977, pp. 1–11.

the 'exact imprint' (*charaktēr*) of 'God's very being' (*hypostaseōs*). The word is used here to mean 'substance': *hypostaseōs* is what the Father and the Son have in common. This lines up with standard Aristotelian and Neoplatonic usage, where *hypostasis* is the reality of something, in contrast with what is merely apparent or illusory. This usage persisted in the earlier early Church. In other words, *hypostasis* was not distinguished from being (*ousia*).[17]

Debates over the person and nature of Christ prompted ever deeper consideration of how to express what the Bible said about Christ. By the middle of the fourth century, *hypostasis* began to be contrasted with *ousia* or being. In the process of speaking about the person of Christ and the Trinity, it was necessary to tease out the relation between 'individual reality' and something more generic: between persons and natures. *Hypostasis* came to refer to the 'person' side of that distinction.[18]

The contention that Greek philosophy bent Christian theology out of shape does not make much sense here, not when Christian theology can redefine terms from 'Greek philosophy' through 180 degrees. Having mentioned *ousia*, or being, we can remain with that word for another example. This term has a rich philosophical heritage, as rich as any concept can have. The standard treatment comes from Aristotle, in the *Categories* I.5, where he distinguishes between the 'primary' sense of *ousia*, which refers to the being of individual things ('for instance, the individual man or human being'), and a 'secondary' usage, which applies to overarching categories ('things [. . .] called substances within which [. . .] the primary substances are included', such as the species 'human' or 'horse'). As Meredith points out, it is clear that neither of Aristotle's two senses of *ousia* apply exactly to God: not in the first sense, in that Father,

---

17 'Hypostasis', in *Oxford Dictionary of the Christian Church*, ed. F. L. Cross and E. A. Livingston, OUP, 2005, pp. 817–18.

18 This led to some awkward misunderstandings between theologians. It seemed to some Latin speakers that *hypostasis* ought to be translated by *substantia*. (In terms of etymology, they are directly comparable.) That works for the earlier meaning but not for the later one. Not grasping this, some Westerners feared that the One God in three *hypostases* of later Greek theology spelt tri-theism (three divine beings), when in fact it spelt three divine Persons.

Son and Spirit are not three aspects of one individual, and not in the second sense, because we are not talking about three gods.[19] Again, Trinitarian theology took the best term it had for what it wanted to say but did new things with it, as the biblical witness required. Christian theologians wished to stress the unity of God in such a way as to say that God is *one* substance in no other way than *as three*. As with *hypostasis*, Christian theology bent existing philosophical definitions of a word into new shapes, not vice versa.

As a final example, consider the doctrine of creation, and particularly the idea that everything in the world was created *out of nothing* (or *ex nihilo*). Far from being a capitulation to Greek philosophy, this rides in the face of everything and anything that the philosophers had ever thought. Christians denied that the universe was formed out of pre-existing matter (as we find in Plato), that the world emanates out of God's own substance (as in Neoplatonism), or that God and the universe stand alongside each other eternally (as in Aristotle).[20] Aristotle stressed what Parmenides had said earlier, that 'from nothing, nothing comes'.[21] The only counter-example would be that accidents come to be in a substance, or that substantial forms come to be in matter. That matter and form should come out of nothing is precisely what all Greek philosophers, however much they disagreed on other points, collectively opposed.

Creation out of nothing is strongly biblical, but we do not find an extended, abstract discussion of the idea in any one place in the Bible. The most explicit statement comes first in the apocryphal, or 'deutero-canonical', book of 2 Maccabees,[22] and later in Romans 4.17, where Paul writes about God 'who gives life to the dead and calls into existence the things that do not exist'. More than that, the doctrine synthesizes a variety of ideas, expressed here and there throughout the Bible: that God created 'all things'

---

19 Meredith, *Philosophy*, p. 96.

20 This story is covered well by Claude Tresmontant in *The Origins of Christian Philosophy*, New York: Hawthorn Books, 1963, trans. Mark Pontifex.

21 Parmenides, *On Nature*. Aristotle, *Physics* 191b. Lucretius in *De Rerum Natura*, book 1.

22 2 Macc. 7.28.

(for instance, John 1.3; Col. 1.16; Rev. 4.11), for example, coupled with the recognition that this involves matter, that nothing is co-eternal with God (for instance, Isa. 43.10; Ps. 90.2; Col. 1.17) and that God is sovereign (for instance, Isa. 46.10; Jer. 32.17; 1 Tim. 6.15). The task of doctrine was to join this together; the result was the doctrine of creation out of nothing. In the words of Rowan Williams:

> Since there is at the heart of this [biblical] speech a conviction that God is that on which every particular depends, the one who creates from nothing, the logic of our discourse about God's action must observe the constraints imposed by the implicit prohibition against describing God as an agent among others. And I hope this can be said without inviting the lazy response that this is an imposition of alien metaphysics on the personalist idiom of the Bible.[23]

Previous examples showed Christian theology bending philosophical ideas into new shapes; with creation it did little less than melt them down and cast them anew.[24] The early Church demonstrates what Aquinas later expressed in an evocative metaphor: 'those who use philosophical doctrines in sacred doctrine in such a way as to subject them to the service of faith, do not mix water with wine, but change water into wine'.[25]

Reading On

English translations of the works of the Church Fathers can be found in three comprehensive series. Two are ongoing: *The*

---

23 'Redeeming Sorrows', in *Wrestling with Angels*, ed. Mike Higton, SCM Press, 2007, pp. 255–74, p. 270.

24 For a terrific survey of this story, see two essays in the definitive treatment of the subject: Ernan McMullin, 'Creation Ex Nihilo: Early History' and Janet Martin Soskice, 'Creatio Ex Nihilo: Its Jewish and Christian Foundations', in *Creation and the God of Abraham*, ed. David B. Burrell, Carlo Cogliati, Janet Martin Soskice and William R. Stoeger, CUP, 2010, pp. 11–23 and 24–39 respectively.

25 *Exposition of the 'On the Trinity' of Boethius* 2.3 *ad* 5, trans. Rose E. Brennan, St Louis: Herder, 1946, correcting 'Scripture' to 'doctrine'.

Fathers of the Church (CUA) and *Ancient Christian Writings* (Paulist Press). A third, earlier series comes in three parts from T&T Clark: *Ante-Nicene Fathers* (1867–73) and *Nicene and Post-Nicene Fathers* in two sets (1886–1900). The T&T Clark collection is freely available online and can be bought in reprint editions quite cheaply. The English is antiquated, and the sources from which it was translated necessarily lag behind the best contemporary textual criticism. It is ideal for quick reference, but for serious study, more modern editions should also be consulted.

The Routledge *Early Church Fathers* series combines accessible introductions to various Fathers with a selection of texts in translation. Particularly relevant for this chapter are Robert Grant on Irenaeus, Geoffrey Dunn on Tertullian and Joseph Trigg on Origen. Mark Edwards takes a critical view of Origen as an uncritical Platonist in *Origen against Plato* (Aldershot: Ashgate, 2002). A cheap translation of the Apostolic Fathers comes from Penguin, translated by Maxwell Staniforth as *Early Christian Writings* (Penguin, 1987). Hans Urs von Balthasar collected a useful anthology of Irenaeus entitled *The Scandal of the Incarnation: Irenaeus Against the Heresies* (Ignatius, 1990).

On philosophy and the early Church, three volumes can be recommended: Anthony Meredith's *Christian Philosophy in the Early Church* (T&T Clark, 2012), Christopher Stead's *Philosophy in Christian Antiquity* (CUP, 1994) and Robert Louis Wilken's *The Spirit of Early Christian Thought: Seeking the Face of God* (New Haven: Yale University Press, 2003).

6

Neoplatonism and the Later Fathers

We have discussed Plato and Aristotle and seen that they are more theological than we might have been led to expect. Pagan Greek philosophy, religious from the start, became *even more religious* before it was eclipsed by Christian theology. It is in this form that it makes its largest contribution to the Christian tradition of thought and spirituality, in Neoplatonism.

The Neoplatonists called themselves simply 'Platonists'. The term 'Neoplatonists' was applied only later and represents a judgement that seeks to distinguish them from a reputedly more authentic 'Platonism', perhaps because they are so religious, mystical and magical. Such an interpretation will be favoured by those who play down the religious and theological dimension in Plato himself. Even within Neoplatonism, these judgements are reflected in the sense that there are 'orthodox' Neoplatonists (perhaps Plotinus and Porphyry[1]) and others (such as Iamblicus and Proclus), who deviate because they are more liturgical or magical. When Plotinus was invited to worship in a temple he replied, 'It is they that should come to me not I to them.'[2]

Neoplatonism is said to begin with Plotinus, at least for those who want a corpus of writings at the origin, or with this teacher Ammonius Saccus, who left no texts. They follow an earlier period, between the immediate legacy of Plato and the Neoplatonists, which is often called Middle Platonism. This influenced Philo, and

---

1 Porphyry is sometimes seen as less orthodox, and more liturgical.

2 Recounted by Anthony Meredith in *Christian Philosophy in the Early Church*, T&T Clark, 2012, p. 37, from Porphyry's *Life of Plotinus* 10, trans. A. H. Armstrong, Cambridge: Loeb, 1969.

in as much as Platonism influenced the New Testament, it was Middle Platonism. As scholars continue work on the interaction of Platonism and Christianity during this period, Middle Platonism is likely to rise in prominence. John Rist has pointed out that much of what is attributed to Plotinus is actually already there in Middle Platonism. Christian writers such as the Cappadocians (the two Gregories and Basil) did not read Plotinus until late and did not find a great deal that could not already have been found in Middle Platonism.

The religious sensibilities of pagan antiquity bear study by anyone interested in the background to the New Testament and early Christianity. We find a tapestry that is by turns vigorous, attractive and repulsive, reflecting the religiosity, aspirations and disillusionments of a culture on the cusp between the order of antiquity and the fragmentation of late antiquity. This period presents a rich diversity of religious movements, with adherents each in his or her own way seeking immortality and personal salvation, and even a 'relationship' to a god, as a saviour and lord.[3]

One of the principle religious–philosophical movements in the first centuries was Gnosticism, which in incipient form was a backdrop for some of the Epistles. Our understanding of such groups advanced considerably in the twentieth century with the discovery of the Nag Hammadi texts, which come from a late Gnostic sect that originally probably had Christian roots. Gnosticism represents a heady mix, drawing on Christian, Platonic and probably proto-Buddhist sources. Pre-New Testament Judaism contained some fairly Gnostic groups, which formed another nursery for this movement.

Neoplatonic Ideas

Taken as a whole, the Neoplatonists are important for stressing a number of ideas which either chimed with Christianity fairly unambiguously, or which could be adapted by Christian thinkers relatively easily. In the first category, we have the description of evil

3 Colin Brown, *Christianity and Western Thought*, volume I, Downers Grove: InterVarsity Press, 1990, pp. 79ff.

as privation, which is to say as lack or failure. As an angle on this, notice that evil can only ever be described in terms of a failed particular good; it has no positive and distinctive essence of its own, common to every instance of evil. To take some mild examples, a fountain pen that will not write is a failed fountain pen, but a carrot that will not write is not a failed carrot. A fountain pen need not be good to eat; a carrot should be. The nature of any particular evil is relative to the nature of the particular good that it fails to be.

As another aspect of the privation approach, consider that a good fountain pen and a good carrot veritably sparkle in their goodness, whereas no one savours a bad carrot, nor pays particular attention to the failed pen. Evil has a certain greyness and pallor of disappointment. A reporter once challenged the devoutly Christian French composer Olivier Messiaen over his opera *Saint Francis of Assisi*: 'There is disappointingly little sin in your work, Monsieur Messiaen.' The composer replied, 'Sin isn't interesting; dirt isn't interesting. I prefer flowers. I left out sin.'[4]

On a related theme, Messiaen's contemporary and compatriot Simon Weil pointed out that works of imagination are inclined to romanticize evil and render goodness dull, whereas the opposite is true in real life:

Imaginary evil is romantic and varied; real evil is gloomy, monotonous, barren, boring. Imaginary good is boring; real good is always new, marvellous, intoxicating. Therefore 'imaginative literature' [except for the very best] is either boring or immoral (or a mixture of both).[5]

Seeing evil as privation also underlines that evil has a certain senselessness to it, either in the realm of natural evils, where we are led to ask God 'but why?', or with human evils, where an investigation will always suggest a moment when someone made a *wrong* choice: of a lesser good over a great good, or of an evil mistaken for a good, or simply an act of abject perversity. This

---

4 'Sin isn't interesting. I prefer flowers', *The Guardian*, 29 August 2008.
5 *Gravity and Grace*, Routledge, 2002, pp. 62–3.

picks up a theme put forward by Socrates: evil is always a mistake. In telling the story about any particular human sin, it may be that we can have some sense of why someone made a particular mistake, perhaps in terms of an evil they themselves suffered, for instance with an abusive person who was himself treated that way in the past. That is another element of evil as privation: acting in an attenuated way follows, in these cases, from having suffered a wrong that has left this person himself somehow attenuated.

C. S. Lewis explored the senselessness of evil cleverly in *The Screwtape Letters*, from the other side, so to speak. Since evil is failure, from the perspective of evil, *good* becomes incomprehensible. Lewis has Screwtape, a demon and therefore the epitome of failed being, write with complete bemusement about what is solid, good and characterful in human life. Concerning the joyful laughter that proceeds naturally from a loving human community, Screwtape writes that 'what the real cause is we do not know', just as the joyful element in music is 'quite opaque to us'.[6]

Casting evil as privation does not deny that evil things happen. By it we are simply saying that the problem with evil is the terribly real failure of something to be properly real: to live up to the reality that is proper to it. If I lose a limb in an accident, I have really lost a limb, but the nature of the evil I have suffered is one of loss. People really can be wicked; their wickedness is characterized by a failure to live up to the moral dignity of being a human being.

The understanding of evil as privation was expounded particularly forcibly by Augustine. The idea delivered him from Manichean dualism, which placed an evil power over and against the good, as both equally real. Pseudo-Dionysius and Aquinas have also been forceful exponents. In recent decades, Herbert McCabe and Terry Eagleton have been important writers.[7]

The characteristic view of the Neoplatonists towards the world was as an emanation or overflow from God. Concerning the value of the world itself, Neoplatonists had a mixed perspective. They

---

6 C. S. Lewis, *The Screwtape Letters*, Letter 11, London: Fontana, 1955.

7 For instance, 'Evil' in *God Matters*, Continuum, 2002 and *On Evil*, New Haven: Yale University Press, 2011 respectively.

tended to treat matter, in particular, as being a long way from the divine source, and therefore as fundamentally quite base. For the Neoplatonists, being proceeds from what he called 'the One', like lava from a volcano. Materiality is a long way from the volcano, where the fire has gone out of the rock. Plotinus, for instance, talked of his shame at being in the body. All the same, even the most otherworldly of the Neoplatonists attacked the world-hating Gnostics. Some Neoplatonists, such as Proclus, went further, recognizing a certain similarity between the highest (the One) and the lowest (materiality): materiality is common to all material things and therefore exhibits a certain sort of simplicity, like the One. This idea of divine simplicity was treated with great sympathy by Christians. It proposes that God is not composed of various facets, as if the divine attributes, for instance, just happened to hang together. In God, rather, everything somehow overlaps: his justice is his mercy, his existence is his essence, and so on.

Finally, the Neoplatonists put a useful emphasis on the *transcendentals*, a set of characteristics grouped together. The list differs from author to author, but they include some or all of the following: being, goodness, truth, beauty and unity. They are called transcendentals because they do not fit in only one of Aristotle's 'categories' of accidents (see p. 44) but 'transcend' them: there can be a good relation, a good position or a good quantity, for instance. The transcendentals are a particularly effective way into divine simplicity. Even as we know them in this word we obtain an intimation of simplicity since the transcendentals are 'convertible': by which we mean that goodness is true, beauty is good, being is good, goodness is beautiful, and so on.

Neoplatonic Figures

We have already encountered one important precursor to the Neoplatonists, the Middle Platonist Celsus, the target of Origen's *Contra Celsum*. His attack on Christianity, *Alethes Logos* (the true *Logos* or doctrine), was written around AD 150. It has not survived but can be pieced together from Origen's line-by-line response of around AD 250. Celsus was not out to attack anything and everything that was not Middle Platonism. He was a synthesizer who respected many different traditions (on the grounds that they more or less agreed with him). In this, he deployed a motif familiar to us from the Fathers: he sought for what in any tradition witnessed to the *Logos*, which is the basis for *any* truth. All the same, Celsus recognized emerging Christianity as a threat, no doubt because he could see ways in which it provided a compelling vision for anyone with Platonic sensibilities.

The pivotal source of Neoplatonism proper was Ammonius 'Saccas'. His 'surname' comes from his humble occupation as sack-bearer at the docks of Alexandria. The date of his birth is unknown, but was probably around AD 160; he died around AD 242. Ammonius did not leave any written works and his chief legacy is to have taught Plotinus. The Christian historian Eusebius claims that Ammonius taught Origen. He was mentioned by Christian figures (who claim him right through to his death) and pagans (who say that he renounced Christianity). He stressed the fundamental unity of Plato and Aristotle's thought, mainly by means of a thoroughgoing Platonization of Aristotle.

His pupil Plotinus (*c.* AD 205–70) was an Egyptian and is usually considered to be the most significant Neoplatonist. He studied Persian and Indian philosophy and almost managed to visit those countries by attaching himself to a military expedition, although it returned before it reached its destination. From those traditions he picked up the idea that the world emanates, or radiates, from the One, which is unknowable. Taken on its own, Christian theology has tended to consider this something of a disaster, since it simultaneously brackets God with creation and tends to render him transcendent in such a way as to be oblivious to the material universe. It also casts creation as something necessary. Combined, however, with creation out of nothing, and a corresponding sense that creation is God's freely chosen gift, the emanationist perspective provided tools for conceptualizing the relation of the world to God as one of *participation*. Moreover, the Neoplatonists combined this outward dynamic with one of return, sometimes paired as the Latin terms *exitus* (coming out, as in *exodus*) and *reditus* (return). The overall structure of Aquinas's magnum opus, the *Summa Theologiae*, is structured this way.

For God actively to have made the world would be supremely undignified, according to Plotinus. We cannot attribute any activity to the One because that would imply duality, for instance between knower and known. On that basis, the emanation of creation must be unwilled.[8] As Meredith notes, Plotinus explicitly rejected an 'artisan' account of creation. 'Making' and 'moving' are signs of 'some failure in quality'; in contrast, the posture of those 'whose nature is all blessedness have no more to do than to repose in themselves and be their being'.[9] Against this, Christians and Jews advanced a view in which God is involved with creation, like a worker or artist. Again, this shows the willingness of Christian (and Jewish) thinkers to reject prevailing philosophy when necessary. This has political and economic freight. Plotinus's One is pavilioned in the indolent repose of an aristocrat who has forgotten *noblesse oblige*; the Christian God is willing to roll up his sleeves: first, metaphorically, in creation and then, in full-blooded reality, in the carpenter from Nazareth.

From Plotinus's 'One' followed various 'hypostases'. The three highest entities for Plotinus were the One, then Mind and Soul: the number three haunts the mystical–philosophical mind. Mind represents the beginning of a 'fall' into multiplicity for Plotinus, with 'Soul' even more multiple, since it begins to relate to material things.

Plotinus sometimes advanced the idea of a single soul which is in all rational creatures. This would become important for a certain Arabic Neoplatonism which was far more radically Neoplatonic than Christianity ever was. The status of the Qur'an in Islam led to the equation of theology with Qur'anic interpretation, such that philosophy became very separate as a result. The parallels with what happened to philosophy and theology in the Christian West after the rise of Protestantism are salutary: only after biblical inspiration and interpretation came to be seen in ways more

---

8 *Enneads* 6.8.8.
9 *Enneads* 3.2.1, cited by Meredith, *Philosophy*, p. 81.

closely paralleling that of the Qur'an in Islam did Western philosophy explode in massively heterodox speculation.

Porphyry (c. AD 233–309) was a student of Plotinus. He edited Plotinus's works into the form in which they survive: the six *Enneads*. This was no mean feat, as Plotinus had terrible handwriting. Porphyry also wrote a biography of his master and of Pythagoras, as well as commentaries on Plato, Aristotle and Ptolemy. One work, in particular, the *Isagoge* (Greek for 'introduction'), became the textbook for teaching logic for Christians for a thousand years. Porphyry was a fierce critic of Christianity, not least because Christians worshipped Christ 'instead of God'. His book *Adversos Christianos* now exists only in fragments.

Iamblicus (c. AD 245–c. 325) was a Syrian and a devotee of Pythagorean thought alongside Platonism. To Plotinus he added an important note of the descent of the divine into the world and therefore a stronger sense of mediation. All Neoplatonism tended to see the universe as a hierarchy of beings. Iamblicus had a particularly lively sense of this, and his philosophy is full of intermediary figures: gods, demigods, angels, demons. In his book *On the Mysteries of Egypt* he interpreted this in terms of *theurgy*: calling upon these mediators to descend into the human and material realm. In this, he treats physicality differently from Plotinus. Iamblicus sensed that the material world can be the arena for encountering the spiritual, which rendered him one of the most appealing Neoplatonists for Christian theologians: matter too can be the dwelling place of God, or the gods. All the same, theurgy upset Christian writers. Thinkers such as Iamblicus wanted to extend such practices to the populace at large. That made these rites all the more a target for Christian scorn (Augustine attacked theurgy at length in *The City of God*) since it could look not dissimilar to the Eucharist.

Our final pagan is Proclus (AD 412–85). He stands somewhat on a limb in terms of the Neoplatonic succession of teachers. Like Plotinus he travelled and was inducted into many mystery religions. Like Iamblicus, he presented a complex system of emanation from the One, and like Iamblicus he was important for Christians for his valuation of materiality, recognizing the simplicity in matter that mirrors the simplicity of God. Much of his work took the form of commentaries on Plato but his most significant book is his *Elements of Theology*. This almost mathematical theology was later abridged as the *Book of Causes*. That work, in turn, was then misattributed in the Arabic world to Aristotle, and later still translated into Latin bearing Aristotle's authority. It seems to have been Thomas Aquinas who recognized the true lineage. The *Book of Causes*, perhaps approached through Aquinas's commentary, is one of the most intoxicating of philosophical texts.

Boethius

In the period of the later Fathers, the Roman Empire was crumbling. We find several tendencies at play. For some, the sense is of a coming drought. Boethius, for instance, looked back to the giants of both Roman and especially Greek philosophy and in translating the Greeks into Latin has the look of someone putting out buckets to catch the last of the rain before a storm passes over. In Pseudo-Dionysius, in contrast, we have less of a sense of looking backwards. For him, the message is that today is a great time to be alive and to think. The image is of someone diving in and out of a pool, whooping and rejoicing. Then there are those, like John of Damascus, and his monastic tradition, whose approach is to see water as for watering gardens, and getting on with that.

Boethius (Anicius Manlius Severinus Boethius, *c.* AD 480–524) is one of the oddest figures in the history of Christian philosophy. He is crucial for having translated some of the works of Aristotle into Latin, ensuring that they retained currency in the West. He hoped to translate all of Aristotle and all of Plato. In this he failed. He also translated the *Isagoge* of Porphyry. His project was curtailed when he got on the wrong side of his employer, the Arian king of the Ostrogoths, Theodoric, and was executed.

In terms of his own original writing, Boethius is important for a number of short theological works, but his last work, *The Consolation of Philosophy*, written in prison, sees philosophy standing on its own feet, without reference to theology. The text is not atheistic: God features. It simply makes no reference to the Scriptures. Some commentators suggest that Boethius had ceased to be a Christian, but others dispute this interpretation.

From Boethius we get some definitions that have echoed down the centuries. Eternity, for instance, is 'the whole, simultaneous and perfect possession of unbounded life'.[10] More technically, a nature is 'the specific *differentia* [differentiating factor] which informs a thing',[11] and a person is 'an individual substance of a nature endowed with reason'.[12]

Maximus the Confessor

Maximus the Confessor represents the sane but enthusiastic integration of Neoplatonism with the Christian tradition, not least in terms of the connection of things in the world with each other and with God. Maximus calls each thing's form (in Aristotle's sense) its *logos*. Each of these *logoi* (the plural of *logos*) is some reflection of the divine *Logos*, the many *logoi* reflect aspects of the one pre-existent *Logos*.

As with other writers, Maximus is as interesting for how he wrote as for what he wrote. Two works take the form of an examination of difficult passages in previous works. The *Ambigua* and *Scholia* take the most difficult passages from the writings of Gregory of Nazianzus (and, to a lesser extent, Pseudo-Dionysius). Maximus thought that more is to be gained by examining what is difficult than what is easy. Here we see the dawn of something like the scholastic method of always facing the objections in the face (although there are precedents, for instance in classical discussions of difficulties in Homer). This is in keeping with Platonic dialectic, where discussion of the difficulties in one another's position helps us to advance together towards the truth. Maximus exemplifies the Christian faith as unafraid of criticism. It has been criticized to an extraordinary degree, and strengthened in the

---

10 *Consolation of Philosophy* V.6.
11 *Against Eutyches and Nestorius* §1.
12 *Against Eutyches and Nestorius* §3.

process. This criticism, for the main, has been constructive and comes from within.

In the later Byzantine Empire, philosophical education carried on as in the West. In fact, it carried on with greater continuity: a wider range of Greek texts from the ancient world were kept in play. Education served to train officials for the state and the Church. We do not find the creative or 'speculative' interest as in the West, a feature that has marked the Eastern Church down the ages.

These were literary cultures and in both the East and the West we find a strong emphasis on teaching rhetoric and logic. The tradition of formulating answers to assorted questions, found in Maximus, flourished again between 1040 and 1070, for instance with John Italos (c. 1025 to after 1082). Another chief output was the writing of commentaries, with the high preponderance on Aristotle. These were not by any means always original. A scholar would reproduce what he considered to be the best of what had gone before and add new comments, without necessarily giving attributions.

Controversy was not unknown. Some of the most able philosophers were put on trial, for heterodoxy in the case of Michael Psellos (1018 to after 1081) or for subordinating theology to philosophy in the case of John Italos (c. 1025 to after 1082). Italos was condemned for rationalism: laying out doctrines that were held to be 'mysteries' in ruthlessly philosophical terms. Italos is still condemned yearly by Orthodox Christians, in a proclamation (the *Synodikon*) made on the First Sunday of Lent. Another philosopher, George Gemistos Plethon, gave up Christianity to become a thoroughgoing Neoplatonist, advocating pagan worship.

Pseudo-Dionysius

A body of literature comes to us from antiquity bearing the name of 'Dionysius'. Claim is clearly being made that this author is none other than the Dionysius converted by Paul in Athens (Acts 17.34). However, the author and the New Testament figure are clearly different people. To make the matter worse, the supposed first-century author was also confused with an early missionary to France, of the same name, who was made a patron saint of Paris. The association between the author and the Dionysius of the New Testament was only broken in the fifteenth century. The real author of this literature (called 'Pseudo-Dionysius' today) seems likely to have lived in the late fifth or early sixth century, probably in Syria. The date is settled by the obvious influence of Proclus, who is often quoted directly, although without acknowledgement. By contemporary standards this is a horrible mess: plagiarism and passing oneself off as someone else. At the time, this was common practice.

We could hardly exaggerate the influence of Pseudo-Dionysius on later Christian thinking and spirituality. He is the 'Denis' mentioned throughout *The Cloud of Unknowing*, for instance, and was a principal wellspring for a flowering of mysticism that stretches through the Rhineland tradition to John of the Cross. Maximus the Confessor took Pseudo-Dionysius up enthusiastically and Pseudo-Dionysius is one of the authors most often cited by Aquinas. He is more of an influence on the structure of Aquinas's thought than even the numerous references would suggest.

The works of Pseudo-Dionysius comprise *On the Divine Names*, *Mystical Theology*, *On the Celestial Hierarchy* (which is as important as any book ever written for influencing thought about angels), *On the Ecclesiastical Hierarchy* (which influenced some interesting later political thought, especially Nicholas of Cusa in *The Catholic Concordance*) and ten letters. The works that have survived refer to two others that have been lost, *Theological Representations* and *Symbolic Theology*.[13]

The best place to start is *On the Divine Names*, which is a riot of a book: a philosophical, mystical and theological maelstrom which presents God as revealed in a great many names and as being beyond them all: God is good, for instance, but also beyond-good, or exceeding-good. These represent two of Pseudo-Dionysius's

---

13 Kevin Corrigan and Michael Harrington, 'Pseudo-Dionysius the Areopagite', http://plato.stanford.edu/archives/fall2011/entries/pseudo-dionysius-areopagite/.

three ways to speak about God: affirmation and eminence. The other way is that of negation, to which we return below. The book is full of arresting ideas, such as a 'yearning' in God which can only be filled by God. For all he was a philosopher, Pseudo-Dionysius has as much place for the will and desire as for the intellect and knowledge. The author of the *Cloud* put this pithily: 'He [God] may well be loved, but not thought. By love may He be gotten and holden; but by thought never.'[14] This represents a profoundly affective aspect to Pseudo-Dionysius's thought: he seized upon desire as profoundly appropriate for the Christian. For all Pseudo-Dionysius is among the most philosophical of Christian writers, he also had a place for practice. He wrote that we do not only learn but also 'experience [*pathein*, literally, 'suffer' or 'undergo'] divine things'.[15] For one thing, he had an extraordinarily liturgical vision of Christian life. He presents us with an intoxicating vision of the liturgy in heaven, and even of the liturgy on earth.

Other of his works also consider the basis for the truth of religious language. The *Symbolic Theology* dealt with what we would call metaphor, with statements about God that communicate even though they are not literally true. A celebrated example comes from Psalm 78.65, where God is described as being like a warrior with a hangover (an implication of the Hebrew not stressed equally by every translation). Among many useful things that Pseudo-Dionysius points to here is that these outlandish metaphors are useful *in their outlandishness*: they hold before us the weakness of our language in talking about God, as well as some truth about him. *Theological Representations* has been lost but we know some of what it said from references in other works by Pseudo-Dionysius. He discussed the relationship between the names we use for God and the names we use for creatures in terms of the creature as an image of God. His argument is that when we use the same word of both, we can use a word of a creature because what it refers to was first true of God. He refers to 'father' and points to Ephesians, to God as the Father 'from whom every

---

14 Chapter 6, trans. Evelyn Underhill, London: John Watkins, 1922.
15 *Divine Names* II.9.

family in heaven and on earth takes its name' (Eph. 3.15). We can say 'father' of an animal because it copies something in God. This is the basis for a position that Aquinas was later to elaborate with great sophistication.

The Mystical Theology is the wellspring of 'negative theology'. Discussion of entering into darkness and silence, like Moses on the mountain, had a particularly profound influence on later thought. Gregory of Nyssa is the other principal exponent of this image in *The Life of Moses*. This approach to God teaches that we know more clearly in this life what God is not rather than what God is. We make progress along this path not only by means of the easy negations (God is not a warrior with a hangover after all) but also of the more difficult and daring ones (God is not 'good' according to our easy sense of goodness; God does not 'exist' according to our easy grasp of existence). This is a way to stress God's transcendence, which some find appealing and others find threatening.

Reading On

A translation of Plotinus's *Enneads*, made by Stephen Mac-Kenna, has been reprinted by several sources and is available online. Penguin published a version abridged by John Dillon (1991). The obvious anthology is *The Essential Plotinus*, translated by Elmer O'Brien (Hackett, 1975). The *Elements of Theology* by Proclus gives us Neoplatonism at its most theological. There is a modern translation by E. R. Dodds (Oxford: Clarendon Press, 1992) and an older (and cheaper) translation by Thomas Taylor (several editions). Taylor (1758–1835) so loved Greek thought that it is said that he and his wife spoke ancient Greek in their household. As the *Book of Causes*, this work received an extraordinary commentary by Aquinas (translated by Vincent A. Guagliardo and others, CUA, 1996). For a selection of Neoplatonic texts, see *Neoplatonic Philosophy: Introductory Readings*, edited and translated by John Dillon and Lloyd Gerson (Hackett, 2004) and Algis Uzdavinys, *The Golden Chain* (Bloomington: World Wisdom, 2004). Mark Edwards translated *Neoplatonic Saints: The Lives of Plotinus and Proclus by their Students* (Liverpool University Press, 2000).

Among secondary literature, consider R. T. Wallis, *Neoplatonism* (Bristol University Press, 1995), Lloyd Gerson, *Plotinus* (Routledge, 1998) and Radek Chlup, *Proclus: An Introduction* (CUP, 2012).

The theological works of Boethius in Latin with English translation from Loeb as *Theological Tractates and the Consolation of Philosophy* (trans. H. F. Stewart, E. K. Rand and S. J. Tester, Cambridge, 1918). It is available online. Good secondary literature includes John Marenbon's *Boethius* (OUP, 2003) and Philip Edward, *A Companion to Boethius in the Middle Ages* (Leiden: Brill, 2012).

For Maximus the Confessor, see *Selected Writings* in the *Classics of Western Spirituality* series, edited by George Berthold (Paulist Press, 1999), *Questions and Doubts*, translated by Despina Prassas (DeKalb: Northern Illinois University Press, 2009) and an excellent small volume *On the Cosmic Mystery of Jesus Christ*, translated by Paul Blowers and Robert Louis Wilken (Crestwood: St Vladimir's Seminary Press, 2003.) The secondary literature on Maximus is strong but relatively modest. It includes Lars Thunberg's *Microcosm and Mediator: Theological Anthropology of Maximus the Confessor* (Chicago: Open Court Publishing, 1995) and Torstein Tollefsen's *The Christocentric Cosmology of St Maximus the Confessor* (OUP, 2008). Melchisedec Törönen discusses the philosophical elements of his theology in *Union and Distinction in the Thought of St Maximus the Confessor* (OUP, 2007). For an all-round introduction to his thought, see Hans Urs von Balthasar, *Cosmic Liturgy: The Universe According to Maximus the Confessor* (Ignatius, 2003).

Niketas Siniossoglou recounts the story of the experiment in 'radical Platonism' in later Byzantine theology in *Radical Platonism in Byzantium: Illumination and Utopia in Gemistos Plethon* (CUP, 2011). The complete works of Pseudo-Dionysius have been translated by C. Luibheid as *Pseudo-Dionysius: The Complete Works* (Paulist Press, 1993). C. E. Rolt's translation of *The Divine Names* and *Mystical Theology* has a more old-fashioned grandeur, which suits these works (SPCK, 1920 and other editions). Good secondary literature includes Andrew Louth, *Denys the*

Areopagite (Continuum, 2002), Fran O'Rourke, *Pseudo-Dionysius and the Metaphysics of Aquinas* (Leiden: Brill, 1992) and P. Rorem, *Pseudo-Dionysius: A Commentary on the Texts and an Introduction to their Influence* (OUP, 1993). On the apophatic way, see Denys Turner, *The Darkness of God: Negativity in Christian Mysticism* (CUP, 1992).

7

The Early Mediaeval Period

We have arrived at the 'Middle Ages'. For those who came up with the phrase, this is a term of abuse. This is the period 'in the middle', strung between two ages that matter: classical antiquity and the Enlightenment. Needless to say, it was Enlightenment thinkers who coined the term (Hegel, for instance, in his *History of Philosophy*). For them, the Middle Ages were a lull, a period of sleep, not least in thought. A similar presumption lies behind the phrase 'the dark ages' (the earlier Middle Ages) and the name 'gothic' for a period of art and architecture, meaning dark, downbeat and a little sinister. As an indication that these assumptions might be mistaken, consider the light and airy elegance of a gothic cathedral and ask whether the period when it was built was really one of gloom and stagnation. As Alfred Crosby wrote, 'In our time the word *medieval* is often used as a synonym for muddle-headedness, but it can be more accurately used to indicate precise definition and meticulous reasoning, that is to say, *clarity*.'[1] C. S. Lewis's friend Owen Barfield was more specific: no one should be dismissive of the scholastics, because they gave us – by gargantuan labour – the words with which we think today. The philosopher or psychologist today is 'consuming the fruits of that long, agonizing struggle to state the exact relation between spirit and matter' with words such as absolute, actual, attribute, cause, concept, deduction, essence, existence, intellect, intelligence, intention, intuition and so on.[2]

---

1 Alfred Crosby, *Measure of Reality*, CUP, 1996, p. 65.
2 Owen Barfield, *History in English Words*, London: Faber and Faber, 1962, p. 123.

The germ of truth in the dismissive attitude towards the Middle Ages is that they began with the collapse of the Roman Empire. Northern tribes despoiled cities all the way to Rome; international travel and trade declined. This did not, however, mean complete collapse. Those 'barbarian' tribes were soon speaking Latin and engaged in scholarship; the Roman Empire no longer provided an international political order, but the pan-European reach of the Church – and of the 'Holy Roman Empire', after Charlemagne – was not far behind. The period was anything but provincial. The eighth Archbishop of Canterbury was Theodore of Tarsus, a Greek-speaker born in modern-day Turkey in AD 602. Scholars moved about, as did the books they wrote, spreading ideas. Alcuin moved from York to Aachen in AD 782; around 845, John Scottus Eriugena followed him, from Ireland. This was not particularly unusual. The pace of interchange picked up with the formation of the itinerant orders of the thirteenth century: the Franciscans and the Dominicans. Born in Southern Italy, Thomas Aquinas held positions in Cologne, Paris, Naples, Orvieto and Rome; born in the Scottish borders, John Duns Scotus taught in Oxford, Paris and Cologne.

Another way to judge the 'darkness' of the Middle Ages is in terms of their output. This period – supposedly between the literary high points of the classical world and the Renaissance – produced literary marvels. Indeed, we can realistically talk of a series of renaissances *during* the Middle Ages when, almost by definition, the received wisdom is that there were none. We have the 'Carolingian Renaissance', for instance, centred around the court of Charlemagne in the late eighth century into the ninth (of which Alcuin and Eriugena were part) and a literary renaissance across Europe between 1000 and 1150. The gothic style burst upon Europe, in the twelfth century, not as some isolated architectural experiment but as part of an intellectual revival in and near Paris, and particularly at the Abbey of St Denis, where scholarship and a delight in the natural world flourished under Abbot Suger.[3] The

---

3 See *On the Abbey Church of St Denis and Its Art Treasures*, ed. Erwin Panofsky and Gerda Panofsky-Soergel, Princeton University Press, 1979.

rediscovery of Aristotle in the thirteenth century could also be said to have provoked a renaissance, if any leap forward on the basis of renewed attention to the past has ever been worthy of that name.[4]

Mediaeval Institutions

For the first portion of the Middle Ages, the engine of thought and scholarly activity were the monasteries. The Dark Ages are called 'dark' because of an eclipse of general learning, which was preserved only in the monasteries. Given that learning *was* preserved there, and that it burned so brightly, those centuries may not have been so 'dark' after all. All the same, the period up to the eleventh century was not particularly one of philosophical innovation. The way in which these monks combined scholarship with a practical Christian life has, however, itself aroused philosophical interest in recent decades, not least from Alasdair MacIntryre in *After Virtue*, which we encountered in Chapter 3. The monks and nuns deserve our attention not so much for what they wrote as for how their lives embodied the teaching that they had inherited.

From the end of the eleventh century, we see the stirrings of a style of thought subsequently known as *scholasticism*. The name means 'that which is taught in the schools'. By 'schools' we mean bands of scholars, clergy almost to a man, gathered around abbeys, such as that of St Victor, near Paris, or cathedrals, such as Paris and Reims.

Around the turn of the thirteenth century, the centre of scholarly gravity shifted. Monastic scholarship became less important relative to the emerging universities in cities such as Paris, Oxford, Cambridge and Bologna. This represents part of the growing urbanization of Europe during this period: monasteries tended to be rural; universities were urban. Universities grew out of those cathedral schools, and a place with a cathedral is a city by definition. At a university, learning was somewhat more

---

4 We could also call it the first 'science and theology' crisis.

'worldly' than at a cathedral. Alongside theology, it was also possible to study law, for instance. Significantly, philosophy was considered to belong to the university's faculty of *arts*, not theology. This brought a degree of independence, not least from ecclesiastical control. This fact about academic planning, which might seem insignificant, marks an important stage in an ever-sharpening distinction between theology and philosophy. What might have started as a move to protect theology, by separating and demoting philosophy, actually gave philosophy a new status through its new independence. The separation meant that when Aristotle's texts were rediscovered they could have their unsettling influence in the universities through the arts faculty, whereas in the monastic schools they tended to be rejected or suppressed.

John Scottus Eriugena

Although the period before the eleventh century did not see a great deal of philosophical creativity, the great exception is the already mentioned John Scottus Eriugena (*c*. 800–*c*. 877). He is important not only for his own ideas but also for the figures he advocated and brought into circulation. These were particularly writers at the high-water mark of Christian Neoplatonism: Gregory of Nyssa, Pseudo-Dionysius and Maximus the Confessor. Eriugena was educated in his native Ireland. Thanks to the quality of scholarship there, he knew Greek as well as Latin, which was unusual for the time. This allowed him to translate important works by each of these authors into Latin.

Eriugena had an expansive mind and an expansive project. He mapped out a structure to reality, and its relation to God, that was both fully philosophical and fully theological. In his own lifetime, he was important for his powerfully philosophical rebuttal of predestination to hell (in *On Divine Predestination*), arguing that God predestines only to life, with human and not divine will leading to sin and damnation. Although he is sometimes called a universalist – believing in the salvation of all – he offered a considered account of separation from God, insightful for working out both sin and its punishment in terms of emptiness.[5] His academic method was strongly characterized by dialectic, by distinguishing options and resolving tensions, as befitted a Platonist.

John liked distinctions so much as to risk courting unhelpful dualisms. His most important philosophical work is the *Periphyseon*, or 'On the Division of Nature'. It presents a thoroughgoing Christian Neoplatonic vision of reality, not least in its sense of outflow and return, which structures the work as a whole. Eriugena's scheme takes in God (who is creating and uncreated), the divine ideas (creating and 'created' in this scheme), the world (created and uncreating) and non-being (which is neither created nor creating). The vision is appealing, not least because he defies the fourth category, seeing God, not non-being, as the goal of all things. He can, however, risk bracketing God with the world, since both stand as examples of 'nature', and also of making God so transcendent as to be (from a creaturely point of view) 'nothing'.

Eriguena was condemned by Pope Honorius III in 1225 for propositions such as the idea that all things are God (which does not do the subtlety of this thought justice) and that the divine ideas are created (which is fairer). That said, John stands as one of the great creative thinkers of the Church. It would be difficult for anyone to be as speculative again. Eriguena's immediate legacy was, nonetheless, felt primarily through his translations. Rendering Dionysius into Latin could safely be said to have started a Neoplatonic revival in the West, with the translations of Maximus also important.

Anselm of Canterbury

For the English, Anselm (*c.* 1033–*c.* 1109) is 'Anselm of Canterbury', where he was archbishop; for the French, 'Anselm of Bec',

---

5 See Paul A. Dietrich and Donald F. Duclow, 'Hell and Damnation in Eriguena', in Michael Dunne and James McEvoy (eds), *John Scottus Eriugena and His Time*, Leuven University Press, 2002, pp. 347–66.

where he was abbot; for Italians, 'Anselm of Aosta', where he was born. He would likely have lived out his time as Abbot of Bec had he not been forced to take up the archbishopric during a visit to England in 1092.

Anselm is a representative of the 'monastic theology' of the Middle Ages (a school both rich and deep, and not studied as widely as it deserves). For him, theology was primarily contemplative. It was of a piece with daily disciplines by which a community of monks, or nuns, helped to prepare one another for the life of the world to come, and indeed to anticipate it here and now, not least in a constant cycle of prayer and worship. We could even say that Anselm is both 'the summit of the early scholastic genius and the ripest fruit of the monastic schools', as David Knowles put it.[6] In some ways, his work even anticipates scholasticism at its most rationalistic.

Anselm famously wrote, 'I do not seek to understand so that I may believe; but I believe so that I may understand.'[7] He cites Isaiah 7.9, not in the form we will find it in our Bibles today, but as it came to him in Latin (via the ancient Greek translation): 'unless you believe you will not understand'. From this, Augustine proposed a pivotal maxim for Christian philosophers: the stance of 'faith seeking understanding'.[8] When the greatest of Protestant theologians, Karl Barth, wrote a short treatise on theological method, he gave it a title taken from Anselm: *Fides Quaerens Intellectum* ('Faith Seeking Understanding').[9]

Anselm's phrase is a wise comment on the necessity of faith, or trust, as a precondition of knowledge. It also suggests a profound mistake in the way many textbooks present Anselm's famous (or infamous) proof for the existence of God. They excise it from the *Proslogion*, where it is part of a prayer to God. If we fail to attend to context our appreciation of any work or argument

6 David Knowles, *The Evolution of Medieval Thought*, London: Longmans, 1988, p. 90.

7 *Proslogion* 1, trans. M. J. Charlesworth, ed. Brian Davies and G. R. Evans, OUP, 2008.

8 Augustine, *Sermon* 43.7.

9 Trans. Ian W. Robertson, SCM Press, 1975.

will be deadened. Anselm was not trying to argue to God from some neutral and uncommitted starting point. Anselm's argument about the existence of God is more accurately seen as a meditation on God's nature than a 'proof'. Anselm was not working out whether God exists or not.

His argument is often called the 'ontological argument', since it deals with questions of being (*ontos*). Turning to the text, we actually find two arguments, one after another, in *Proslogion* 2 and 3. Both deserve to be called 'ontological'. We might consider the second argument first. It proposes that a world of contingency must rest upon a creator who does not need further explanation: which is to say, who is not contingent but necessary.

The first, more celebrated proof, begins by defining God as the most perfect being that can be conceived. Anselm then notes that an *existing* being is more perfect than one *only in the mind*. Now, if God were only in the mind then a more perfect being than God could be imagined: namely, just such a being as this 'God', but who also actually existed. On that basis, God *must* exist, because God is, by definition, the most perfect being that can be conceived.

Philosophers down the ages have attempted to poke holes in this argument. In particular, it rests on a direct comparison between existing in reality and existing in the mind, which makes many uncomfortable. However, as a meditation on what it means for God to be God, it is thought-provoking, not least because it presents God's *perfection* as intimately bound up with his *existence*. This captures the intuition, put forward by many other Christian philosophers, that God is supremely *real*. It is something of a tragedy, then, that Anselm's argument is so often taken out of its setting, as a meditation on the mystery of God's profound reality, to become abstract and mental.

For a certain sort of philosophy of religion, claiming to follow Anselm, God has been relegated to an item in the human mental category of beings – possible and real – among which he happens to be the most perfect. When Anselm sought to approach God through the perfection of his being, it is unlikely that he saw God as one more being among beings. Indeed, as the creator of beings, God cannot be one more being among them.[10] There is a crack one might fall through in Anselm's argument; the 'Perfect Being Theology' put forward by philosophers of religion in recent decades has fallen through it.

Anselm believed in order that he might understand. However, his writings can sometimes seem too overbalanced towards understanding. We come across this in his treatise on the Incarnation and atonement, *Cur Deus Homo* ('Why God became Man'). In Anselm's words, his purpose is 'to prove by rational necessity [. . .] that no man [or woman] can possibly be saved without Him [Christ]' and that this is what necessitates Christ's Incarnation and death.[11] Our quotation has omitted some words from this passage. In them, Anselm tells us that he will argue with Christ 'removed from sight, as if there had never been anything known about Him'. This represents Anselm's method at its most dangerously rationalist. It assumes that we can stand in God's shoes and work out what he would have to do, without reference to what he *has* done. An abstract theology such as this stands at odds with an understanding of theology as reflection on revelation and on God's dealing with us, in the tangibility of history: the dealings of the God who acts out of love and freedom.

If this initial statement provokes fears, Anselm goes on to allay some of them. Although only the death of a saviour simultaneously human and divine could redeem humanity,[12] this does not force God to become incarnate and die in any absolute sense. Christ could have avoided death if he had wished, but since it was

10 MacIntyre refers us to Anselm's 'Reply to the Fool', where Anselm points out that he is not talking about a finite creature who happens to be the greatest among them, but to the 'greatest conceivable'. This perhaps allows us to approach the ontological argument in a way that takes seriously the unutterably profound distinction of God from creatures (*God, Philosophy, Universities*, Continuum, 2009, pp. 38–40). Beyond this, we might note that the second 'ontological' argument, in *Proslogion* 3, works to distinguish God from 'things' since, in radical contradistinction to created things, God has his being necessarily whereas they have theirs contingently.

11 Preface, trans. Jasper Hopkins in *Complete Philosophical and Theological Treatises of Anselm of Canterbury*, Minneapolis: Arthur J. Banning Press, 2000, p. 296.

12 *Cur Deus Homo* I.10; II.7.

the only way (Anselm thinks) to redeem the world, and since God wanted to do that, he voluntarily submitted to death.[13] If God was under any necessity, it was subsequent to his will, not prior to it. God freely entered into a situation from which certain necessities then follow: 'When He created man, He was not ignorant of what man was going to do. And, nevertheless, by creating man by His own goodness, He freely bound Himself, as it were, to accomplish the good which He had undertaken.'[14]

Anselm was addressing significant questions here. Every philosophical theologian is faced with a question as to what, if anything, constitutes the set of parameters within which God must work. One aspect of a possible response is to say that there are things that God 'cannot do', but that they are impossible only because they are nonsense. God cannot do them because they are *not things that can be done*: there is no square circle, for instance, either for God to make or *not* be able to make. As C. S. Lewis put it, 'meaningless combinations of words do not suddenly acquire meaning simply because we prefix to them two other words "God can"'.[15] Another angle is to say that any 'limitations' come from God himself: God cannot lie because God is the truth itself; God cannot be evil because he is goodness itself. As Richard Hooker put it in the seventeenth century, '[t]he being of God is a kind of law to his working: for that perfection which God is, giveth perfection to that he doth'.[16] For some theologians, the regulatory function of God's nature is profound; for others, such as William of Ockham, it is practically non-existent. As a final angle on divine freedom, there is the question of how 'constrained' God is by the way he has made creation. Aquinas develops a sensible line here, saying that God is not bound by his creation *in itself* but that God *is* a 'debtor' to his own nature, to be consistent to himself in all his actions, including those towards creation.

---

13 *Cur Deus Homo* I.10.
14 *Cur Deus Homo* II.5.
15 C. S. Lewis, *The Problem of Pain*, London: Collins, 2012, p. 18.
16 *Laws of Ecclesiastical Polity*, Book I.2.2.

Returning to Anselm, he writes that he wants his readers to understand the faith by means of 'rational necessity'.[17] Up to a point we can understand this as exploring what follows from God's own nature, and of what follows from the nature of a world that God has chosen to create. All the same, Anselm's opening description of his project – to think as if we did not know about Christ, to think as if we could sit in God's chair and think God's thoughts – has too little sense that God is free and beyond human thought. There are any number of ways in which God could have redeemed the world. God is not only free and beyond our thoughts, he is also 'ingenious' beyond our capacity to imagine, such that the 'rulers of this age' (usually held to be the demons) could not fathom God's plan (1 Cor. 2.8). We cannot expect to be able to do so either, especially not in advance. As Aquinas would say a century or two later, the best handle we have on why God acts this way rather than that is not *necessity* but *fittingness*.

In short, *Cur Deus Homo* is rather a mess, and this matters because it has been an influential mess. On occasions Anselm wrote as if God were strongly bound by the logic of necessary reasons.[18] On other, rarer occasions, he introduced the notion of fittingness, but somewhat askew to the rest of the argument.[19] In another place, Anselm seems to suggest that nothing bears upon the divine will in any way: 'it is improper to say that God cannot do something or that He does something by necessity [. . .] a thing is necessary or impossible only because He wills it to be so'.[20] We might see this treatise as a work in progress, and seek in it for a middle way. Some, however, have latched on to one of its extremes or the other: they have either discounted the sense in which God's will and freedom operates within the contours of his

---

17 *Cur Deus Homo* I.25.

18 Knowles notes that the scope of Anselm's 'necessary reasons' reaches even as far as the doctrine of the Trinity – although Knowles himself interprets 'necessity' here to mean no more than 'formally admissible' or 'probable' (*Evolution*, p. 92).

19 '[I]n the case of God, just as an impossibility results from any unfittingness, however slight, so necessity accompanies any degree of reasonableness, however small, provided it is not overridden by some other more weighty reason' (*Cur Deus Homo* I.10).

20 *Cur Deus Homo* II.17.

nature and wisdom or, on the other hand, subjected God to necessity to such an extent that, in the atonement in particular, God the Father seems to have painted himself into a corner, and slaying his Son is the only way out.

The problem lies in Anselm's opening invitation for us to argue in the abstract, to argue 'as if': in this case, 'as if' we did not know that Christ was born, died and rose again. This note of virtuality was to become important for later thinkers. The Dutch ethicist Hugo Grotius approached ethics, even as a Christian, 'as if God did not exist';[21] for Dietrich Bonhoeffer, this is the way for the twentieth-century Christian to live: God would have us live 'as men who manage our lives without him'.[22] Grotius did not disbelieve in God (and neither did Bonhoeffer). Rather, he wanted a system of international ethics and law that could be accepted universally because it rested on what was obvious about the world, even independent of any reference to God, or of any particular tradition of faith. What is 'obvious without reference to God', however, has not necessarily proved a good foundation for ethics, especially on the global scale that interested Grotius. If the nations that took their bearing from religious faith have erred down the centuries, and they have, then those that explicitly rejected Christianity have fared worse: we need only think of the three largest slaughters of the twentieth century, by the Chinese communists, the Soviet communists and the Nazis. The 'neutral' and abstract approach to international ethics that characterizes the Enlightenment, stemming from Grotius, proceeding 'as if God did not exist', was not able to tame the excesses of human hatred and folly during the twentieth century when, more than ever before, humanity tried to live precisely as if God did not exist.

To conclude, Anselm's *Proslogion* does not necessarily teach the reader that God is the biggest thing among things, although some have taken that message from the text and made it their own.

---

21 *De iure belli ac pacis*, Prolegomena 11.

22 Dietrich Bonhoeffer, *Letters and Papers from Prison: Enlarged Edition*, several translators, SCM Press, 1971, p. 360.

Similarly, his *Cur Deus Homo* presents us with several angles on divine necessity, from which we need not suppose that God's will operates outside of the contours of his nature and wisdom, or that God is strongly constrained by 'rational necessity'. Influential thinkers, however, have taken these messages from these texts. Anselm's thought will always repay careful attention. However, to have written one text that led to significant subsequent mistakes is unfortunate; to have written two might be considered careless.[23]

Peter Lombard

Peter Lombard (*c.* 1096–1164) is named after the place of his birth. This is common among the philosophers we encounter from the Middle Ages. With Peter, the reference is to a region (Lombardy, as with Scotland in the case of Duns Scotus). For Thomas Aquinas ('of Aquino') or William of Ockham (a village in Surrey) the reference is to a town or village. Peter Lombard is a good example of how even a child of poor parents could excel academically in the Middle Ages, and rise to fame. He stands as another of the principal stars in the firmament of the 'cathedral schools' that flourished before the universities.

Lombard is important not so much as an innovator in ideas as in teaching. For that purpose, he compiled an anthology called the *Four Books of Sentences*. These enormous chains of biblical and patristic texts became the definitive textbook of theology and stood as the benchmark for teaching theology for the next four hundred years. The books are arranged by subject: Book 1 on the existence of God, the doctrine of the Trinity and providence, Book 2 on creation, angels, sin and the Fall, Book 3 on Christ, the atonement, the virtues and the Ten Commandments, and Book

---

23 A third wrong turn comes from his distinction between an inclination for the just and an inclination for the beneficial in *On the Fall of the Devil*, a distinction that was to be taken up by Duns Scotus and obscures the point that justice is beneficial for human beings and that God seeks both justice and our benefit. A fourth problem is Anselm's tendency to put undue emphasis on the divine essence relative to the divine Persons.

4 on the sacraments and the four last things (death, judgement, heaven and hell). The *Sentences* also provided the benchmark for judging theological accomplishment. To become a teacher or 'master' one had to produce a work to establish one's own voice, within the context of faithfulness to the tradition. This was literally your 'master piece', launching you on a teaching career. It took the form of a commentary on the *Books of Sentences*.

Numbering and referencing

So many significant works of the later Middle Ages take the form of a commentary on the *Sentences* that a note on referencing is worthwhile. The four books are composed of many chapters. In the thirteenth century, these were collected into groups of 'distinctions' by Alexander of Hales. Some of the distinctions have more than one part, but the numbering of chapters carries on across them; it does not start again with 1 when we come to a new distinction.

A commentary on the sentences (or on anything else subdivided by book, including works of Aristotle such as the *Metaphysics*) is often named using the Latin word 'in', here meaning 'upon', with the number of the book in the title itself. A commentary on the first distinction of the second book of the *Sentences*, for instance, would be called *In II Sententiarum, distinctio 1*, or *In II Sent*, d. 1 for short.

Some scholastic commentators subdivided their distinctions into articles, rather than chapters, and then further subdivided their articles into questions. The towering example of a work divided this way, although not itself a commentary on the *Sentences*, is Aquinas's *Summa Theologiae*. First there is a larger sub-division into parts, with room for confusion: the *Summa* does not quite fall into three parts, or into four, but somewhere in between. The parts are called the 'first part', the 'first part of the second part', the 'second part of the second part', and the 'third part'. (All of the second part concerns ethics but the

---

first half deals with the groundwork, such as habit, law and passions, and the second with the details, such as the various virtues and vices.) Each part discusses a series of topics (such as 'the simplicity of God'), each of which is called a question. The simplicity of God is the topic of Question 3 of the first part. Each question is then divided into articles, which pose specific questions, such as 'Whether God is a body?' (Article 1) or 'Whether He is composed of matter and form?' (Article 2).

Finally, turning back to works originally written in Greek, it is worth noting that books are sometimes numbered with Greek *letters* rather than with Roman or Arabic *numerals*, for the sake of authenticity. *Nichomachean Ethics* Γ is the third book of Aristotle's work. References to Plato are often given with the name of the dialogue, a number and a letter from the beginning of the alphabet. The numbers refer to the page in a complete edition of Plato's works published by Henri Estienne in 1578; the letters locate the quotation more specifically. A similar system applies to Aristotle. The edition in question is that by Bekker. The letters, only A and B, refer to the two columns on each of Bekker's pages.

Peter Abelard

Alongside the question of where people taught, studied and wrote (cathedral, monastery or university), we should consider what they wrote. The definitive characteristic of developed scholastic writing is a 'disputational' form. Arguments were advanced, and ideas were clarified, by a method of posing objections and answering them. The pioneer was Peter Abelard (1079–1142), who wrote a discussion in 1117 entitled *Sic et Non*: 'Yes and No'. Peter set an example of looking at a topic from a variety of angles. 'Do angels have bodies?', we might imagine a scholastic theologian asking. The typical method would be to consider what could be said for either position, 'yes' and 'no'. We might reach a clearer sense of an answer in terms of 'it depends what you mean by a body'.

Abelard stands out among his contemporaries for both his brilliance and his petulance. He was enormously able, and he knew it. His intellect, ambition and libido got the better of him. His biography has it all, including romance and castration. Not for nothing did he call his own written account of his life *Historia calamitatum*: 'The Story of His [here meaning 'My'] Adversities'. We can draw a not entirely facetious parallel between this title and the self-important, and self-pitying, autobiographies of present-day celebrities: *My Battle, Weeping all the Way* and so on.

This 'disputational' style should be at least half familiar from the modern idea of a debate. In the classroom of the Middle Ages, a subject might be taught by one person posing both sides of a 'debate' – the objections and the replies – or in the form of an exchange between two teachers or 'masters'. A student would be expected to be able to think on the spot, listing arguments for or against a position. The syllabus for a course of studies might work through a text, such as a book of the Bible, or be designed to cover a certain area of theology systematically. On other occasions, the topic was posed to the teacher in order to put him to the test, or to provoke what we might think of as a 'party piece' dealing with what we would today call 'hot potatoes'. Such discussions were particularly tabled for feast days, offering some light relief.

Abelard is sometimes held up as one of the first theologians with a 'rationalist' philosophical style and even as representing something like an anticipation of the Enlightenment. Certainly, he illustrates a new confidence in human reason, and attention to its workings. He was also, however, a man of faith and piety. His hymn 'O what their joys, and their glories must be!' (*O Quanta, Qualia*) is among the most beautiful of mediaeval lyrics, on the subject of the joys of the saints. In his *Introduction to Theology*, he describes authority as the foundation and reason as secondary, as the buttress.[24] In ethics, Abelard is significant for having put a new emphasis on the

---

24 *Introduction to Theology* Book 2. Quoted in Knowles, *Evolution*, p. 123.

intention of the agent. This approach was to become increasingly important in subsequent centuries. It divides thinkers to this day.

If we encounter Abelard in theology today, however, it is as a coat hook for certain positions, in particular an approach to the atonement that puts the emphasis on Christ's passion as a moral example. However, Abelard is a complex figure and in this he is a reminder that thinkers are generally quite complex. Teachers of intellectual history find it useful to seize upon one aspect of a writer's thought in preference to others; they have a story to tell and it makes for a good narrative to associate a particular idea with a particular person. If, however, we turn to Abelard on the atonement, for instance in his Commentary on Romans, we see that the picture is not quite so clear. He was not so much intending to lay out a complete, systematic account, but rather to burrow away at what Paul was saying. Abelard was clearly worried about inconsistencies within other models of the atonement, in particular theories based on ransom or satisfaction. He therefore wanted to lay serious emphasis on the way in which Christ's passion works by way of example. There is an important sense, however, even in the crucial 'exemplar' passage of his commentary (on Rom. 3.26), that the Incarnation itself has a salvific dimension in addition to any example the Christ offers, and that the crucifixion functions as a singular 'gift of divine grace' in a way that cannot be collapsed to any one model, the exemplar model among them. The commentary on Romans is a good place to see Abelard's mind at work. It is also an illustration that even a very philosophical thinker such as Abelard developed his philosophy with very theological tasks in mind, such as the clearer exposition of the Epistles of Paul.

Perhaps, in the hands of some, Abelard among them, the burgeoning scholastic approach was better at finding the problems in theological theories than it was at putting something positive and constructive in their place. In general, that comment applies more to thinkers closely aligned to logic, such as Abelard, and less to the thinkers whose philosophical interests lay more with metaphysics, such as Aquinas.

Rediscovery of Aristotle

Towards the end of the eleventh century, Christians started coming across the tip of an iceberg of philosophical texts: the majority of the works of Aristotle, otherwise lost to the West. The cause was largely military crusades and the conquest of cities in the Middle East and in Spain. As we noted in the chapter on Aristotle, relatively few of his works survived in the West after the collapse of the Roman Empire: the *Categories* and *On Interpretation*, both logical works translated by Boethius. When the Platonic academy was closed in AD 529, probably by the Emperor Justinian, its scholars fled, settling in Odessa (today in South East Turkey), later moving to Baghdad, taking their texts with them. In Baghdad, the Caliph paid enormous sums for these works to be translated into Syriac and Arabic, enlisting the work of Syriac Christians. When Aristotle was reintroduced to the West, it was largely in the form of these Arabic translations. Spain and Sicily were the most significant centres of translation into Latin, not least because of their geographical proximity to the Islamic world. This work, for all its zeal, left theologians working, in some cases, with Latin translations of Arabic translations of Syriac translations of the original Greek. The Latin versions they produced were remarkably accurate, given the distance from the original. They were not, however, perfect, and this only began to be put right when scholars such as William of Moerbeke (*c.* 1215–*c.* 1286) were able to see Greek originals.

Richard Rubenstein describes the discovery of Aristotle as being like the discovery of an object from outer space. His corpus, 'some three thousand pages of material ranging over the whole spectrum of learning from biology to physics to logic, psychology, ethics, and political science [we could add metaphysics] seemed to be a bequest from a superior civilization'.[25] Aristotle made the world strange again. The body of texts and ideas that a scholar ought to know about was suddenly massively enlarged; things were unlikely to go on as they had before. There was a new point of reference on the

---

25 *Aristotle's Children*, Orlando: Harcourt, 2003, p. 4.

THE LOVE OF WISDOM

intellectual map, and no one was quite sure how to take bearings, or even whether to embrace it or reject it. Part of this came down to a crisis of confidence and the question of what to make of the Christian tradition now that this alien capsule had descended bearing witness to a grasp of science (as it seemed) far more advanced than their own. As Rubenstein notes, Aristotle seemed to know about *everything*: science (about which Christians might feel rather inferior) as much as metaphysics (about which they were more confident); and if Aristotle exceeded them over science, that might mean that Christian metaphysics was not so sure either. Inasmuch as there was a crisis in this period, it was one over 'theology and science' as much as it was over anything else. That is worth remembering when we are told that the nineteenth or twentieth centuries posed an incomparable scientific challenge to the Christian faith.

Aristotle's texts represented the core of this new inheritance, but also important were some works of high Neoplatonism, often mistaken for works of Aristotle, such as the *Book of Causes*, and Arabic commentaries, especially those by Averroës (Ibn Rushd). Averroës responded to the work of Avicenna (Ibn Sina), who had presented a vision of Aristotle harmonized with Plato and Neoplatonism. Avicenna's works were themselves influential on Christian philosophers, not least for his work on the distinction between essence (what something is) and existence (that something is). Avicenna put the emphasis on the former. That led to an interest in the potential over the actual, since essence names something that might be, whether or not it actually exists. That chimed, to some extent, with a Platonic interest in the divine ideas. In contrast, the commentaries by Averroës on Aristotle tried to free the interpretation from any Platonic cast.

Averroës was a strident advocate of the eternity of the world and of the idea that all human beings share one soul. This was to have a significant impact on later Christian mysticism. Saying that what Aristotle called the active intellect is one for all people opened the way to saying that it is also identical with God, for instance in the works of Meister Eckhart (*c.* 1260–*c.* 1328).[26]

---

26 Agnes Arber, *The Manifold and the One*, London: J. Murray, 1957, p. 39.

Such notions formed the backbone of the positions condemned by Archbishop Stephen Tempier in 1270 and 1277. Averroës, as a 'rationalist', was also an important catalyst for the widening distinction between theology and philosophy. The distinction is reasonably subtle in his own work, but later Christian Averroists pushed it to absurdity in order to justify their position. Siger of Brabant (c. 1240–80), for instance, taught that something can be true 'philosophically' (such as that the world is eternal) and its opposite true 'theologically'. That allowed him to uphold an Aristotelian (or Averroist) position where it mattered most to him, in philosophy, while hoping to get the theologians and those who cared for such things off his back. He did not succeed. Siger also taught that God only knows general things, not 'particulars'. He is part of an extreme philosophizing tendency in Europe at this time, always roundly condemned. Boethius of Sweden is another example. He went so far as to follow Aristotle in denying the resurrection of the dead and in teaching that only philosophers could be happy. Here we could contrast Aquinas who, in the words of Étienne Gilson, 'would follow Aristotle when he was right, but no further, and because he was right, but on no other ground, [whereas] the Averroist would consider Averroës, Aristotle and human reason, as three different words for one and the same thing'.[27]

The condemnations of the 1270s were incisive in Christian philosophical history, not least because of the backlash they provoked, in which Christian thinkers were keen to distance themselves from the condemned positions. Some of Templier's thrust was to contradict any sense of limitation on God's power. The reaction was a new-found enthusiasm for *voluntarism* in Christian theology: a stress on the will and power of God above all else. This was to be a remarkably unhelpful drift. We will come to voluntarism later, but for now we can turn to the figure who better than any other responded to Aristotle with warmth and good judgement (alongside the Neoplatonic texts also circulating), and immeasurably enriched the Christian tradition in the process: Thomas Aquinas.

---

27 *Reason and Revelation in the Middle Ages*, New York: Charles Scribner's Sons, 1938, pp. 79–80.

THE LOVE OF WISDOM

Reading On

As a general introduction, see Gillian Evans, *Philosophy and Theology in the Middle Ages* (Routledge, 1993). Deirdre Carabine has written on Eriugena in *John Scottus Eriugena* (OUP, 2000). The major works of Anselm have been translated by Gillian Evans and Brian Davies for OUP (2008), with a more extensive collection of texts than the parallel Penguin collection. Jasper Hopkins's translations are available online, as well as in print, as *Complete Philosophical and Theological Treatises of Anselm of Canterbury* (Minneapolis: Arthur J. Banning Press, 2000). Jasper Hopkins provides a good way in with his essay 'Anselm of Canterbury' in Jorge J. E. Gracia and Timothy B. Noone (eds), *A Companion to Philosophy in the Middle Ages* (Blackwell, 2003). The existentialist philosopher Karl Jaspers writes perceptively about Anselm in *Anselm and Nicholas of Cusa* in his *Great Philosophers* series (New York: Harcourt Brace Jovanovich, 1974).

For a study of Lombard, see Philipp Rosemann, *Peter Lombard* (OUP, 2004). His *Commentary on the Epistle to the Romans* has been translated by Steven Cartwright (CUA, 2011). For an analysis, see Thomas Williams, 'Sin, Grace and Redemption' in *The Cambridge Companion to Abelard*, edited by Jeffrey E. Brower and Kevin Guilfoy (CUP, 2004). Penguin published Abelard's exchange with his inamorata Héloïse, translated by Betty Radice (1974). His story was told by the great Irish translator of mediaeval Latin Helen Waddell in *Peter Abelard: A Novel* (New York: Henry Holt and Company, 1933).

Richard Rubenstein recounts the rediscovery of Aristotle in *Aristotle's Children: How Christians, Muslims, and Jews Rediscovered Ancient Wisdom and Illuminated the Middle Ages* (Orlando: Harcourt Brace, 2003). For the Arabic backstory to mediaeval Christian theology, see the *Cambridge Companions* to *Arabic Philosophy,* edited by Peter Adamson and Richard Taylor (2005) and *Classical Islamic Theology,* edited by Tim Winter (2008).

8

Thomas Aquinas

For those who take to Thomas Aquinas (1225–74), no other thinker compares. Josef Pieper was one such enthusiast (and he remains one of Aquinas's best recent proponents). As he put it:

> There are in the writings of St Thomas numerous chapters whose sentences move in such rhythmic cadence towards their *conclusio*, their final 'therefore', that one can think of no more fitting comparison than that with the determined stride of the final measures in a organ fugue by Johann Sebastian Bach.[1]

Aquinas was born into a wealthy noble family in Southern Italy, in the town of Roccasecca. He was enrolled at the Benedictine abbey of Monte Cassino, one of the most powerful ecclesiastical institutions in Europe, with every prospect of him becoming the abbot in due course. Thomas horrified his family when he announced his intention to leave the monastery, a supremely appropriate place for a well-to-do cleric, to become a Dominican friar, a wandering preacher, which was supremely inappropriate. The legend goes that his brothers imprisoned him, although he eventually won his release.

Aquinas's biography puts him on the fault lines of contemporary Europe. He was born in the country but spent his adult life in the city. He was taught in a monastery, the rural intellectual powerhouse of a passing age and imbibed its 'monastic theology', which was rooted in Augustine and Christian Platonism. After that, however, he was sent by the Dominicans to a city, to Naples,

---

1 Josef Pieper, *The Silence of St Thomas*, New York: Pantheon, 1957, p. 28.

and to a university, which was to become the centre of scholarship in an age just beginning. There he encountered the work of Aristotle.

Aquinas was a reconciler but not an accommodator. His inclination was to see the goodness and truth in everything he could, while never selling out. Beneath his approach lay his conviction that God is the truth of all truth and the good of all goodness. On that basis, he was open to learn from the widest range of sources, while also holding that all truth had to be brought back to God and incorporated into a robustly Christian vision. His aim was to construct the richest possible theological vision of the world, elucidated with the best tools available, and on that basis to hold fast both to revelation and to the contemporary intellectual challenges of his age, and to address the latter in terms of the former.

Part of Thomas's greatness lies in the moment at which he was born and in his willingness to seize its opportunities. Theologically, for instance, ongoing dialogues with the Greek church at the time gave him an unusually wide access to the writings of the Greek Fathers. In his compilation of snippets of commentary on the four Gospels (the *Catena Aurea* or *Chain of Gold*), he quotes from 57 different Greek Fathers but only 22 Latins.[2] Across his works as a whole, the tally of his abundant references might proceed in something like this order: the Bible, Aristotle or Augustine (tied for second place), Pseudo-Dionysius, John of Damascus and Boethius. One of the joys of reading Aquinas is to be introduced on every page to the most acute and perceptive comments of writers from the preceding millennium, assembled by the supreme magpie among theologians.

Aquinas was also a synthesizer when it came to his philosophy. He was well informed about philosophical history, for all his information about the thought of the ancient world was necessarily mostly picked up second hand. He was heir to two principal philosophical schools: Aristotle and Neoplatonism. The former he received through the burgeoning university system,

---

2 Jean-Pierre Torrell, 'Thomas Aquinas', in Jean-Yves Lacoste, *Encyclopaedia of Christian Theology*, Routledge, 2005, pp. 1572–7, p. 1274.

in some cases falling upon texts of Aristotle 'hot off the press' from the translators working with newly acquired Arabic editions. His Neoplatonism was absorbed more obliquely. In the first place, he was a pupil of Augustine, and Augustine is one of the great wellsprings of Christian Neoplatonism. Also important were Arabic commentaries on Aristotle, some of which continued a tradition of reading Aristotle in the light of Plato that stretched back to antiquity. Furthermore, Aquinas also knew a supreme expression of Neoplatonism: the *Book of Causes*, a light adaptation of *The Elements of Theology* by Proclus. Then there is the Christian writer from the Patristic period most deeply inspired by Neoplatonism, and Proclus in particular: Pseudo-Dionysius. If Aquinas had done nothing else, he would be remembered for having made something thoroughly Christian of Proclean Neoplatonism. Pseudo-Dionysius, magnificent though he is, can sometimes read as someone whose centre of gravity lies just a little too far from the Christian centre ground. Mention of Arabic sources and commentators here reminds us that Aquinas also stood on the boundaries between religious traditions. He read Jewish and Islamic authors in Latin translation and although he was critical when he thought he needed to be, he approached them as fellow pilgrims on a quest for the truth.

The debt to Aristotle is everywhere obvious in Aquinas, not least because Aquinas gives a reference when Aristotle is cited. The debt to Neoplatonism is less obvious. In 1956, Robert Henle produced an impressive survey of Aquinas's discussion of Platonic texts.[3] It only gave half the picture, however, since Henle proceeded as one *could* reasonably proceed for the Aristotelian influence, but cannot for the Platonic: he used a concordance and looked for the name of Plato and references to Platonism. By and large, however, Aquinas mentioned the Platonic system by name only when he wished to criticize it. Platonic themes inform the

---

3 Robert John Henle, *Saint Thomas and Platonism: A Study of the 'Plato' and 'Platonici' Texts in the Writings of Saint Thomas*, The Hague: Martinus Nihoff, 1956.

structure or substrata of his thought, but this is so close to him that he does not name names. This is only a particularly intense example of a general principle in mediaeval philosophy, pointed out by Étienne Gilson: 'Plato himself does not appear at all, but Platonism is everywhere.'[4]

Fran O'Rourke has written brilliantly on this topic. His conclusion could be summarized with the phrase that Aquinas worked out Platonic structure in terms of Aristotelian detail.[5] With this approach, Aquinas turned to each thinker at his best. Aristotle gave us a wealth of vocabulary with which to describe creatures and their relations. These often rest on perceptive distinctions: between the four causes, for instance, or between substance and accidents. However, Aristotle had remarkably little to offer by way of overarching metaphysical structure at the grandest level. He has no answer for why the world is the way it is: it just is. His god, such as it is, is relatively unrelated to the world. In contrast, Plato was concerned above all with the overarching structure: the origins of the universe and how it comes to be that anything exists, or is beautiful, or good. Plato was a theorist of the relation of the world to that which transcends it. Aquinas turned to Aristotle for language to describe the detail. His sense that the world and everything about it comes from God, however, finds its natural expression in Platonic language.

Interest in creation underlays Aquinas's use of both Plato and Aristotle. Pieper wrote that if Aquinas were to be given a name in the Carmelite style (such as 'St John of the Cross' or 'St Thérèse of the Child Jesus'), it should be Thomas *a Creatore*: of the creator.[6] Thomas's order, the Dominicans or Order of Preachers, was founded by Dominic in 1216 with the principal aim of converting the Albigensians. This version of the ancient Gnostic heresy had taken hold in southern France in the eleventh century and become dominant in parts of Languedoc a century later. Like the

---

4 Étienne Gilson, *History of Christian Philosophy in the Middle Ages*, New York: Random House, 1955, p. 144.

5 'Aquinas and Platonism', in *Contemplating Aquinas: On the Varieties of Interpretation*, ed. Fergus Kerr, SCM Press, 2005, pp. 247–9.

6 *Silence*, p. 32.

earlier Gnostics, the Albigensians held that the material world was the work of an evil power, and that redemption involved renunciation of materiality in quest for a pure, spiritual existence. Aquinas was attracted by the religious order that, in opposing the Albigensians, most of all stood against this hatred of the created world. Having joined it, he was further shaped by its work and theological traditions. Aristotle featured here almost in the guise of a *natural scientist*. His many works on aspects of the natural world struck a chord with a culture newly concerned, for instance, to decorate its churches with carvings of foliage. His exhaustive discussions of the processes of reason chimed with the intellectual culture into which it was introduced. More significant still for Aquinas was the combination of these two elements, and the sense that human knowledge is always bodily, sensual knowledge: knowing through the senses. Far from the body dragging us down, as the Albigensians thought, it is integral to what we are. Aristotle helped Christian theologians to think such thoughts. The business of knowing might in a sense be immaterial – a thought is not a physical thing – but for Aquinas human knowledge is embodied all the same. We only know anything, even about God, as far we are led by sensible things (*ST* I.12.12). Aquinas uses a word here, *manuduci*, which literally means 'lead by the hand' by sensible things.

The Relation of Philosophy and Theology

Aquinas lived a busy life, full of travelling and organization, including drawing up the curriculum for the Dominicans across Europe and composing new liturgy for the Pope. Despite all this activity, Aquinas's writings unfold at a leisurely pace set by the subject matter in hand and a spirit of contemplation. We mistake the man if we do not place prayer at the centre of his life. Near its end, during one of his long periods of prayer, the crucified Christ is said to have appeared to him and said 'you have spoken well of me, Thomas'. Aquinas died at the monastery of Fossanova, east of Rome, in the modern province of Lazio, on 7 March 1274.

When his canonization was later being considered, it emerged that the monks had not sung a requiem for him on the day of his death, as every convention would have dictated. Instead they sang a Mass with interspersed quotations from the Bible that asked not for forgiveness of sins, but which praised God for the life of 'a just man made perfect': the Mass *Os Iusti*, proper to saints who have confessed the faith.

From the days of his early masterpiece *De Esse et Essentia*, Aquinas pressed to the heart of philosophical questions. All the same, he resisted the growing tendency to divorce philosophy from theology and give philosophy its own autonomy. As he writes in the first question of his greatest work, the *Summa Theologiae*, reason can only get us so far, and even then it might make mistakes. Arguments over the relation of theology and philosophy have, however, haunted every version of the school founded on his works, which is customarily called 'Thomism'.

Output

Aquinas produced a prodigious output. At his death, aged 49, he had written about eight and a half million words. It is said that by the end of his life he was dictating to several secretaries at once, loading each one up with a paragraph to copy down before turning to the next, *and a different project*, picking up there where he had left off with that secretary a couple of minutes before.

In the broad theological imagination today, Aquinas's work is dominated by two surveys of Christian theology: the earlier *Summa Contra Gentes*, written as a manual for missionaries, and the later, and not quite finished, *Summa Theologiae*, written for trainee friars. We also have the beginning of a mini-*summa* in his *Compendium Theologiae*. His plan for it was to discuss the Apostles' Creed, the Lord's Prayer and the Beatitudes, thereby covering faith, hope and love. As it stands we have the first part, and the beginning of the second. Alongside these *Summae*, he wrote a series of treatises on important questions, with names such as *On Evil*, *On Divine Power* and *On Truth*. His set of discussions of virtue are full of insights for Christian life today. The set *On Fraternal Correction*, for instance, was quite obviously written by someone who had spent his life in community and knows the importance of reputation and the finer details of what destroys morale. Aquinas also wrote many commentaries on books of the Bible and the works of Aristotle. None of these are as well known as they should be. Hidden among the discussions of passages of Aristotle that are of little interest today are relatively unknown passages on matters of great importance. His most significant biblical commentaries cover the Psalms, Job, Jeremiah and Lamentations, along with most of the New Testament. In his commentaries on Paul, Aquinas can appear to have a pedantic, long-winded style, which nonetheless lays out the structure of Paul's argument in crystalline detail. Alongside whatever theological points Aquinas makes of his own, the contemporary reader will usually find a first-rate guide to the intricacies of Paul's prose. Perhaps his most useful work for the weekly preacher, however, or for Bible study, is his *Catena Aurea* or 'Chain of Gold'. Here Aquinas collected excerpts from what he considered to be the best Patristic commentaries on the Gospels that he could find. As often as not, the sections line up with lectionary readings. A preacher stuck for something to say about a Gospel passage is likely to find ready insights. Aquinas was a preacher (some of his sermons survive) and his love for the Scriptures extends well beyond his many commentaries. Scholars have counted 25,000 quotations from the Bible in the *Summa Theologiae* alone.

Complete System?

Few thinkers have had a greater influence on later Christian thought than Aquinas. Although he is the touchstone of orthodoxy for Roman Catholics (and others), he was considered dangerously progressive during his lifetime and immediately after. His star has particularly risen over a 'long twentieth century', stretching from an encyclical letter from Pope Leo XIII (*Aeterni Patris*) in 1879 to the present day. Almost as soon as Leo was made pope, he set about a plan for 'the restoration of Christian philosophy'.[7] He saw Aquinas as central to this project and urged theologians across his church to return to the Dominican as a model. Leo wrote with a fervour that recalls his predecessor, John XXII, who had commented that Aquinas 'enlightened the Church more than all the other Doctors together; someone can derive more profit from his books in one year than from a lifetime spent in pondering the philosophy of others'.[8]

The course of this revival has taken twists and turns. At first, 'Thomism' proceeded much as it had before, but with renewed confidence. A prominent figure was the Dominican Reginald Garrigou-Lagrange (1877–1964), who advanced the cause of a great edifice of theology, built on Aquinas's works so vigorously as to have earned himself the nickname 'the sacred monster of Thomism'.[9] The theologians of the next generation, however, (some of whom Garrigou-Lagrange had taught) struck off in a very different direction. Garrigou-Lagrange, like his predecessors, had promoted not so much the texts of Aquinas himself as an exhaustive scheme based on his works: the Thomism called *Neo-scholasticism*. This made little distinction between the thought of Aquinas and the interpretation of Aquinas. In a sense, that could represent quite a sophisticated position. It made no naive attempt to lay hold of Aquinas's thought separate from the way it had been taken up into a tradition. More problematically, this tradition had become deadened to a real and widening gap between the ideas we find in Aquinas's own writings and the position of influential commentators, such as Francisco Suárez (1548–1617) and Thomas Cajetan (1469–1534). The theologians of the generation after Garrigou-Lagrange took it upon themselves to put

---

7 Since then it has become almost commonplace for popes to write in praise of Aquinas. Pius XI wrote, 'We consider that Thomas should be called not only the Angelic, but also the Common or Universal Doctor of the Church; for the Church has adopted his philosophy for her own, as innumerable documents of every kind attest' (*Studiorum Ducem*, 1923; see also Pius X, *Doctoris Angelici*, 1914).

8 Consistorial address of 1318, quoted in *Doctoris Angelici*.

9 Richard Peddicord has written a biography, *Sacred Monster of Thomism*, South Bend: St Augustine Press, 2004.

this Neoscholasticism under the spotlight and question where it was faithful to Aquinas and where it was not. Leo XIII played a part in this because he perhaps unwittingly provoked work on a new, more scholarly edition of Aquinas's works. As these volumes arrived in libraries around the world, scholars found inspiration to revisit the texts themselves. From this, a much wider renewal and reform of theology followed. Resting on the two pillars of a return to Aquinas and a return to the Fathers, its protagonists called it *ressourcement* ('going back to the sources' or, as we say today, 'resourcing'), while its detractors called it *Nouvelle Théologie*. Marie-Dominique Chenu (1895–1990) led the work of this movement on Thomism. On the Patristic front, principal figures include Henri de Lubac (1896–1991) and Hans Urs von Balthasar (1905–88). Yves Congar (1904–95) and Jean Daniélou (1905–74) are both also important. These five figures represent some of the leading figures of twentieth-century Catholic theology.

Inasmuch as scholars in previous generations, the Neoscholastics, had read the works of Aquinas himself, they generally had little interest in his historical setting or sources; he was the timeless voice of the tradition. His sources, even the Patristic ones, were of little interest in themselves. Today we think of the Patristic period as the jewel of a more or less 'catholic' inheritance. For the Neoscholastics, the Fathers were on a journey towards a true account of things; their faith was a work in progress. To a twenty-first-century mindset, that is one of the reasons they are so stimulating to read, and fun to teach. That sense of development, however, stood against the Neoscholastic sense of an inviolable tradition. After all, by later standards, the theology of the Fathers is incomplete at best, and at worst they 'got things wrong' (such as Origen on the pre-existence of souls). Aquinas was seen as having synthesized all that was of value from them. With that accomplished, no great reason remained for reading them. We see this in the choice of readings in Catholic daily prayer. Today, after the reforms following the Second Vatican Council, the writings of the Fathers take pride of place among what is placed before the Church day by day, second only to the Bible. Before the reforms, however, a priest or nun was more likely to be presented with a legend from the life of a saint than with a passage of Patristic theology. The *ressourcement* agitators not only put a renewed emphasis on the texts of Aquinas, they also put a new stress on Aquinas as a historical figure. With this they placed him in a lineage that stretched before and after him. With this they helped to reinvigorate the study of doctrinal history.

Such attention to history fostered a new interest in Christian thought as something creative and developing, and as a story and tradition to inhabit rather than a reference library to consult. To see what is at stake, we might consider two different approaches to the nature of law. In France, following the Napoleonic reforms, law tends to be viewed as a complete and sufficient system. It is codified and hangs together according to an overarching, top-level logic. New laws find their place within a grand scheme. In contrast, the English perspective sees law as a tapestry of parliamentary acts, enacted in response to particular situations, and with a sense of growing up from ground level, by precedent. Law is a tradition to be inhabited, something in which to argue. There is more to law than its written form, and even what is written and collected makes no claim at being complete. That would be a vain hope, but also an unnecessary one. When a judge hears a case, she is involved in something creative, by which she draws upon precedent, perhaps interpolating existing laws, to establish justice in some new situation.

The former, 'Continental' approach is an Enlightenment project, whereas the English scheme is more mediaeval. (In a variety of ways, it is tied up with monarchy.) Just as legal codes on the Continent are more comfortable with a sense of completion and self-sufficiency than is the English approach, Continental theologians are typically more attached to writing systematic theologies, and teaching from them, than English theologians, whose more natural form has been the essay, written for a specific time and place.

In law, the English scheme rests on an assumption of something akin to natural law. The enacted, or 'positive', law does not create justice but mirrors it. Since there is an order of equity that transcends any human codification, human law cannot be complete and does not need to be: justice is out there, to be appealed to when necessary, when a gap in the law has to be filled. In theology, the 'unsystematic' approach works with a similar relation of incomplete embodiment. The theology that human beings might write can represent something of the eternal truth – theology as it exists in God's mind – but it palpably cannot hope to codify it with any degree of completeness, nor need it. Theology at any particular moment need only seek to be an adequate expression of the faith for that particular moment and situation, confident that 'the faith' is there to be appealed to: as it is set out in the Scriptures, as it is woven into the history of Christian thought, and ultimately, as found in God.

The Neoscholastics thought of theology in a codified sense that parallels French law. They saw Aquinas as the great systematizer, and saw themselves as building on his works to produce ever more complete accounts. The Catholic theological reformers of the twentieth century questioned this. They presented Aquinas as closer to the approach characterized by comparison to English law. His work, even at its most seemingly exhaustive, was an exercise in exploration not completion. After all, even the largest projects of Aquinas had particular situations in mind: the *Summa Contra Gentiles* was written for missionaries; when the time came to write an 'introduction' to theology for friars in general, he wrote something new, the *Summa Theologiae*. By bulk, the majority of his works jump off from specific texts, from the Bible or the tradition, or from particular topics, rather than setting out to cover all of conceptual space.

We see how little Aquinas sought to create a complete and timeless system from his boundless interest in new ideas. Time after time over the course of his career he fell upon a new text or question with relish: in his *On the Hebdomnads* of Boethius early on, or in his commentary on the *Book of Causes* later in his life. That stands profoundly at odds with the outlook of the Neoscholastic scheme that took his name: so much at odds, indeed, that we might wonder whether it did not take his name in vain. In contrast to Thomas's openness, Neoscholastic Thomism tended to approach new texts and new questions like a castle with moat and drawbridge or, to change the metaphor, with the Teflon coating of an expensive frying pan. Neoscholastics told themselves that this outlook was one of confidence: who needs to think about Kant or Hegel, or embryology, when we already have the complete picture? In the twentieth century, it became more and more clear that this outlook was in fact profoundly defensive. Alasdair MacIntyre, perhaps the most significant Roman Catholic philosopher of his generation, presents this Neoscholastic withdrawal as the singular tragedy of his intellectual tradition.[10]

To crown it all, Aquinas quite deliberately left his *magnum opus* (the second *Summa*) unfinished and incomplete. Around 6 December 1273, he broke off writing, following a vision. 'All that I have written seems to me nothing but straw', he wrote, 'compared to what I have seen and what has been revealed to me.'

Throughout his works he presents a *participatory* vision of truth according to which human expressions of truth can be accurate and even adequate in their own way, but only as expressions of something rooted in God, which transcends them. He followed the insight of the Fourth Lateran Council: human expressions of truth have a likeness to divine truth, but only on the basis of a yet greater dissimilarity. His acute awareness of that dissimilarity rules out any sense that Aquinas sought a complete system. He underlined the point with an eloquent practical gesture when, after that vision, he laid down his quill once and for all.

This raises profound questions as to what anyone is *doing* with Aquinas in contemporary theology, or with any other historical author for that matter. We live in the middle of a revival of interest in Aquinas, but that phenomenon masks a distinction between contrasting approaches. For one group, the Neo-neoscholastics, Aquinas gives answers; for the other group, Aquinas is a good person in whose company to think. As an example, for the former group, Aquinas rules out the possibility of the ordination of women, whereas for the latter group he might provoke exploration down avenues that lead to the opposite conclusion. Members

---

10 MacIntyre argues that John Henry Newman's Anglican heritage was part of the solution. See *God, Philosophy, Universities*, Continuum, 2009, pp. 137–8.

of both groups consider that they are being faithful to Thomas, but might come to opposite conclusions on a particular topic.

Aquinas's Philosophical Approach

The structure of the *Summa Theologiae* runs as follows:

Part I – God; creation
Part II:I – The goal of human life; passions, sins, law and grace
Part II:II – The virtues
Part III – Christ; the life of the Church.

Anna Williams, and others, point to a more or less Neoplatonic structure, picking up the themes of *exitus* and *reditus*, proceeding and returning. Aquinas starts with God, first as One and then according to the internal and 'necessary' processions of the Trinity, as Three. He then considers external and contingent processions, which is to say the creation and the properties of angels and material beings. That concludes the first part. The second part considers what it means to be human in terms of action, and that involves an extended discussion of the ethical life. This is thoroughly teleological: it is oriented to God as the goal of human life. All action should be good action, and all good action is both a reception of something from God and, in a sense, a journey back to him. Then, in part three, we have the great theological drama of the coming forth of God *within creation*, in the Incarnation, the story of human redemption and the eschatological return of creation to God as fully redeemed. In the incomplete conclusion of the third section, he discusses the role of the Church in this *exitus–reditus* scheme: as the means of redemption and, as the body of Christ, also its goal, as oriented to the final vision of God, but even now the place of his visitation.

Aquinas's thought is full of distinctions, his account of 'how the world hangs together'. Among other categories, this takes in substance and accidents, form and matter, existence and essence, potentiality and actuality, being and action, necessity and contingency, genus, species and individual, and the four causes.[11] We have covered much of this material in the chapter on Aristotle, for Aquinas gives each his own particular colouration.

Aquinas might make distinctions but this does not make him a dualist, as if what are distinguished (existence and essence, form and matter, and so on) exist by themselves. Just because we can distinguish pairs of aspects to something does not mean that we can separate those aspects. For instance, we can distinguish between form and matter, but a material thing is not an amalgam of two independent and opposed realms of form and matter, or rational spirit and irrational stuff. We are simply recognizing aspects to things, aspects indeed which could not be manifest but for the inextricable link between them. We cannot know form other than through matter; there can be no matter other than bearing some particular form. (On this point Aquinas differed from other scholastic theologians. He did not believe that formless matter, or 'prime matter', could exist by itself, without a form.) Similarly, no accident can exist separate from its existence in some substance. As have noted, we do not encounter the ability to play the oboe other than as a property of a real human being.

The form/matter distinction, and substance/accidents distinction, come into their own in relation to the soul. That subject is a good example of Aquinas combining the best of Plato and Aristotle, and in this case erring towards the latter.

As we saw in opening chapters of this book, Plato recognized human immortality but at a price: the soul in Plato is too easily immortal and spiritual, rendering the body its prison. In contrast, the strength of Aristotle here is for the soul to be perfectly integrated with the materiality of the body: the soul is the material person viewed from the perspective of what that materiality adds up to, namely the form. As a consequence, the soul in Aristotle is a little too worldly for Christian purposes. Immortality is not in view. The soul of a human being on death is as intrinsically perishable

---

11 For a pithy summary of these topics, perhaps a little too pithy for the beginner, see his *De Principiis Naturae* (*Concerning the Principles of Nature*).

as the form of a jug when it is smashed. Aristotle's account of the soul was almost ready for theological use, but not quite.

Aquinas tweaked Aristotle's description of the soul in a Platonic direction. The human soul is the form of the body, but it is an unusual sort of material form, since God made it immortal. That, for Aquinas, is closely associated with rationality. The soul describes what a human being is, and what a human being can do. We can reason, and indeed reasoning is the summit of what we are for Aquinas. Reason of itself can be thought of in isolation from a body, as with the angels, meaning that the reasoning soul can be imagined to exist separated from the body.

Aquinas placed his tweak at the beginning of human life. He held that every human soul is specially created by God in each individual case, and *that* is what invests it with immortality. That, however, may be a red herring. After all, *everything* is created by God, including rocks and the forms of rocks, sheep and the form of sheep, people and their souls, without having to deny that they also come into existence according to natural process that makes sense on a worldly level. For my part, I would prefer to place the divine intervention at the end of bodily life, rather than its beginning. Perhaps Aristotle was right, from a pagan perspective, to say that the human soul is the sort of thing that would perish at death, as the form of a jug perishes when it is smashed or the 'soul' of a tree when it dies. Aristotle, however, did not know that, at death, God graciously preserves who we are – our form or soul – until the resurrection. However we account for the preservation of the soul, this stress on resurrection is important, and was important for Aquinas: the soul is the form of a body, and it is 'unnatural' for it to exist separate from the body. The souls of the righteous may be in the hand of God (Wisd. 3.1), but even there they yearn for restored materiality.

These various categories and distinctions put forward by Aquinas deal with aspects of *being*: being expressed through form and through matter, through substance and accidents, and so on. We get close to the heart of his metaphysics when we note that, for Aquinas, being naturally overflows into doing, or what Aquinas would call *action* or *act*. At a first glance, Aquinas's philosophical scheme can seem quite abstract and intellectual. At a closer look, it turns out to be full of energy and action. Being is acting, so even a book, for example, is acting: it is performing the first and foundational act of any existing thing, which is be-ing, and being in its own particular, bookish, way. This remarkable and somewhat counterintuitive position makes sense for Aquinas on the basis that the being of any particular creature, books included, is its own particular trace of its creator. Its being is an imprint of God's being, and God for Aquinas is *all action* or *pure act* (an idea we encountered in the chapter on Aristotle). At the heart of every creature, therefore, is its first and deepest of actions, which is simply to be.

Action is an imitation of God, who is not only *all act* but also *all perfect*. Because of that, Aquinas sometimes refers to a creature's being, its first and innermost act, as its 'first perfection', and to its outward actions as its 'second perfection': 'just as the act of being and the nature of a thing are considered as belonging to its first perfection, so operation is referred to its second perfection'.[12] Elsewhere, Aquinas describes three perfections: first to *be*, second to *act*, and third to *attain*.[13] Just as God is the source of being (the first perfection), he is also the goal of being (the third perfection). He is also the one being imitated in the second perfection: just as God is both good and the one who pours out goodness, so we most perfectly show goodness when we not only are good (along the lines of the first perfection, of being) but also pour that goodness out (in act, along the lines of the second perfection), and especially as we act towards others so as to direct them towards their true good and goal, namely God (their third perfection).[14]

For the English speaker, probably the most perfect expression of the idea of a second perfection, of act, following from a first perfection, of being, is found in a sonnet by Gerard Manley Hopkins.

---

12 *Summa Contra Gentiles* (hereafter *SCG*), trans. Anton C. Pegis and others, New York: Hanover House, 1955, 5 vols, II.46.3.

13 *ST* I.6.3.

14 *ST* I.73.1; *SCG* II.45.4.

(He wrote the accents in so as to give the poem the particular rhythm he wanted.)

> As kingfishers catch fire, dragonflies dráw fláme;
> As tumbled over rim in roundy wells
> Stones ring; like each tucked string tells, each hung bell's
> Bow swung finds tongue to fling out broad its name;
> Each mortal thing does one thing and the same:
> Deals out that being indoors each one dwells;
> Selves—goes itself; myself it speaks and spells,
> Crying Whát I do is me: for that I came.
> Í say móre: the just man justices;
> Kéeps gráce: thát keeps all his goings graces;
> Acts in God's eye what in God's eye he is—
> Chríst—for Christ plays in ten thousand places,
> Lovely in limbs, and lovely in eyes not his
> To the Father through the features of men's faces.

Ethics

Being expresses itself in act. In another way, act shapes who we are. Admittedly, for Aquinas what basic kind of thing we are is settled in advance by our substantial form (to be a tree, a book or a human being). *What sort* of a human being we are, however, depends on the accrual of accidental forms, which either shape us towards virtue or towards vice. We have already encountered this idea in Aristotle: virtues and vices are 'habits', formed by actions as they become 'second nature'. The link between *being* and *doing* runs in both directions. Each human being is born as a work in progress. We are made open and set on a journey. The old question 'What are you going to do with your life?' lines up with another: 'What do you want to be when you grow up?' We are very closely associated with our actions and their consequences.

Ethics in Aquinas is all about becoming the right sort of person, for whom doing the right thing becomes natural. That approach allows goodness to be exercised in a way that is sensitive to context. As George Herbert put it in a poem about the 'honest man':

Who, when great trials come,
Nor seeks, nor shuns them; but does calmly stay,
Till he the thing and the example weigh:
All being brought into a sum,
What place or person calls for, he does pay.[15]

Virtue can judge what is demanded in each particular situation in a far more subtle and supple way than the rival tradition of memorizing examples or cases (called 'casuistry') from large manuals of ethics. The emphasis Aquinas places on virtue is also part and parcel of his presentation of a good life as easy and joyful, not arduous and draining. For the person formed in virtue under God's tutelage, goodness comes naturally, rather like the skilled dancer being able to execute difficult steps with hardly a second thought. Aquinas sometimes faces an objection that lingers in Christian ethical thinking to this day: 'isn't the essence of virtue to be heroic and demanding?' His reply is almost a little sarcastic: 'no, the essence of goodness isn't to be hard; it's to be good. Don't mix them up.' Rather like that skilful dancer, the virtuous person is happy and at ease in being virtuous. As Fergus Kerr has put it, the ethics of Aquinas most of all comes down to 'beatitude and virtue'.[16]

Analogy and Participation

One of Aquinas's most significant contributions to philosophical theology is in the area of religious language. He returned to the topic several times across his corpus, but the passage to consider is *Summa Theologiae* I.13. Here Aquinas confronted, head-on, a problem posed down the history of religious thought: how can we have anything to say about God, when God inconceivably

---

15 From 'Constancy'.
16 *After Aquinas: Versions of Thomism*, Wiley-Blackwell, 2002, p. 111.

surpasses human knowing? How can our words capture anything
of what God is like? The bark of a dog can express little about its
mistress, yet we and the dog sit on the same side of the creature–
creator distinction. As Augustine put it: 'The total transcendence
of the godhead quite surpasses the capacity of ordinary speech.'[17]

I asked what our language could 'capture' of God. The word
was used inadvisedly, and deliberately so. Aquinas stands with
theologians down the ages in saying that knowledge of God rests
on God's action, not ours. We are principally concerned with
God's revelation, not our speculation, with God's donation not
our 'capture'. This section of the *Summa* is not primarily an exercise in natural theology: in working out what to say about God
separate from revelation. But even with the emphasis on what
God has revealed in human language, our fundamental problem
remains, which is how human language can bear upon God. We
say that 'God is good', but it remains to be asked what we mean
by 'good' in that statement.

Aquinas considers two wrong turns, one of which was already
popular before his time, and one which was to become popular
after. The first option is to stress God's transcendence and to do
that so much as to say that the divine reference for a word and
the human reference for a word have nothing in common. This is
called *equivocity* or *equivocal* use of language. We say that God is
wise but we have no sense of what 'wise' means in that statement.
We are compelled by the Scriptures to say 'God is wise', but what
that wisdom amounts to is completely opaque to us. This position aligns with the *apophatic* or 'negative' tradition in theology,
which stresses that our knowledge of God is knowledge of what
God is not. To say that God is 'living' would indicate no more
than that God is not dead.

Although Aquinas has a healthy respect for divine transcendence
and the apophatic tradition, this approach to religious language
will not do for him. Whatever the scriptural writers thought they
were doing, they thought they were being more communicative

17 *On the Trinity* VII.7, trans Edmund Hill, Hyde Park: New City Press, 1991,
p. 227.

than this when they wrote about God. To refer to the 'living God' meant more than saying that God is not dead. Moreover, as Paul wrote, some things about God are clear even from creation, if we have the eyes to see: 'his eternal power and divine nature, invisible though they are, have been understood and seen through the things he has made' (Rom. 1.20).

The opposite position is *univocity*. On this view, we use a word of creatures and of God in exactly the same way. The points made by the apophatic theologians, albeit to an extreme, help us to see the problems with univocity. Even to share a word between one creature and another (humans and gorillas are both 'social', for instance) involves stretching a word, not using it univocally and, it goes without saying, God is more different from us than we are from gorillas. For another thing, many words apply to our fellow humans as accidents: this person, thank goodness, is wise, but he only happens to be wise. God does not just happen to be wise; God is wisdom itself. We do not understand what it means for someone to be wisdom itself, so when we call God wise we cannot be using the word in the same way as when we apply it to a creature.

Having ruled out equivocity and univocity, another approach is to suppose that words say nothing about God in himself but only about God's effects in the world: when we say that God is good we say nothing about God himself but only that God causes goodness in the world. The position is associated with Alain of Lille. Aquinas criticizes it as he criticized equivocity: when the scriptural writers wrote about the living God they meant more than saying that God is the cause of life in creation, although that is true. He points to a further problem: it cannot explain why we say some things about God and not others. We say that God is good but not that God is a body, and yet God is the cause of both: of goodness and of bodies.

Alain's account will not work, but it points us in the right direction because it points to causation. It is not, writes Aquinas, that God is good because he is the cause of goodness in things but, rather, that he causes goodness in things because he is good (I.13.2). This gives Aquinas all he needs to construct his account of religious language. We can use our human vocabulary, learned from creaturely things, to speak about God, because God is the cause, or creator, of those creatures. Everything about them has been given to them by God. Their goodness, wisdom, strength, and so on, is given to them by God as an image or trace of God's own goodness, wisdom or strength. We call this a *participatory* account: everything the creature has comes as a participation in God.[18] Evil only is excepted. Evil is precisely a failure of the creature to receive from God, a turning away from his gift.

This trace or participation is what allows our talk about God to be more than equivocation and also what means that it is not univocation either: these names say something about God's very self, Aquinas writes, but they certainly do not capture everything about him (I.13.2). Our language relates to God in a similar way to how creatures relate to God, as a sort of likeness. The name for a likeness to God in things is participation and the name for a likeness in language is *analogy*. This involves applying a word from one domain to another domain, but not 'improperly' because it refers to a real 'likeness' (I.13.6).[19]

The basis of all of this comes from the doctrine of creation, and the idea that

> God possesses beforehand in himself all the perfections of creatures, being himself absolutely and universally perfect. Hence every creature represents him, and is like him, so far as it possesses some perfection; yet it represents him [. . .] as the supreme principle of which they both fall short and derive some likeness (I.13.2).

Aquinas distinguishes *what* a word like wisdom means and *how* it means it: the reality it names and how it names it. What 'wisdom'

---

18 An introduction to participation as the key to Christian metaphysics is forthcoming and due for publication in 2014.

19 Awareness of analogy and its workings is helpful for negotiating human life. Take the word 'confidential'. It can mean slightly different, although analogically related, things in different settings. Awareness of this means that our confidentiality can itself be more 'sophisticated'.

refers to applies first of all to God. God is more wise, and true, good and alive, than any creature is. The creature does have a share in these properties from God but they belong to the creature in a derived and secondary sense. What I mean by 'wise' applies more perfectly to God than to any creature. The opposite applies to *how* it means it. The 'flavour' the word has for us, or the handle we have on it, comes to us through creatures. My sense of wisdom is primarily creaturely wisdom. My sense of what it means to be alive is creaturely life. This is the only sense of these words that I have. This way of meaning applies primarily to creatures and only secondarily to God. God is wiser than my grandmother, it goes without saying, so I say 'wise' of God more truly than I do of her, but my sense of what 'wise' means was learned from people like my grandmother.

Reading On

Aquinas wrote two compendious treatments of the Christian faith. Questions in the earlier *Summa Contra Gentiles* are laid out in a less intricate structure than in the later *Summa Theologiae* (sometimes known in the USA as *Summa Theologica*). This may make for accessibility but it sacrifices charm. It has been translated into English (South Bend: Notre Dame University Press, 1975) in five cheap volumes. The later, magisterial *Summa Theologiae* was translated into English twice in the twentieth century. The later translation runs to 60 volumes with facing Latin and English, plus index (Blackfriars, from 1964, reissued by CUP, 2006). The earlier edition was published from 1920 to 1942, originally in 22 volumes (London: Burns, Oates & Washburne) and is available online.[20] Although Timothy McDermott's *Summa Theologiae: A Concise Translation* is likely to offend purists, his abridgement is remarkably sensitive and makes an ideal way to begin to explore the later *Summa* (London: Eyre and Spottiswoode, 1989). The introductory *Compendium of Theology*, which is another good

---

20 Quotations in this book are taken from this translation.

place to start for his theology, has been translated by Richard Regan (OUP, 2009).

Hardly any anthology exists of greater value for the theologian than Josef Pieper's small collection *The Human Wisdom of St Thomas: A Breviary of Philosophy* (translated by Drostan Mac-Laren, Ignatius, 2002). Morris Stockhammer's *Thomas Aquinas Dictionary* indexes a wide range of topics as quotations (New York: Philosophical Library, 1965). Penguin's *Selected Writings*, translated by Ralph McInerny (1998), is one of several good anthologies of important texts, alongside Timothy McDermott's edition of *Selected Philosophical Writings* (OUP, 1998).

Three remarkable essays on Aquinas by Josef Pieper are collected in his *The Silence of St Thomas* (New York: Pantheon, 1957). He wrote a general introduction in his *A Guide to Thomas Aquinas* (Ignatius, 1991). G. K. Chesterton was not a scholarly theologian but he was an instinctual Thomist, as witnessed by his *St Thomas Aquinas* (London: Hodder & Stoughton, 1933). The Scottish Dominican Fergus Kerr has produced a number of accessible books on Aquinas. The most basic is *Thomas Aquinas: A Very Short Introduction* (OUP, 2009). *After Aquinas: Versions of Thomism* (Wiley-Blackwell, 2002) sets out the twists and turns of how Aquinas has been received, appropriated and deployed down the centuries. His *Contemplating Aquinas: On the Varieties of Interpretation* (SCM Press, 2003) brings together some excellent essays. For Aquinas as a spiritual writer, see Jean-Pierre Torrell, *Christ and Spirituality in St Thomas Aquinas*, translated by Bernhard Blankenhorn (CUA, 2011). The works of Aquinas have received many brilliant more advanced studies. If two are to be recommended they might be Oliva Blanchette's *The Perfection of the Universe According to Aquinas: Teleological Cosmology* (University Park: Pennsylvania State University Press, 1992) and John Wippel's *The Metaphysical Thought of Thomas Aquinas: From Finite Being to Uncreated Being* (CUA, 2000). Marcus Plested has charted a remarkable story in his *Orthodox Readings of Aquinas* (OUP, 2012), which does much to dismantle many of the stock distinctions made between the Eastern and Western Churches.

9

Late Scholasticism

John Duns Scotus (*c*.1265–*c*.1308) is one of perhaps three British theologians to have achieved widespread fame. Unfortunately for the British, none of these figures covers us in honour. The other two are the Scottish monk Pelagius (mid-fourth century to early fifth century), who gives his name to the Pelagian heresy (salvation by hard work rather than by grace), and William of Ockham (*c*.1300–*c*.1350), a flag-bearer for *nominalism*, which we will consider below.

Like Ockham after him, Scotus was a Franciscan friar. He held teaching positions in Oxford, Paris and Cologne. In comparison to his predecessors, the balance between philosophy and theology in his work seems to veer by turns to one and then the other. On occasions, philosophy sets the running, and especially logic, to an extent unfamiliar in Aquinas, for instance. On other occasions, he runs philosophy down in favour of revelation. This is less contradictory than it might seem. Scotus makes a sharper distinction than his predecessors between *nature* and *grace*, or between what is *natural* and what is *supernatural*. By 'supernatural' here we do not mean the creatures encountered in horror films but the sense that there is something beyond the order of this world. Even with that clarification, we should treat the nature–supernature distinction with care, since if we admit it lightly we may already concede a break between the two that some would consider too sharp.

Grace and Nature: Revelation and Ethics

If we see the natural and the supernatural as fundamentally alien to one another then a particular understanding of revelation follows, one which plays down the sense in which the Scriptures are a human document with a 'natural' story, as well as a divine document with a 'supernatural' story. The Church had always held the Bible to be inspired and, indeed, to be 'the word of God'. The shift in the late Middle Ages was not so much to hold it in higher veneration – that would hardly have been possible – but rather to set the Bible in sharper contradistinction to the rest of human thought and culture (although that part of ecclesiastical thought and culture which we call the authoritative tradition or 'magisterium' came to be seen as increasingly like revelation and less like the rest of thought and culture). Previously, placing Scripture alongside reason made sense, since revelation, reason and the world proceeded from God as part of the same well-ordered plan. Both creation and revelation were seen as an expression of what God is like and could therefore be expected to line up with one another. Philosophy could be respected, as far as it went, because any investigation of the nature of things would bear witness to their author, namely God. We can distinguish between reason and revelation, and rightly so, but we should also recognize that all revelation involves reason (since God speaks into a human situation, in human history, with human words) and all reason is a form of revelation (since both the intelligibility of what we know and our capacity to know are participations in the divine Word).

Philosophy or 'reason', however, only goes so far. God therefore reveals to us not only truths beyond human knowledge (such as that the world is of finite age, a truth beyond human exploration for most of human history, or that God is three) but also what we might otherwise have worked out (for instance that God exists, or that God is one, or that we should tell the truth and should not steal) but only after a long time, and only by a few and with possibility of error along the way.[1] Aquinas makes this point in the very first

---

1 *ST* I.1.1.

article of the *Summa Theologiae*, stressing both the *overlap* of reason and revelation, and their differences. In contrast, Scotus began one of his major treatises, the *Ordinatio*, by setting theology off from philosophy, '[p]hilosophers maintain the perfection of nature and deny supernatural perfection', while 'theologians understand the deficiency of nature and the perfection of the supernatural'.[2]

Seeing revelation as detached from reason belongs alongside seeing God's will as detached from his reason. We see this worked out at its most extreme is Scotus's ethics. Just before his time, the natural-law approach had flourished. Alongside Scripture, ethics was also grounded in the reasoned exploration of the nature of reality: of human beings, of human communities, and of the universe more widely. Admittedly, a fallen world is going to illustrate ethical priorities as much through lapses, and in the breach, as through positive examples. For Scotus, the natural-law approach would not do; for him, any sense that the nature of things might illustrate what is right and wrong would curtail the all-important freedom of God. As a voluntarist (from the Latin *voluntas*, meaning 'will' or 'choice'), Scotus put priority on the will in contradistinction to reason and wisdom. On that account, Scotus held that only the first two (or maybe three) of the Ten Commandments belong to the natural law (in its usual sense) and are self-evidently correct. These are the commandments that deal with God. In contrast, the other commandments hold only because God has chosen to say that they hold. For Scotus, God could just as well have said 'thou shalt murder'. That freedom is a mark of God's *greatness*, since greatness consists more than anything else in his freedom and power.

Scotus came to define freedom as *synchronic freedom*: the ability, in the very moment that we are going to do one thing, to choose not to do it, or to do the opposite. This is the beginning of a profound shift in Western thought over the nature of freedom: from freedom *to* to freedom *from*. Previously, to be free was to be able to do what one did easily, and easily to do what is right.

---

2 Prol., §5, quoted by Olivier Boulnois, 'Duns Scotus, John', in *Encyclopedia of Christian Theology*, ed. Jean-Yves Lacoste, Routledge, 2004, pp. 458–63, p. 459.

Today, freedom is largely seen as brute choice, which must involve freedom not to do even what is right. This is a Scotist legacy.

Scotus would not allow that we could work out how to live from examining what it means to be a human being – that natural-law approach – because that would curtail God's freedom, understood as 'freedom to' do whatever he wants, even given what he has already done. God is free, according to Scotus, to decree that stealing is wrong, or that it is right, that murder is wrong, or that it is right.

A generation or so after Scotus, William of Ockham would take this reappraisal of ethics as far as it could go, arguing that all ten of the commandments rest on God's arbitrary will, such that he could have said 'You will enter into eternal life by hating me.' On a similar basis, resting on the absolute power of God, Christ could just as well have been incarnate as a rock or a donkey.[3] A proper response to this overwrought voluntarism is relatively easy to envisage. God did not dream up any of the commandments on a whim or as an expression of his brute freedom. The commandments are expressions of God's *nature*. It is no infringement of God's excellence that he cannot commend evil, since it is no infringement of God's excellence that he cannot *be* evil. Indeed, it is very much part of God's excellence that he is 'light and in him is no darkness at all' (1 John 1.5).

The voluntarist understanding of creation leads to a certain attitude towards the world. Since its form rests on the arbitrary will of God, the world does not reveal the nature of God. Creation is no longer a manifestation of a million aspects of the divine life, as it was in previous theology. The result, as one author has recently written, was a tendency to observe the world 'in a detached manner (indeed like investigators from another galaxy)'.[4] Moreover, since

---

3 Although this example is widely cited, for instance by Josef Pieper in *Scholasticism*, New York: Pantheon Books, 1960, p. 143 and Oliver Crisp in *Divinity and Humanity*, CUP, 2007, p. 84, the *Centiloquium Theologicum* from which it is taken may not be authentically by Ockham. See Gijsbert van der Brink, *Almighty God: A Study of the Doctrine of Divine Omnipotence*, The Hague: Peeters, 1993, p. 83, n. 62. The notion is, however, in keeping with his thought.

4 John Milbank, 'The Thomistic Telescope: Truth and Identity', in *Transcendence and Phenomenology*, ed. Peter Candler and Conor Cunningham, SCM Press, 2007, pp. 288–333, p. 292.

the world embodies no particular divinely revealing order, it can be approached, even manipulated, in a pragmatic fashion, and since it reveals no particular order, our behaviour towards it came to be ruled by agreement between ourselves, imposed upon the world rather than discerned there. This marks the rise of contract as a basis for rule and law.[5] Further still, although the early voluntarists clearly saw the world as God's creation, and its parts as disposed purposefully by God according to his own inscrutable will, that element could, and did, drop out with time. Dwelling in the world was no longer thought to bring any particular communion with God; that it is a *creation* was simply something to be believed. Increasingly, as we have seen in later history, it was not believed.

This secularizing tendency joins up with another. From 1300 onwards, we see theology given its own realm, increasingly separate from philosophy. That was inevitable, since theology was now primarily to do with the Scriptures in distinction from philosophy, the truth of the Scriptures coming from beyond in a way that circumvented reason, a bolt from the blue. No doubt, this move was intended as a complement to theology and revelation. It stressed that the Scriptures are in a realm of their own (although no one had doubted that before). The effect over time, however, worked in the opposite direction. Creating a domain for Scripture in sharp contradistinction to reason also created a domain for reason in contradistinction to Scripture. Within a few hundred years, an appeal to reason independent of Scripture and its interpretive penumbra in the theological tradition would make sense. A division that had attempted to shore up the all-sufficiency of Scripture left us with the all-sufficiency of reason. The more Scripture came to be seen as that bolt from the blue, a time-capsule containing facts, the more it could be ignored by those who so chose.[6]

Again, this maps on to a sharp division between the natural and the supernatural, often worked out in terms of the proper destiny of the human being. From the time of Scotus onwards, the idea

5 Milbank, 'Telescope', p. 297.
6 Significantly, this narrative about the rise of neutral, untheological reason is accepted both by those who celebrate it (such as Honnefender) and those who deplore it (such as Boulnois, Milbank and Pickstock).

became important that human beings have an entirely 'natural' destiny and set of desires, which can be understood in worldly terms. A supernatural destiny, to the vision of God, is then an overlay: something separate that God bestows but which our nature does not call for. Neoscholastitics such as Bañez, Suárez and Cajetan attributed this position to Aquinas. Although passages in his writing can be advanced to support it, many do not, and the logic of the whole is not in favour of a realm of 'pure nature' in contradistinction to an overlay of grace. Henri de Lubac was to point this out with this book *Surnaturel* in 1946. To be fair to those who proposed the nature/grace distinction, they wished to stress the gratuity of grace and also the certainty of God's existence, supposing that it could be proved even by 'natural' reason, 'without' grace. It had conceded, however, the idea of a purely natural account of the world, for which grace was an extra. Modern atheism could be said to have grown from this: it is the rejection of that extra.

Gilson recounts a parallel scheme, with the emphasis on Ockham's consummation:

At the top of the world, a God whose absolute power knew no limits, not even those of a stable nature endowed with a necessity and an intelligibility of its own. Between His will and the countless individuals [. . .] in space [. . .] and [. . .] time, there was strictly nothing. No intelligibility [no overarching order] could be found in any of God's works. How could there be order in nature, when there is no nature? [. . .] Instead of being an eternal source of that concrete order of intelligibility and beauty, which we call nature, Ockham's God was expressly intended to relieve the world of the necessity of having any meaning of its own [. . .] Ockham's philosophy took deep root in the European universities of the fourteenth century. Scholastic philosophers then began to mistrust their own principles, and mediaeval philosophy broke down [. . .] the best minds were surprised to find reason empty and began to despise it.[7]

_____

7 Étienne Gilson, *The Unity of Philosophical Experience*, New York: Charles Scribner's Sons, 1937, pp. 85–6, 90–1.

Scotus rejected natural-law ethics, because it seemed to restrain the freedom of God to decree whatever moral code he wanted: not least since that choice is now based in his will rather than being rooted in expressing his nature. Scotus also rejected the virtue approach to ethics, but this time because it seemed to run counter to the freedom of the human being. The root of that second rejection lies in Scotus's distinction between a desire (or 'affection', or capacity) in every person for benefit (or advantage), and another, very separate capacity for justice. By nature, we desire our own flourishing but, according to Scotus, in order to be moral we need to transcend that desire and choose, instead, to be just: to choose to do the right thing, not what makes us happy.

This approach stands profoundly at odds with the scheme of Aquinas and others before Scotus. For Aquinas, the origin of all that is good, in any and every way, is God. God is the source of all that is good: as excellent, as beneficial or as moral. Because of that, the excellent, the beneficial and the moral also co-inhere in the world. Any human being's best happiness and fulfilment comes by choosing the morally good, not the morally bad. If our sense of self-interest leads us to do what is wrong, then that is because we do not properly know where our interest really lies. If, however, we are skilled at discerning the true goodness of things (which is the virtue of prudence) then our desires (which are always, by definition, for self-interest) can become a good guide in conduct. In contrast, for Scotus, benefit and moral goodness are at best unconnected, and are often at loggerheads. Scotus bequeathed a masochist ethical scheme where choice is so central that doing good cannot be based on what comes naturally; at its most authentic, goodness is marked by sacrifice. This moral vision continues to be significant to this day, both for those who try to live by it, and for those who reject the moral life in no small part because of its association with relentless abnegation.

When, centuries later, Kant sided with duty over self-interest, he was siding with Scotus. In *Religion within the Bounds of Mere Reason*, Kant went so far as to say that if we did the objectively right or good thing, but out of self-interest – for instance if we refrained from cruelty because we were worried about our reputation – then that would not in fact be a good act, because it was done out of self-interest and not out of obedience to duty. The point is not far from Scotus's own position. In contrast, Aquinas would reply 'thank goodness for a proper sense of the value of a good reputation'.

Ockham and Nominalism

The English Franciscan friar William of Ockham (*c.*1287–1347) was one of the most radical of mediaeval thinkers, pressing various ideas to their furthest extent: principally voluntarism, which we have already encountered, and nominalism, which will feature prominently in this section. This radicalism was not well received. Fifty-one propositions from his works were pronounced to be erroneous by one papal commission and heretical by another. He died excommunicated from the Church.

Ockham's most striking feature is his *nominalism*. As Maarten Hoenen has defined it, 'nominalism is the theory holding that there is nothing outside the human mind corresponding to general terms such as man or living thing (universals)'.[8] That is to say, if we give the same name, 'human being', to seven billion creatures, it is simply *because we give them that same name* ('name', as we noted above, is *nomen* in Latin, from which we get 'nominalism'), not because we are recognizing something common that they all share. There is no metaphysical reality (called a 'universal') which they all share.

Nominalism reflects a fateful shift in Western thought away from things towards our knowledge or conceptualization of things. We will see this time and again: for Descartes certainty in thought was to be found in reflection upon our own thinking; Kant urged us not to seek foundations for goodness or truth in a transcendent source beyond the order of this world but rather in the structure of thought itself; much philosophy in the early twentieth century

---

8 Maarten Hoenen, 'Nominalism', *Encyclopedia of Christian Theology*, ed. Jean-Yves Lacoste, Routledge, 2004, pp. 1131–8.

shifted from thinking about 'external' object, such as being or goodness, towards thinking about the structure of language.

Before we consider nominalism, it will be useful to lay out the lineaments of realism, its opponent: the idea that all creatures of a particular type have something real in common, namely the form proper to that species, which makes them what they are. Realism admits of a variety of interpretations, and we have already encountered two quite different varieties. For Plato, the form of the individual participates in a separate, eternal Form; for Aristotle, things are determined by their forms but there are no forms outside of individual things. We could call Plato's position 'strong transcendent realism', since he assumed the existence of the form of things outside of the things, as exemplars in another realm; we could call Aristotle's position 'moderate, non-transcendent realism', since he held that things of the same kind shared the same form, but that this form, for all it was real, is not found outside of concrete things. We have also seen a third position, that of Augustine, who laid the foundations for Christian realism. His position might be called, inelegantly, 'strong transcendent realism with a grounding in the divine ideas', since forms exist in things and in their exemplar, but that exemplar is no longer a separate, eternal form but rather dwells in the mind of God.

The Christian realist is with Ockham in denying eternal exemplar forms, separate with God. Ockham went further, however, and he did so as a *voluntarist*. He denied any centrality to a link between the innermost reality of a created thing and something in God's mind, of which it is an image. Indeed, by the time of Ockham, voluntarism so put the emphasis on the divine will rather than the divine intellect, that the divine ideas were all but eliminated from theology. Nominalism followed in its wake. Creation now rests on the inscrutable, radically free will of God, not in the divine intellect (admittedly joined by the will). In the language of Aristotle's four causes, the idea of God as the formal cause of things hardly features in any significant way; he is only the efficient cause. Nominalism also rests on voluntarism from a human point of view, since the commonality of a common name is now said to come from the human will, and no longer from things themselves. It rests on the will choosing to impose a name, rather than on the intellect perceiving a pre-existing truth.

If Ockham's name is widely known, today it is for his famous 'razor'. As he formulates it in his commentary on the *Sentences*: 'Nothing ought to be posited without a reason given, unless it is self-evident, or known by experience or proved by the authority of Sacred Scripture.'[9] He deployed it for nominalist purposes. Ockham thought that we could be able to do without real universals, and therefore that we should. The question for us here is what we mean by the phrase 'known by experience'. While we cannot conduct an experiment and find a real universal, or any other metaphysical entity, lying under a microscope or caught in a net, we *can* ask ourselves whether our experience of the world and of life makes more or less sense according to this view or that. We cannot trap a universal in a jar, but that does not mean that reality does not impinge on us in such a way – an empirical way – that the existence of universals makes sense.

This invocation of experiment is relevant. Ockham's nominalism favoured experiment, and members of the Franciscan order to which he belonged played an important part in the growth of early modern science. In part, this was because science requires a certain disenchantment of the world to happen first. This idea sometimes goes by its German name, as popularized by Max Weber: 'Die Entzauberung der Welt'. We have already touched on this. For Thomas, the world is entangled with the divine ideas. Although he held all knowledge to be sensual, which in a sense favours experiment, Aquinas actually had no great interest in 'scientific' questions.[10] Ockham, however, even more than Scotus, viewed the world as floating relatively free from anything but the will of God. On that basis, nature does not tell us anything about God, but neither therefore is anything about nature known in advance

---

9 *In I Sent.* dist. 30, q. 1, trans. Paul Vincent Spade in 'Ockham's Nominalist Metaphysics', in *The Cambridge Companion to Ockham*, ed. Paul Vincent Spade, CUP, 1999, pp. 100–17, p. 104.

10 His teacher, Albert the Great, however, showed an aptitude for natural science when he said that in matters that are open to empirical verification, he required empirical verification. See Josef Pieper, *Scholasticism*, p. 115.

on account of a larger theological picture. That idea opened the way for science. The only way to know anything about the world was to make a scientific study, and since the world is a more 'secular' place than it was before, there is less sense of an impiety in putting it to the test.[11]

Nominalism is a widespread position today. That is, in part, because it has changed the terms of the discussion. Nominalism is part of a drift towards thinking that the world makes sense entirely on its own terms: there *just are* objects that we call chairs; who needs embarrassing metaphysical categories such as 'form' to describe them? In this, nominalism steps towards materialism twice over. In the first place, it evacuates the universe of metaphysical categories, by rendering them redundant or by shifting them to be part of our *mental* furniture rather than part of the objective structure of the universe. Nominalism also drifts towards materialism in a more subtle sense. A typical nominalist critique of realism might ask the realist if she really believes that there is an archetypal lock and an archetypal key floating in the ether, of which every lock and every key is a copy or image. If so, how does the realist cope with the massive divergence between various locks and various keys? Keys can look so different that a common archetype can be difficult to conceive. If there is no common *form* to locks or to keys, in the physical sense of 'form', how can they share in a common metaphysical form? The very question, however, rests on a nominalist shift towards supposing that physical things *just are* and that metaphysical claims come as a secondary overlay. Asking what *physical* features they have in common (e.g. what all keys, or all locks, or all doors have in common in terms of shape) is what nominalism conditions us to ask: this is the nominalist frame of reference. Nominalism has deflected us from seeing, conceptualizing and responding spiritually to the world.

---

11 For the mediaeval background to modern science, see Edward Grant, *The Foundations of Modern Science in the Middle Ages: Their Religious, Institutional and Intellectual Contexts*, CUP, 1996. For a recent example of the division, consider the independence assumed by Karl Barth between theology and science (*Church Dogmatics* III.1, Preface).

The realist, in contrast, holds that what all locks and keys have in common is not primarily a set of physical properties, but a set of *spiritual* properties, for all those spiritual properties are worked out in matter. What is the carpenter exploring or seeing when he makes a chair? Not just the basic geometry and common physical features of chairs but also the very idea of solidity and support, even of domesticity. Chairs interest us because those features (support, domesticity and so on) are embodied in them. A locksmith, for her part, is not primarily on a quest for this or that shape, for these right angles and those notches, for their own sake. She is interested in opening and closing, hiding and revealing, barring the way and opening it. Realism, odd though it might seem to the twenty-first-century mind, is the *more* practical philosophy. It explains what the carpenter is about in making a chair and what the locksmith is trying to do. Realism embraces what the artisan is actually about.[12]

Realism is also the implicit metaphysics of the storyteller. The locksmith is interested in locks and keys as they enter into stories and it is a realist view of the form of a lock or a key that determines how locks and keys feature in stories, and paradigmatically in fairy stories or children's stories. To know the truth of locks and keys, or doors and chairs, we should understand how they enter into human narratives, both mundane and poetic. In contrast, nominalism deflects us from asking these questions, or seeing the world this way.

With this said, we can turn back to our earlier comments, in the chapter about Plato, over how to *see* the Forms. The forms of all things proceed from God as their creator, but some forms press more deeply into the mystery of who God is than others. If we want an intimation of the forms in the way Plato did, we should

---

12 Realism is part of a larger metaphysical picture, and its eclipse is part of a larger metaphysical eclipse, not least over causation. Realism sees the locksmith not only as the efficient cause (the one who does something) but also as the *formal* cause: the repository of a real adding-up-to-something, which he imparts to his materials. Beyond that, realism also keeps the *final* cause in mind: performing a certain task, embodying a certain domesticity in the case of the chair, barring and opening in the case of the lock and key.

keep our eyes and hearts particularly open in those moments associated with what is deepest in God: the birth of a child (since the Son is eternally begotten of the Father), the repose of a child on its parent's shoulder, leave-taking or return, the threefold repetition of folk stories (the Holy Spirit is the 'second difference', who puts the seal on difference), the glance down a road when, for a moment, we perceive not simply a road but a trace of the truest Road (which is Christ himself, who is the Way).

We might find it, unexpected, in the turn of the much-mentioned key in its lock. For centuries, Christians have placed book ends around the Magnificat in the days leading up to Christmas: a different antiphon for each of the last days of Advent. One runs

> O Key of David, and Sceptre of the House of Israel, who opens and no one shuts, who shuts and no one opens; Come and bring forth the captive from his prison, who sits in darkness and in the shadow of death.

Here is the realist contention: that all secure possession, opening and shutting, revealing and concealing, find their origin in God, and in particular in Christ, who is the 'key of David, who opens and no one will shut, who shuts and no one opens' (Rev. 3.7).[13] Every key is an embodiment of this.

At the root of the realist claim is the intimation that the nominalist denies: a profound sense of the order of the world, that its parts add up to wholes, that each individual also represents and embodies something larger. The dispute between realism and nominalism is not likely to be one that can be settled by argument. The realism–nominalism debate lies about as close to first principles as we can come. It is a dispute about how we see the world, either as individuals or as communities. A discussion can proceed, however, by asking about consequences: in particular, whether it is really possible to live as a nominalist. We can ask with Leszek

---

13 Cf. Isaiah 22.22–24, where some of our carpentry images also find an expression: the promised saviour is that sure 'peg' upon which 'the whole weight of his ancestral house, the offspring and issue, every small vessel, from the cups to all the flagons' can safely be hung.

Kołakowski, 'Can one survive intellectually if we believe that the world contains nothing except individual objects?'[14]

Quantity

We noted in Chapter 3 that when Christian theologians wished to describe God as infinite, they had to rehabilitate the notion of infinitude, for instance by aligning it with simplicity rather than multiplicity. If we look at Aquinas using concepts of finitude and infinitude, we find them understood as primarily a *qualitative* matter. After about 1300, however, both finitude and infinitude started to be understood by theologians in more and more *quantitative* terms. This has two consequences. First, it made God more distant from the world than before. God is on the same scale as we are, and therefore infinitely distant. Moreover, if we associate both God and creatures with quantity, then a direct comparison can be made, and creatures come off badly. In a qualitative model, such a comparison cannot be made so directly. God's otherness becomes the basis for his closeness; the absolute distinction between God's action and my action is what means that they do not compete – they are not 'in the same space' – and can therefore overlap. Consider that an apple and an orange are too similar for something to be both at once, there is a paradigm of competition, whereas being a piece of paper and being a declaration of love are so different that one thing can be both. That is why the utter difference between God and creatures allows the Incarnation to be possible, rather than preventing it. In contrast, after the quantitative and therefore *comparative* model takes hold, theologians started having to propose that God had to become less God in order to become human: the 'kenotic' mistake.[15]

---

14 Leszek Kołakowski, *Why is there Something rather than Nothing?*, Penguin, 2008, p. 34.

15 See Stephen Sykes, 'The Strange Persistence of Kenotic Christology', in *Being and Truth: Essays in Honour of John Macquarrie*, ed. Alistair Kee and Eugene Long, SCM Press, 1986, pp. 349–75.

The quantitative turn, then, tends to run created things down, distancing them from God, whereas a qualitative account allows us to rejoice in a good apple (as God does) as being perfect in its own way: it is a perfect apple rather than an entirely failed god. All the same, in the opposite fashion, quantity also seems to bracket God too closely with the world. God and creatures now belong on that same axis: the axis of quantity. A quantitative approach tends always towards seeing God as a being among beings, different only in degree. Little, in the end, domesticates God quite so much as calling him very big, or even infinitely 'big'.

For Aquinas, each sort of thing has being in its own sort of way. Every creature *exists* but the existence of one is coloured by its essence, and the existence of another by *its* essence. They are beings, but the relation between them is *analogical*. The relationship between the being of a creature and the being of God is even more profoundly analogical. In contrast, Scotus held to the *univocity of being*. That is to say: being is being is being, where ever we find it, whether in this creature, or in that creature, or in God. This is a particularly forceful way to say that God is a being among beings. Scotus wrote what no one before could have written: that any of us could stumble upon a being and recognize it as a being but be unsure whether it is God or not. The root of this, as Anne Ashley Davenport has shown, is that being for Scotus was basically mathematical: each thing, including God, is *so much being*. This places the category of being prior to God, at least logically, which is never a good idea. It also left Scotus with the difficult question of asking how God and creatures could be spoken of in the same way ('univocally') when, as even he admitted, they are so different. His solution was to make the element of being that they share amount to almost nothing. God and creatures are things, but all they share is this business of being a thing, of existing. That approach is part and parcel of Scotus's voluntarist lack of interest in God as *formal cause*, as sharing himself in the characterfulness of the flower, the fox, the fir tree. There is nothing here of *participation*, which was so central for Aquinas: nothing of the idea that *what* something is (and *that* it is) amounts to a sharing, or participation in God. Instead, like the plaintive words of a song by The Verve (from the album *Urban Hymns*), 'we have existence and it's all we share'.

Reading On

Three volumes of Scotus's more accessible works, all translated by Allan Wolter, are *A Treatise on God as First Principle* (Chicago: Franciscan Herald Press, 1983), *Philosophical Writings* (Edinburgh: Nelson, 1962) and *Duns Scotus on the Will and Morality* (CUA, 1986). Introductions include Richard Cross, *Duns Scotus* (OUP, 1999) and Antonie Vos, *The Philosophy of John Duns Scotus* (Edinburgh University Press, 2006), the first short and the second long. For a critical reception of Scotus, see Catherine Pickstock, 'Duns Scotus: His Historical and Contemporary Significance', *Modern Theology* 21 (2005), pp. 543–74. A selection of the philosophical works of Ockham was translated by Philotheus Boehner (Hackett, 1990).

10

The Renaissance and Reformation

Renaissance means 'rebirth'. The meaning and reference are so broad that it can be helpful to think of it as more like an adjective than a noun: as much as it singles out any particular period, it refers to a moment characterized by a particularly intense rediscovery and renewal, often in the realm of thought and culture.

When and what counts as the Renaissance, or a renaissance, depends to a large degree on who you are and what you value. For a certain Protestant-minded account of history, the Renaissance is represented most perfectly by Erasmus (1466–1536) and his work on the text of the Greek New Testament. The century most deserving the name Renaissance is the sixteenth. The centuries before, if considered at all, are seen as a period of limbering up, or of missed opportunities. According to the Catholic-minded account, the high point of the Renaissance is the fifteenth century, in the painting, sculpture and Neoplatonic scholarship of Italy. On such a view, the Renaissance had a long and glorious beginning, taking in the poetry of Dante (c. 1265–1321) and Petrarch (1304–74), and the realistic painting of Duccio (c. 1255–c. 1318) and Giotto (c. 1266–1337).[1] For a more liberal-minded thinker,

---

1 There is merit in this view. Compare paintings in a well-stocked art gallery and you will see that the thirteenth- and fourteenth-century artists Duccio and Giotto mark the beginning of a lineage that continues to blossom in the fifteenth century with the likes of Masaccio and, later, Fra Angelico. Between Giotto and Masaccio, however, Italian art lurched back to a style again called 'gothic': the 'international gothic'. A good explanation of this odd twist is the devastation of the Black Death. The sense of confidence and of rejoicing in the world as God's good creation, begun with the earlier artists, took a blow because of such widespread horror. It revived only later, with Masaccio and the later artists. On this view, the Renaissance began in the thirteenth century.

the 'Renaissance' might be seen principally as the prelude to the Enlightenment, or the first rays of its dawning.

What counts as the Renaissance (or a renaissance) depends on what counts as scholarship, culture, or whatever else is having its rediscovery and renewal. As we saw, the birth of gothic architecture in France in the mid-twelfth century was a renewal of architecture as great as any other in history. The arrival of Aristotle provoked a 'rebirth' on the basis of renewed attention to the past: the very definition of a renaissance. The influence of the court of Charlemagne in the late eighth and early ninth centuries is justly called the Carolingian Renaissance.

This observation illustrates a point from the philosophy of history: history is subjective and never more so than when it comes to what we call a period or when we take it to begin or end. When does the Patristic period end (the time of the Church Fathers): with Leo the Great, or Maximus the Confessor, or with Bernard of Clairvaux, or even with Thomas Aquinas? When, for that matter, did the period of the early Church end: with the death of the biblical writers (an extreme and unhelpful view), or with the definition of the canon of the New Testament, or with the fourth ecumenical council, or the seventh, or with the end of the Patristic period (whenever that was), or are we perhaps still in the time of the early Church?

The distinction between really pivotal stances in philosophy often revolves around the answer to questions such as these. The entire framework of theology is different depending on whether we take the early Church (where the parameters were established and the sources of Christian theology provided) to stretch to AD 100 or to AD 451. The lion's share of one's philosophical position can be captured in your sense of whether the great watershed of thought falls in, say, 1510, dividing the Middle Ages from the modern period, or in 1300, dividing a 'patristic' age of intellect and mediation from a modern age of will and competition. Scarcely less important is one's judgement as to whether the notion of a 'postmodern' era amounts to very much, which is partly to ask whether the end of the twentieth century represents a break from the previous centuries, or its intensification.

Nicholas of Cusa

Among renaissance theologians, none is likely to fascinate the reader more than Nicholas of Cusa (1401–64), in whom a Neo-platonist theology of a Thomist variety flourished like a year's last bloom. The work to read is *On Learned Ignorance*, a text in the negative or apophatic tradition with a strong sense of God's simplicity and plenitude. As with Aquinas, Cusa stressed that the key to divine incomprehensibility lies in divine simplicity: we simply cannot imagine what it means for God's essence and existence (and so on) to be the same. Cusa calls this 'the coincidence of opposites'. In God, identity and difference coincide; he is the knower and the knowing, one and more-than-one, and so on.

God is the subject of the first book: he is the *absolute maximum*. The second book deals with the created universe, where we find being from God contracted to finitude: creation is the *contracted maximum*. Cusa expounds his account in terms of 'enfolding' and 'unfolding': 'God is the enfolding of all things in that all things are in Him; and He is the unfolding of all things in that He is in all things.'[2] Cusa continues in intoxicating form for page after page, always staying just the right side of the dividing line between Christianity and pantheism.

The third and final book concerns Christ. Cusa was a profoundly Christological thinker. In Christ, God and creation are joined; Christ is simultaneously the *absolute maximum* and the *contracted maximum*, which Cusa expounds in terms of his metaphysics of enfolding and unfolding. The idea of Christ as the microcosm of all creation is important here, as it had been 800 years before in Maximus the Confessor, to whom Cusa bears comparison. Like Maximus, he made a great deal of the Johannine idea that 'through him all things were made', and proposed an account of redemption founded on the Incarnation and based on the union of divinity and humanity.

---

2 *Learned Ignorance* II.3, trans. Jasper Hopkins, Minneapolis: Arthur Banning Press, 1985.

Dominicans, Franciscans and Jesuits

The fifteenth and sixteenth centuries were ones of consolidation for the religious orders which played a leading role in Roman Catholic theology: the Dominicans and Franciscans joined, after their foundation in 1540, by the Jesuits. The Dominican school in Spain deserves mention, especially as it flourished in the university city of Salamanca. There, Francesco de Victoria (c. 1485–1546) addressed newly urgent questions of international law. Previously, human law had been considered a national matter. Victoria built on the idea of natural law to cover 'the law of nations' (*ius gentium*). His work is credited as the beginning of the international law invoked today in face of atrocities such as genocide. Victoria and his colleagues are an important stage in the development of a particularly significant overlap of theology and philosophy: political theology.

Bartolomé de las Casas (1474–1566), eventually another Dominican, also addressed the enormous moral questions working themselves out on the world stage. He is particularly known for his defence of the indigenous peoples of the New World, who were subject to forced conversion and slavery. In response, las Casas spent decades arguing for their rights, in law courts and university debating chambers, and before bishops, kings and emperors. He brought the full weight of Thomist philosophical theology to bear on the question. In particular, he addressed himself to what it meant to recognize reason in another human being, and what that compels us to offer in response. In this way, he opposed the proposition that the indigenous peoples of the New World were 'natural slaves', a term taken directly from Aristotle (*Politics*, 1254b). Las Casas made substantial but far from complete progress. As a result of his work, the Spanish crown promulgated laws protecting the native Indians, although these were later repealed, and Pope Paul III renounced forced conversion. Las Casas stands as an example of acute philosophical training put to work for the best of causes.

Cajetan was the master of the Dominican order between 1508 and 1518. His commentary on the *Summa Theologiae* set the running for how it was to be interpreted for centuries to come. This is a good example of the power of commentary to determine how a text is to be understood. (Both Luther and Barth provoked a lasting sea-change in theology by means of commentary on the Epistle to the Romans.) Perhaps Cajetan's most significant work is his short *Analogy of Names* (1598). It provided an understanding of analogy, attributed to Aquinas, which has in recent years been subject to sustained attack as inaccurate.[3]

Part of the problem with this work was an attempt to squeeze a wide-ranging vision in Aquinas, which is in part worked out afresh in each particular situation, into a general scheme. Pieper argued that it is a peculiar characteristic of Aquinas that he does not settle on a uniform technical vocabulary. Theologians and philosophers, we can note, differ over whether the ideal means of expression for their subject approaches 'everyday language', even if that is everyday language of a rather particular sort.

Cajetan charted a 'Scotist' (following Scotus) course over analogy, such that the meaning of 'analogy' shifted significantly, away from naming a likeness only in view of a 'yet greater dissimilarity' between God and creatures (as the Fourth Lateran Council has insisted), towards something far closer to thinking that we had God comprehended. In the words of Placher, 'Unsystematic references have become a systematic theory [. . .] Far from offering a series of reminders concerning how we cannot understand what we mean when we speak of God, analogy now functioned as a way of explaining just what we do mean.'[4]

This shift away from the complexity of analogy, with its sense of revelation and veiling, was taken even further by the Jesuit, Francesco Suárez. Gavin Hyman has characterized Cajetan and Suárez as being driven by a search for certainty in a way that anticipates Descartes (who by a method of total scepticism tried to find that which is unshakable as a foundation upon which to rebuild

---

3 For instance, by Conor Cunningham, in *Genealogy of Nihilism*, Routledge, 2002, p. 181.

4 William Placher, *The Domestication of Transcendence: How Modern Thinking About God Went Wrong*, Louisville: Westminster John Knox Press, 1996. Quoted by Gavin Hyman, *The Predicament of Postmodern Theology: Radical Orthodoxy or Nihilist Textualism?*, Louisville: Westminster John Knox Press, 2001, p. 37, n. 31.

thought).[5] Hans Urs von Balthasar saw a highly significant consequence: in search of the simplest, clearest and most certain object for thought, they proposed being stripped of any characteristics or designations (again following Scotus).[6] As a result, being was exalted above God, at least conceptually. Being became the most fundamental idea, with both God and creatures as variations upon it. This led to an understanding of God that is profoundly dominant in modern (and contemporary) theology, both academic and everyday: as a thing among things. In a phrase attributed to Herbert McCabe, we all too easily see God as if he were just like the President of the United States, only bigger and invisible. Moreover, in as much as being now becomes thinkable in abstraction from God, this shift marks the beginning of secularity per se.

When it comes to authority in the Church, something significant is also happening at this time. The earlier tradition had by no means downplayed the Bible. It was held to be the word of God, divinely inspired and inerrant. The shift was over an attitude towards maxima and minima. Previous approaches to interpretation saw a plenitude of meaning in the Bible. In view of its divine inspiration, the meaning of the Scriptures overflowed. As a result, it could be interpreted on many levels. The possibility of a certain playfulness here, and even of a certain waywardness, was held in check by the requirement to argue with reference to the interwoven whole of Scripture, and more than that, of living within that interwoven whole. In contrast, the 'modern' approach (exemplified since at least the sixteenth century) is one of the cautious minimum. This involved looking at the biblical revelation as a communication of facts, and the process of interpretation as a search for certainty.

In this, both Protestant and Catholic theology developed along lines at once both similar and opposed. Seemingly opposite tendencies – we might say mistakes – rest on common, unquestioned assumptions. The Protestant position was to see revelation as involving propositions communicated infallibly by Scripture. Catholics, in contrast, saw

---

5 Hyman, *Predicament*, p. 37.

6 Suárez, *Disputationes Metaphysicae*, dist. 1, 1.19. Cited by Hyman, *Predicament*, p. 37, n. 35.

just such propositions communicated infallibly by a twofold route: by Scripture and tradition, the latter increasingly conceived in terms of the papal office. In one sense, they were diametrically opposed, but they defined themselves against one another within a common, and new, sense of what it meant for authority to operate: as securing the facts, not as securing the framework within which to live.

Platonic Influences

If the thirteenth century had seen a return to Aristotle, the fifteenth century saw a return to Plato and a more mystical form of philosophy. The focus was Medici Florence. As a phenomenon, it has the quality of a slightly over-ripe bowl of fruit, of a good thing taken too far. There was a renewed spirit of optimism, and a delight in creation, not least in the human being as the image of God. Giovanni Pico della Mirandola's (1463–94) *Oration on the Dignity of Man* has been called 'the manifesto of the renaissance'. Celebration, however, could tip over into hubris and an insufficiently developed sense of sin and the suffering of the masses. Marsilio Ficino (1433–99) translated the complete works of Plato into Latin for the first time, along with many works of Neoplatonism.

We see Christian theology delighting to confront, face to face, the Platonic inheritance which previous Christian thinkers had examined, moulded and been inspired by while remaining ignorant of its wellspring in the works of Plato himself. In Florence at that time, we see Christianity, with its traditions of liturgy and mysticism, considering all that was liturgical and mystical about ancient religions and proving that it could beat them at their own game. That is the positive angle. We also see theologians at risk of being swept away on a tide of pagan Platonism; we see less than judicious judgement on texts, that strays into magic, and – indeed – Christians becoming magicians (as with Dr Dee in the court of Elizabeth I). Much was celebrated simply because it was old, such as the Kabbala and the writings known as the 'Hermetic corpus'. Judged historically, it has proved to be a stew of Platonic, Pythagorean, Stoic and Eastern sources. It found a particular advocate in the Italian Giordano Bruno (1548–1600). His theological scheme postulated an infinite and eternal universe and verged on pantheism. He was burnt at the stake.

Plato was to influence Anglican theology, in a gentler manner, in the form of the Cambridge Platonists: a group of theologians associated with Emmanuel College in particular, whose writings had a heady quality at the time but appear rather more tame today. The Platonic influence never quite went away in the Church of England. I have been told that leaflets could be found at the entrance to Canterbury Cathedral in the early twentieth century, which explained, for the sake of visitors from overseas, that while the Church of England and the Roman Catholic Church share much in common, their principal difference is that the Roman Catholic Church is Aristotelian, while the Anglican perspective is Platonic.

It is easy to be dismissive of Renaissance writers, and their humanist movement, as naive and insufficiently Christian. It is also easy to be suspicious of that name, 'humanism', or intimidated by it, given that today it labels an explicitly atheistic rejection of Christianity and religious belief. A good response follows a wise principle: do not cede the territory too quickly. 'Humanism' was Christian for centuries before it was associated with atheism. One task for Christian mission today is for Christians to rediscover what it means to offer a fulsome and compelling account of human dignity and flourishing, and to be the means for its achievement.

Renaissance means 'rebirth' (*ri-nascere* in Italian). It was a rebirth by return to what went before: a rebirth in architecture, for example, through careful, even scholarly, attention to the architecture of classical antiquity. We have seen the same with the return to Aristotle. In painting, the return was to realistic depiction, as in the portraits of Imperial Rome, and to perspective, as practised by Masaccio for the first time in over a millennium.

The point is a general one. Little is as revivifying for thought as a return to the great thinking of the past. Rarely does anything exciting happen in theology, or philosophy, that is not to some significant degree grounded in a renewed encounter with the tradition. There is more, however: not only can we read from the past for the sake of the present and the future, we *should* read from the past in that way and for that sake. Texts are forever jumping out of their boxes and once they have jumped out, we cannot force them back in, to be only what they once were. Texts need deciphering. We can only decipher them – as Hans-Georg Gadamer pointed out, and Friedrich Schleiermacher and Paul Ricœur – by bringing what we know to bear upon the text, and what we are and have experienced. That makes Augustine's *Confessions*, or Aristotle's *On the Soul*, or Mark's Gospel for that matter, a perennially new text, for each new reader, and new for each community, in the position it finds itself at any given time. All that, and yet each of these texts is also the same from generation to generation. They both bind us together and provoke us afresh.

Michel de Montaigne (1533–92) was responsible for a revival of scepticism, which cast a long shadow across the early Enlightenment. We can see this as a form of weariness in the face of increasingly elaborate complete systems. Also significant were the European 'wars of religion'. On the face of it, they brought wrangling over fine intellectual points into disrepute. Scepticism promised to draw the heat from these disputes with its challenge 'who really knows?' That said, recent scholarship has helped us to re-evaluate those conflicts. No one claims that those wars were anything other than awful but an alternative assessment has been offered over their origins. Previously, the story of those wars has been told as the eventual triumph of the moderate modern nation state over intrinsically violent religion. Historians such as William Cavanaugh, however, have cast them as the triumph of the intrinsically violent nation state over religion.[7] From a philosophical point of view, this illustrates the importance of *story* for our moral sense, indeed for our sense of who we are and where the options lie. If we take the nation state as basic then we tell a story about religion in its terms (perhaps as a rise and fall). Cavanaugh helps us to see that a story has also to be told about the nation state. The task in such a case is to tell the story constructively, with a proper sense of continuity as well as discontinuity, as neither an unmitigated tragedy or a unsullied romance.

---

7 Among other books, William Cavanaugh, *The Myth of Religious Violence: Secular Ideology and the Roots of Modern Conflict*, OUP, 2009.

Luther

Of the Reformers, Martin Luther (1483–1546) in particular spoke severely against philosophical method, calling philosophy 'the Devil's whore'.[8] This was of a piece with his emphasis on a 'theology of the cross', marked by paradoxes such as 'the death of God', which shatter the hubristic self-sufficiency and confidence of human thought. Luther condemned those who 'learn from Aristotle' and not from 'the crucified and hidden God'.[9] As an example of this, we find Luther laying in to the syllogism, raising concerns similar to those voiced earlier in this book. 'No syllogistic form is valid', he wrote, 'when applied to divine terms'.[10]

Luther's scorn was turned on both Aquinas and Scotus. (During this period, the word 'Duns' was receiving its contemporary ring of 'fool' or 'stupid person'. Duns Scotus was in view.) That Aquinas and Scotus could be aligned in this way shows the extent to which the details and differences of scholastic theology were becoming eclipsed. Aquinas, certainly, could apply the syllogism, even to as unlikely a source as a Pauline Epistle (often with considerable effect) but as Denis Janz notes (drawing on a panoply of the best twentieth-century scholars of Aquinas), the role of the syllogism in the writings of Aquinas overall was strictly limited.[11] His 'demonstrations' are worked out within the context of faith, not in cold abstraction, as contingent, not necessary; they were expository not logical.[12] Crucially, his writing was concerned with progress in the Christian life: it is 'exhortative and pastoral'.[13] We are dealing with 'likenesses' to the truth, not with the truth as fully comprehended.[14] All of this

8 A recent collection has picked up this phrase as its title: see the reading suggestions for this chapter.

9 *Martin Luthers Werk: Kritische Gesamtausgabe*, volume I, p. 613, quoted by Denis R. Janz, 'Syllogism or Paradox: Aquinas or Luther on Theological Method', *Theological Studies* 59 (1998), pp. 3–21, p. 8.

10 *Werk*, I, p. 226, quoted by Janz, 'Syllogism', p. 7.

11 Janz, 'Syllogism', pp. 8–14.

12 Jean-Pierre Torrell, *Saint Thomas Aquinas*, p. 226. Quoted by Janz, 'Syllogism', p. 14.

13 Janz, 'Syllogism', p. 14.

14 *SCG* I.8.1. Quoted by Janz, 'Syllogism', p. 10.

means that the position of Aquinas on the usefulness and scope of the syllogism was not anything like so far from Luther's own.

Luther's philosophical training was strongly coloured by the thought of William of Ockham, mediated through figures such as Gabriel Biel. Various authors have pointed this out and, in slightly different ways, have commented on quite how important it was for the shape of his later, reforming theology.[15] In particular, Luther was a nominalist (see pp. 151–6),[16] and even when he rejected some of the theological conclusions that had been built on nominalism, he still thought within its framework. For instance, Luther is known for stressing a *forensic* account of justification: it is principally about God changing the way he thinks about the sinner, rather than making the sinner righteous. This sort of concern for how something is labelled, rather than its substantial being, is characteristic of nominalism. As Eric Mascall put it (perhaps exaggerating for emphasis), 'For nominalism there can be no such thing as a supernatural transformation of a man's being in its ontological depths *beneath* the observable level, for on nominalist principles there is nothing beneath the observable level to transform.'[17] (Since contemporary Catholics belonged within a similar intellectual heritage, many were also arguing from similar principles.) In addition, we might add, accounts of salvation strongly

---

15 Louis Bouyer, *The Spirit and Forms of Protestantism*, London: Harvill Press, 1956; Heiko Oberman, *The Harvest of Medieval Theology: Gabriel Biel and Late Medieval Nominalism*, Cambridge, MA: Harvard University Press, 1963; Steven Ozment, *The Age of Reform 1250–1550: An Intellectual and Religious History of Late Mediaeval and Reformation Europe*, London: Yale University Press, 1981.

16 Heiko Oberman, *Luther: Man Between God and the Devil*, New Haven: Yale University Press, 1989, pp. 119–123.

17 *The Importance of Being Human*, p. 68. For Mascall, the fundamental problem is that nominalism rules out any sense that 'anything whatever can really inhere in a creature and at the same time be wholly a gift from God', which rules out accounts of salvation as participation in the divine nature (2 Peter 1.4). That said, more recent scholarship on Luther has suggested that he did sometimes conceive of justification in these terms in his early work. Similarly, Jon Mackenzie has suggested that Luther does retrieve a particular sense of *substance* in his later writings, worked out metaphorically in terms of place: as a 'place where one can stand firm and settle down' ('Luther's Topology: Creatio Ex Nihilo and the Cultivation of the Concept of Place in Martin Luther's Theology', in Janet Soskice (ed.), *Creation 'Ex Nihilo' and Modern Theology*, Wiley-Blackwell, 2013, pp. 83–103, p. 91).

based on the Incarnation – the 'ontological model', which stresses the vivifying effect of God sharing our human nature – were ruled out for the nominalist mindset since they did not believe in natures at all, human or otherwise. Similarly, an emphasis in the Reformers' doctrine of salvation on the all-powerful but inscrutable divine will finds its roots in the other principal strand of late mediaeval philosophy, closely related to nominalism, namely voluntarism.

Luther was to have a profound influence on philosophy, beyond any simple disavowal of what had gone before. Jacques Maritain discussed Luther in his *Three Reformers* (the other two, controversially, are René Descartes and Jean-Jacques Rousseau), where he pointed to Luther as the father of the individualism that was to dominate Western culture, not least in a philosophical culture that concentrates principally on the subject, or human 'I', rather than on the world and community. This, Maritain argues, followed from Luther's all-consuming concern for the individual 'cut off from the universal body of the church [. . . and standing] solitary and naked before God and Christ'.[18] More positively, on similar grounds, Luther can be claimed as the wellspring of what is best in Christian existentialism (see Chapter 13): an insistence that we cannot let abstraction or speculation take us away from attention to the concrete action of God in Christ, or from the question of our own standing before God. In the words of a recent exploration by Jon Mackenzie, Luther warns us never to forget that 'God encounters human persons', on account of which, 'The theologian cannot simply speculate beyond the creative event towards a general paradigm by which to encompass the salvific activity of God because God does not interact with his creation generally, but rather particularly.'[19] This warning should only go so far: God *does* interact with creation generally, in the sense that he interacts with *all* of creation, and this is not an illicit topic for thought. The point is that this interaction is only ever itself particular, so thoughts of

---

18   Jacques Maritain, *Three Reformers*, London: Sheed & Ward, 1928, p. 35.
19   Mackenzie, 'Luther's Topology', p. 98.

what is general should not deflect attention from the offer of grace addressed to each individual, not least to oneself.

Reading On

For Nicholas of Cusa, start with *On Learned Ignorance*, translated by H. Lawrence Bond with other works in *Selected Spiritual Writings* (Paulist Press, 1997). Cusa's groundbreaking work on church polity is *The Catholic Concordance*, translated by Paul E. Sigmund (CUP, 1996). For an account of his remarkable life, see Erich Meuthen, *Nicholas of Cusa: A Sketch for a Biography*, translated by David Crowner and Gerald Christianson (CUA, 2010). Jasper Hopkins translated the complete works of Cusa into English (Minneapolis: Arthur Banning Press), including a translation of *On Learned Ignorance* with a helpful 'appraisal' (1985). At the time of publication, this complete edition was also available on Hopkins's website.

Charles Taliaferro and Alison Teply collected writings by 'Cambridge Platonists' in *Cambridge Platonist Spirituality* (Paulist Press, 2004). On the return to ancient sources at the Renaissance, see Edgar Wind, *Pagan Mysteries in the Renaissance* (New Haven: Yale University Press, 1958), Florian Ebeling, *The Secret History of Hermes Trismegistus: Hermeticism from Ancient to Modern Times* (Ithaca: Cornell University Press, 2007) and Frances Yates, *Giordano Bruno and the Hermetic Tradition* (Routledge, 2002).

Among volumes on the Reformers and philosophy, see Jennifer Hockenbery Dragseth (ed.), *The Devil's Whore: Reason and Philosophy in the Lutheran Tradition* (Minneapolis: Fortress, 2011) and Graham White, *Luther as Nominalist* (Helsinki: Luther-Agricola-Society, 1994).

II

The Enlightenment

We come to the Enlightenment. The name itself is propaganda: it sets out its story as being, by definition, a journey from darkness to light. We have already noted this in another set of terms, which arise from this period: 'gothic', 'Dark Ages', 'Middle Ages'.[1] In this narrative of succession, all that is vanquished and an age of reason dawns, separated by a radical break from what preceded it.[2]

The trend in scholarship today is to dispute how radical this break was, and to note elements of continuity between the Enlightenment and what went before, on at least two levels. First there is the contention that much of what is most significant about Enlightenment thought follows from moves made in the early fourteenth century: univocity, voluntarism and nominalism. These were the primary revolutions; the Enlightenment is their apotheosis.[3] The second point is that the Enlightenment has been a victim of the success of its own rhetoric. Yes, these thinkers rejected much of the theological metaphysics of the Middle Ages, and yes, they contrasted faith with reason and wanted more of the latter. All the same, that rhetoric today obscures quite how religious and theological many Enlightenment thinkers were. John Cottingham has worked on this in relation to Descartes, and John

---

1 One part of this shift is to think of what has gone before and more or less homogeneous. However, the very method of scholastic dispute shows that the authorities do not always agree. The tradition was at worst more fragmented, and at best richer, than the Enlightenment critics would allow.

2 I am grateful to Jeff Phillips for discussions about this period.

3 Olivier Boulnois, *Être Et Représentation*, Paris: PUF, 1999, Catherine Pickstock, 'Modernity and Scholasticism: A Critique of Recent Invocations of Univocity', *Antonianum* 78 (2003), pp. 3–47. Also important is Graham White, *Luther as Nominalist*, Helsinki: Luther-Agricola-Society, 1994.

Milbank has rehabilitated the theological aspects of David Hume (who, in spite of his reputation as an enemy of religious belief, is recorded as having said that he had 'never met an atheist').[4]

A hallmark of the Enlightenment is its concern with epistemology, the philosophy of knowledge. During this period, epistemology becomes 'first philosophy'. Before, the foundational question had come from ontology: 'what is real?', now it was 'what can we know, and how can we know it?' In a sense, the Enlightenment even ushers in a period of faith. Reason was redefined to exclude much that was theological; that found a new realm in a parallel growth in fideism and pietism: faith *as opposed* to reason.

Descartes

René Descartes (1596–1650) is often called the father of modern philosophy, particularly for placing the mind rather than external reality at the centre of his philosophy. Although a revolutionary, Descartes was not a solitary. As MacIntyre points out, he was partly able to be the polymath he was because of the wide circle of friends with whom he corresponded.[5] Again we see the place of friendship and dialogue in philosophy.

Anyone who has taken high school mathematics has come across Descartes, through the more familiar adjectival form, 'Cartesian'. Cartesian geometry describes shapes, movement, acceleration, and so on, in terms of a grid laid out in three spatial dimensions, along axes usually called x, y and z. We probably take this for granted and do not give it a second thought. However, it was new when Descartes proposed it. Before Descartes, objects had priority over space; after Descartes, space has priority and it just so happens that this or that object is here or there. Originally a 'philosophical'

---

4 John Cottingham, 'The Role of God in Descartes's Philosophy', in *A Companion to Descartes*, ed. Janet Broughton and John Carriero, Wiley-Blackwell, 2010, pp. 288–301, and *Cartesian Reflections: Essays on Descartes's Philosophy*, OUP, 2008. John Milbank, 'Hume Versus Kant: Faith, Reason and Feeling', *Modern Theology* 27 (2011), pp. 276–97.

5 Alastair MacIntyre, *God, Philosophy, Universities*, Continuum, 2009, p. 114.

idea, his vision of space now conditions the ordinary thought of non-philosophical people.

Part and parcel of Descartes' scheme was to make a distinction between two sorts of 'substance': matter, which is characterized by this sort of extension in three dimensions, and mind, which is characterized by consciousness and has no place or dimensions. Here, as ever, a theory of being (ontology) goes alongside a theory of knowledge (epistemology). Matter now has all the inert simplicity of being a lump of clay in three dimensions; mind is now where the meaning is. The contrasting, more theological, picture would be to say that matter is always itself mysterious, overlaid with stories, beyond searching out. It is elusive, uncertain, holy even. Descartes' later contemporary Pascal reacted in this way, with an invitation to see the landscape as built up from layer upon layer of meaningful materiality: 'A town or a landscape from afar is a town or a landscape, but as one approaches, it becomes houses, trees, tiles, leaves, grass, ants, ants' legs, and so on, *ad infinitum*. All that is comprehended in the word "landscape".'[6]

Descartes' separation of materiality and mind is reflected in his interest in optics, where he did important work. His dualism put the knowing mind at the centre of a world that lies open before it. Later commentators have pointed out that a tradition proceeds from Descartes that regards vision as mastery. A tendency to see matter as inert goes hand in hand with a sense that objects can rather easily be circumscribed by human knowledge, which comes to dominate them in the process.

At the heart of Descartes' scheme is the way he defined a substance: as something that can exist independently of all else. Aspects of this definition were present in earlier philosophy, not least in the etymology of the word 'substance' itself (see p. 43) but in earlier Christian thought nothing is ever entirely independent. Existence is always something shared from God. Knowing does not start with us either; it is always the presence of something from the world in the mind.

---

6 *Pensées*, 65, trans. J. Krailsheimer, Penguin, 1967.

For all Descartes rejected much of the earlier philosophical tradition of Christianity, he was not an un-theological thinker. Indeed, the extent to which his thought is woven through with theological concerns is increasingly recognized. Among his theological ideas, Descartes is known for returning to the ontological argument of Anselm and recasting it in more mathematical terms, relating perfection to infinitude. According to Descartes, the finite is only thinkable in terms of the infinite, not vice versa.

No line of Descartes' is more familiar than *Cogito ergo sum* ('I think, therefore I am': the earlier French version ran *Je pense, donc je suis*), to be found in his *Discourse* and later in the *Principles*. The line is so famous that it has been given its own name. On the basis of the first word, it is known as Descartes' *cogito*. Descartes put it forward as part of his attempt to find a secure foundation for philosophy according to a method of scepticism. Descartes asked how much we can doubt. Almost everything, was his answer, even what I think I perceive. The only thing about which I cannot be unsure, even in my moment of most far-reaching doubt, is that I am doubting, which is to say that I am *thinking*. Whatever else I am unsure about, I cannot be unsure that I am thinking. The result is sometimes called 'the turn to the subject', since the thinking person (the 'subject') lies at the heart of the philosophical endeavour according to this scheme. It is also called the 'epistemological turn', since our sense of *knowing* is put forward as the secure foundation for our sense of *being*, whereas previously this relation had worked the other way round.

Malebranche

Nicolas Malebranche (1638–1715) was a priest and member of the religious order known as the Oratory (like Newman). With him we again encounter someone raking over the coals of causation. For a start, Malebranche was interested in the play of something like causes in the mind of God. He wondered how God's 'sincere will' for the salvation of all people intermeshed with God's wisdom, which orders the world in such as way that some outcomes are 'practical' and others, including universal salvation, are not.

Over causes in the world, Malebranche represents an approach, called 'occasionalism', that had been bubbling under in Christianity since it was first introduced from Islamic sources in the Arabic texts that accompanied the rediscovery of Aristotle.[7] In Arabic philosophy the associated idea was known as *Mutakallimun*: in Aquinas's example, the idea that 'fire does not give heat, but God causes heat in the presence of fire'.[8]

The occasionalist holds that every effect is directly caused by God and God alone. Imagine that you are standing in the reception of a hotel. You reach out your hand to call for the lift but just as your finger reaches the call button, someone in the lift on the seventh floor presses the ground floor button. It descends, as you wished, and the call button lights up, but not *because* you wished it. For the occasionalist, every effect that seems to be caused by a creaturely agent is like that descent of the lift, and God is like the person on the seventh floor.

Thinkers were driven to occasionalism by a desire to extol God's agency and in order to solve certain knotty problems. (On either front, they sacrificed a great deal in the process.) One such knotty problem was the relation of mind and body. Philosophers more or less accepted Descartes' definition of them as fundamentally distinct substances but could not account for their relation: namely how thoughts affect the body. (According to the Aristotelian view that they rejected, with the soul as the form of the body, this problem does not arise.) The occasionalist makes God the only cause of everything. The relation of thought and bodily action rests on the fact that God causes both the thought and the action directly. This may be criticized as not so much explaining the relation as explaining the relation away.

The tragedy with occasionalism is that it is so nearly right. God is indeed a cause in all effects, even in a profound sense the principal

---

7 In particular in his *Treatise on Nature and Grace* (1680).
8 *SCG* III.69.

cause of all effects, since he is the cause of every agent. In the very moment in which I act, God gives me both my being and my power to act. With this in mind, one of Aquinas's favourite quotations is Isaiah 25.12, which the Vulgate translation he knew rendered as 'Lord, you have wrought all our works in us.'[9] The occasionalist mistake is to think that an effect can only have one cause. That had become easier once the panoply of Aristotle's causes had been stripped back to one: first, there is only efficient causality; next, there is only one efficient cause for any effect. This is the outworking of the shift from a paradigm of cooperation to a paradigm of competition which, once again, began to emerge in the thought of Scotus.

Typically, however, God's way is to share: in this case, to be the agent who nurtures agents as agents.[10] I really cause, in imitation of God and not independently of him. God causes on his overarching level, and I cause on mine. This is usually taken to mean that God not only gives me the power to cause, as a sharing and imitation of his, but also that I receive a freedom that is an image of God's freedom. This is important since, otherwise and certainly on the occasionalist account, God is *directly* responsible for every evil in the world.[11]

The Port-Royal Set

Causation was again of interest to a group of French thinkers centred around the convent at Port-Royal, south west of Paris, run by the Abbess Angélique Arnauld. She was installed thanks

---

9 For an exposition and refutation of occasionalism, see *ST* I.105.5.

10 'It is not superfluous that other causes should produce effects which God could produce by himself. This has nothing to do with inadequacy in the divine power, but comes rather from the immensity of his goodness, by which he wishes to communicate his likeness to things not only in that they exist but also in that they are causes of other things' (*SCG* III.70).

11 For Aquinas, God causally 'concurs' in everything about an action that is good but not in that which is evil. Indeed, it is evil inasmuch as the agent has chosen to deflect the action away from the possibility of the full concurrence of God. See *ST* I.49.2; I.118.2 *ad* 5.

to family pressure at the age of 11 but treated her position as no sinecure and turned the institution into a religious and intellectual powerhouse.

This group showed sympathies with the Dutch Catholic theologian Cornelius Jansen, whose work had been condemned for its hard-line adherence to Augustine of Hippo over grace and predestination,[12] in other words, concerning the causal effects of God upon human beings over repentance. Angélique's brother, Antoine (1616–98), defended the now-dead Jansen against charges of heresy.

Arnauld was a creative thinker, engaged in dialogue with the thought of Descartes, Leibniz and Malebranche. He found inspiration from Aquinas but rejected significant parts of his scheme; hylomorphism is an example. 'After having learned of those things [form and matter]', he wrote, 'we seem not to have learned anything new, nor to be in a better position to make sense of any of the effects of nature.'[13] His most enduring work is his *Logic, or the Art of Thinking*, written with another Port-Royal figure, Pierre Nicole.[14]

Arnauld also picked up familiar themes from Descartes and Malebranche over the relation of the soul and body. He followed Augustine to a more dualistic account than the Aristotelian account of Aquinas, and turned to an occasionalist solution to the problems that posed. Arnauld held that the bodily sensation only entered into the soul because God helpfully happened to cause the sensation in our souls corresponding to each sensation.[15] These are answers to problems which go away if we see the soul as the form of the body. Despite the handicap of rejecting Aristotle, thinkers around this time kept stumbling upon the important idea that when God acts upon and in us, he does not act arbitrarily but in accordance with our nature. If God ever 'chooses for us' it is not a manipulation, since God directs us in the way we should

---

12 His followers, the Jansenists, were expelled from the Catholic Church. Their hymns, frequently beautiful, are worth looking out.

13 *Art of Thinking*, CUP, 1996, p. 20. Quoted by MacIntyre, *God*, p. 125.

14 Trans. Jill Vance Buroker, CUP, 1996.

15 *Examen d'un Ecrit.*

choose if we were to choose best and most humanly. In the words of the Augustinian collect for peace in Anglican Morning Prayer, this makes God's service 'perfect freedom'.

A final member of the Port-Royal circle is Blaise Pascal (1623–62). He is remembered for a profound experience of God on 23 November 1654. He wrote lines to describe it and had the paper stitched into his coat:

> Fire. 'God of Abraham, God of Isaac, God of Jacob', not of philosophers and scholars [. . .] God of Jesus Christ [. . .] He can only be found by the ways taught in the Gospels. Greatness of the human soul [. . .] Joy, joy, joy, tears of joy [. . .] Jesus Christ. I have cut myself off from him, shunned him, denied him, crucified him. Let me never be cut off from him!

Pascal was a considerable mathematician who carried out important work in the theory of probability and algebra. He brought that thinking on probability into an apologetic argument known as his 'wager': that it would be foolish not to put one's faith in God since the associated earthly losses are slight ('nothing', as he puts it) but the gains are eternal ('if you win you win everything').[16] The wager might suggest a rationalist side to Pascal (close to the 'God of the philosophers'), which finds its complement in his deeply affective commitment to God, as expressed in the 'memorial' stitched into his coat.

Pascal's 'thoughts' (*Pensées* in French) were collected in a volume bearing that name. It makes good introductory philosophical reading for anyone interested in theology. His attitude towards practices and habits prefigured a concern of contemporary theological ethics. He wrote that if we want a particular virtue, for instance the virtue of faith, we do well to grow into it through following the practices of good role models who possess that virtue. Those seeking to believe should behave 'just as if they did believe,

---

16 *Pensées*, 233.

taking holy water, having masses said, and so on. That will make you believe quite naturally . . .'[17]

Leibniz

Gottfried Wilhelm Leibniz (1646–1716) was another of history's great polymaths. His work on calculus was contemporary with Newton's, and just as perceptive. Like Newton, he did important work on moving bodies (kinetics); like Pascal he invented a calculating machine. His work on other fields, such as law (in which he obtained his doctorate), is less well remembered. Leibniz knew many of the principal intellectual figures of his time, including Pascal, Arnauld, Malebranche and Spinoza.

Leibniz is remembered for his idea of *possible worlds*. In his time, this was put forward as part of a theodicy, or defence of God in face of evil and suffering (in his essay entitled *Theodicy*, of 1710). According to Leibniz, God knows an infinite number of possible worlds, and that he has created this particular world shows that it is 'the best possible world'. That does not mean that it is perfect in every respect, only that it is as perfect as a world can be. This approach did not fare well, least of all in the hands of Voltaire, following the Lisbon earthquake of 1755. This took the lives of tens of thousands of people and can be said to mark the beginning of modern atheism.

Today the language of possible worlds is used as part of a certain sort of contemporary philosophy ('modal logic'), where statements of fact and logic are worked out in terms of what is or is not true in hypothetical 'possible worlds'.[18] A necessary truth is one that is true in every 'possible world'; a contingent truth holds in only some possible worlds; an impossible proposition holds in none. By and large, philosophers who take this approach use it as a mental device, although some physicists propose an interpretation of quantum mechanics by which extraordinarily many

---

17 *Pensées*, 418. Quoted in MacIntyre, *God*, p. 121.
18 The definitive work in this field is David Lewis, *On the Plurality of Worlds*, Blackwell, 1986.

parallel universes really do exist. This 'multiverse' theory is sometimes advanced by contemporary atheists, since it allows us to
account for certain remarkable features of the universe without
recourse to God: for instance that it is just so configured to allow
for the development of life. As theory, however, it requires as
much faith as belief in God, and perhaps more, since it makes no
difference to any perceptible feature of life. It is the most brutal
of brute facts.

If *actual* parallel worlds form part of an explicit atheism
for some writers, even notional 'possible worlds', in the sense
deployed in modal logic, carry an implicit atheism. This account
treats God as an object within a larger scheme (the sum of possible worlds), and any such god is no God at all. The word 'God'
retains only a shadow of its true meaning. This language of 'possible worlds' is strangely popular among contemporary Protestant
philosophers of religion. Alvin Plantinga, for instance, casts an
argument in terms of 'the proportion of logical space occupied
by the possible worlds in which there is such a person as God'.[19]
Such an approach imagines that we can treat God and the world
as fundamentally unrelated categories or concepts, with a mental
rather than ontological relationship. This is an outworking of the
trend, since the fourteenth century, to cut the world free from
God, and also to elevate the potential over the actual. The disas-
trous significance of this turn towards the concept of 'possible
worlds' is worth driving home. It ignores the fact that God is not
part of any larger grouping or category (which is one reason why
the designation 'he' implies no sense that God is male), nor can
he be subsumed under any overarching scheme.[20] In answer to the
question as to whether God belongs in any genus, Aquinas wrote,
'On the contrary, in the mind, genus is prior to what it contains.

19 Alvin Plantinga, *Where the Conflict Really Lies*, OUP, 2012, p. 29. Plantinga
recast Anselm's ontological proof in terms of modal logic and possible worlds in his
God, Freedom and Evil, Eerdmans, 1973.
20 One way to put this is to say that God does not belong inside thought but,
rather, thought belongs within God.

But nothing is prior to God either really or mentally. Therefore God is not in any genus.'[21]

Returning to Leibniz, he proposed that the world is built from the metaphysical equivalent of atoms: an infinite number of entities called monads, which themselves have no extension in space. Although not material, materiality emerges from their conjunction. This does not make Leibniz a monist – believing in only one all-encompassing substance or type of thing – because these monads are themselves substances, and all substantially different from one another. Reality emerges from the combinations of these monads, and yet in a sense there is no combination, at least not in the sense that one thing influences another. According to his theory of 'pre-ordained harmony', the behaviour of each monad unfolds entirely on its own terms, and yet God has determined the nature of each such that the coordination unfurls as we would expect if they really did influence one another. For Leibniz, this is a solution to the mind–body problem (mind and body each being determined by a particular type of monad).[22] Comparing this account to Malebranche's solution, we might call Leibniz's a sort of immanentized occasionalism. (The word 'immanent' is significant in philosophical theology. It means 'dwelling within', from the Latin for 'to remain in place'. It is frequently contrasted with 'transcendent', meaning 'dwelling without or beyond', but with the sense in the root – *tra-* + *scendere* – of something that lies beyond but which nonetheless *descends*. 'Immanent' is not to be confused with 'imminent', which means 'arriving soon'.)

Spinoza

Baruch de Spinoza (1632–77, in the Latinized form Benedictus de Spinoza) is among the most creative of philosophers, and among those who have sought to build a new account of the world from the ground up, while being compelling enough not to be dismissed as cranks.

---

21 *ST* I.3.5 *sed contra*.
22 Expounded in *A New System of Nature*.

Spinoza's family were Portuguese Sephardic Jews who had fled to the Netherlands to escape the Inquisition. Few other countries in Europe at the time would have offered him the freedom to make the claims that he did. Although he came under no political censure for his theological radicalism, he was expelled from the Jewish community for 'abominable heresies'. The letter of his expulsion sets out to 'excommunicate, expel, curse and damn' him and forbids his fellow Jews from communicating with him or reading anything that he had written.[23]

With Spinoza we again see how difficult it is to put philosophers into categories. Spinoza is a pantheist, since everything is God, but he could also be called a materialist, since God is equated with the material world. As Diané Collinson points out, in postulating only one substance, Spinoza was taking very seriously the idea that a substance is something that exists independently, and nothing exists independently of God.[24] On that definition of substance, the world is not a separate substance from God, so it is the same substance. As is often the case, Spinoza's doctrine of God is seen to rely on his doctrine of creation. Spinoza's radical re-evaluation follows from letting philosophy set the running, in this case his definition of substance. A more theological account of substance, Jewish as much as Christian, might build a sense of the non-independence of creation into a definition of substance, in such a way as will not bracket creatures with creator: creatures are dependent after the manner of a creaturely independence and independent after a manner of creaturely dependence. The relation is not easy to articulate, but it can partly be achieved. Spinoza, however, takes absolute independence to be the criteria for substance, and on that basis subsumes God and the world within the same whole.

According to Spinoza, the world (or world-God) resembles divinity, as previously conceived, in being ultimate and therefore not contingent. For Spinoza, this means running in mechanistic fashion according to laws of necessity. He also saw the world as

---

23 Steven Nadler, *Spinoza: A Life*, CUP, 2001, p. 120.
24 Diané Collinson, *Fifty Major Philosophers*, Routledge, 1988, pp. 61–2.

infinite in extent. Given that divine infinitude had come also to be seen as quantitative, this was another grounds for equating God with the world. That equation would not have been suggested by earlier accounts of divine infinitude, which were principally qualitative rather than quantitative, as we have seen. In this infinite world-God, everything happens somewhere: the potential (what could happen) is emptied out into the world of the actual. The effect is somewhat the opposite: each actual event becomes simply a location on the infinite map of potentiality.

Spinoza elaborated his philosophical vision in terms of 'substance, attribute and mode'. There is that single substance, the infinite substance called *Deus sive natura* (God or nature). This substance, however, is made up of an infinite number of attributes. Of these, two are open to the human intellect, the two substances proposed by Descartes (although seen in his case as exhaustive): extension, which applies to the physical world, and thought, which applies to the mind. These two attributes are not distinct, precisely because they are modes of the one infinite substance.

God is not separate from the world, which in a sense makes the world rational. Again, an elevation is accompanied by a demotion: the world is rational but divine rationality is robbed of purpose or will, and evolves deterministically. To be fair, Spinoza claims freedom for God or nature, but it is unclear how this can follow.

The true human good for Spinoza is knowledge. He paints a picture of blessedness as coming from knowledge of God, which must mean understanding the universe as an ordered whole. In rather a Platonic fashion, this proceeds by an ascent from knowledge of physical things through mathematics and philosophical categories. The truest knowledge of the things in the world is knowledge of them in their necessity and in the necessity of their relations. Spinoza called this the view *sub specie aeternitatis* (according to the perspective of eternity). It is the closest that human beings can come to knowledge of God-or-nature. It leads to delight and a Stoic contentment, which Spinoza called 'the intellectual love of God'.

From one perspective, Spinoza was a renegade and a blip. Although he drew on the work of others, especially Leibniz, his system is an outlier. In another sense, he is an extraordinarily influential figure. Indeed, the significance of his influence on other Enlightenment figures is only just emerging.[25] His influence on recent thought is particularly strong within the strand of postmodernism associated with Gilles Deleuze, who worked on Spinoza for his doctoral dissertation and called him the 'prince of philosophers'. In the Jeeves stories, P. G. Wodehouse makes Spinoza Jeeves's favourite reading.

Deism

For Spinoza, God is about as closely equated with the world as we could imagine. In contrast, however, at the same period of history we also encounter deism, where God is hardly thought to be involved with the world at all. This goes hand in hand with a certain view of the universe fostered by early modern science. It became popular in Britain through the work of Lord Herbert of Cherbury (1583–1648) and his *De Veritate* ('Concerning Truth'). Deists saw the world as an intricate machine which runs on its own laws. They looked to God as the creator of the world, and framer of those laws, but as little else. The key to their position was supposing that the world has an independence, such that it runs itself once made, rather than hanging on God at every moment, like a child at the breast. To say that the universe has its own integrity is one thing. Previous Christian orthodoxy had said that. However, it also said that the world is characterized by a thoroughgoing contingency, on account of which it has to be seen as receiving its being afresh from God at each moment. In turning away from this, the deists looked to nature and reason rather than revelation, when it came to God and religion. Their faith tended to be highly individualistic, rejecting collective, institutional forms of religious life. They also scorned miracles. Some deists continued to live within an existing religious tradition, usually a Christian one, but they would be unlikely to believe in answers to prayer or to hope for a life in a world to come. Deism became particularly

---

25 Jonathan Israel's work is an example.

prominent in the newly independent United States, inspired for instance by Thomas Paine's *Age of Reason* (1793–94). As he put it in the minimal creed that opens that book, 'My own mind is my own church.' Thomas Jefferson (1743–1826) is another representative. He exemplifies the almost exclusively moral character of deist religion. His 'Jefferson Bible' (or *The Life and Morals of Jesus of Nazareth*) consisted of an arrangement of passages from the Gospels, cut out by razor and re-assembled. Jefferson omitted the miracles and anything otherwise supernatural: he opened with the birth of Jesus, not with the Annunciation, and ended with Jesus laid in the tomb.

In a deist scheme, God is distant and yet not transcendent. God is so much like a human craftsman as to be a maker among makers: that familiar being among beings. We get a sense of this, if we consider the alternatives, and do so on two fronts. The first concerns transcendence: is God beyond the realm of creation, so utterly distinct as not to be a being among beings? The second question concerns immanence: is God at the heart of everything, the cause and creator of all that is with a freshness at each moment that exactly resembles the first moment of time? As a student once put it to me: is God transcendent, as in Genesis 1, or walking and moulding the earth, as in Genesis 2? Often our options are presented as having to take a position on a line running from transcendence to immanence. On this view, the more we see God as one, the less we see God as the other. However, we can in fact conceive of God as transcendent or not, and as immanent or not, and these *are not* yoked decisions: to be transcendent does not mean not to be immanent; there are four options, not two; Genesis 1 and Genesis 2 are both in the Bible. As examples of the various positions, consider the following chart.

Conception of God	Transcendent	Not Transcendent
Immanent	Orthodox Christianity	Pantheism
Not Immanent	Pagan Neoplatonism	Deism

For Neoplatonism, God is only transcendent, held away from the material world by a distance that puts him beyond thought, perhaps even beyond being. For the pantheist, at the opposite extreme, God and the world are one: God is immanent without any remainder that would involve transcendence. For Christianity, as exemplified by Augustine or Aquinas, God is utterly transcendent and yet at the same time present as the causation in every cause, the life within all life, the being within all being. He is 'closer to me than I am to myself', wrote Augustine, and yet God is God and creation is creation. Deism does not offer the immanence of Christianity or (differently) pantheism; for the deist, the world derives from God in the past but it now runs on its own terms, according to laws which it uncomplicatedly possesses on its own account. Neither, however, does deism offer the transcendence of Christianity or (differently) pagan Neoplatonism; its god is part of the scheme and tamed to human rationality.

Christians take it for granted that God is transcendent, not part of the furniture of the universe. Comparing this with the Presocratics, or even Aristotle, we can appreciate just how revolutionary this is. Plato got so far, and provided us with much that has been useful for conceptualizing transcendence. All the same, as Étienne Gilson argued, only with the Judaic revelation was it seen that this ultimate truth is also personal: God is 'he who is', not 'that which is'.[26]

Hobbes

Thomas Hobbes (1588–1679) was a polymath, like Descartes, Locke and Spinoza. He turned his hand to optics, mathematics and ballistics in addition to the fields for which he is better known today: ethics, psychology and, particularly, political philosophy. His political thought is set out in *Leviathan* and follows from a frank and pessimistic assessment of human psychology. Left to our own devices, Hobbes thought, we would be at each other's

---

26 Étienne Gilson, *God and Philosophy*, New Haven: Yale University Press, 1941, p. 40.

throats, probably slitting them. At the root of his political scheme lies a thought experiment, of considering what life would be like in a hypothetical world before politics. The answer is that life would be 'solitary, poor, nasty, brutish and short'. This contrasts with the French philosopher, Rousseau, of a century later, who imagined our primordial condition – that of the 'noble savage' – as preferable to that of today.

For Hobbes, human beings possess little by way of natural moral instinct. Their only guiding principle is self-interest.[27] To say this is to perpetuate the distinction made by Scotus, and Anselm before him, between a desire for advantage and a desire for justice, as *fundamentally separate*. Hobbes takes this further: he can hardly imagine that we are much guided by the latter.

Against such a background, Hobbes proposed a distinctive source for the authority of the state. Faced by the dismal prospect of a 'war of all against all', people relinquish their freedom for the sake of freedom.[28] Better to be ruled over by a sovereign, even a rather tyrannical one, so long as he is able to restrain the desire of others to exploit me and steal my goods. In the process, I lose much of my chance to exploit or steal, but that is a worthwhile sacrifice.

Hobbes was not philosophizing in a vacuum. His purpose was in part to legitimate the current political order, even though its reach was draconian. *Leviathan* is a good illustration that the politics we espouse, or are willing to put up with, is grounded in a profound way in our philosophical assumptions about the nature of humanity and indeed of reality itself: is it ruled by a paradigm of peace or of violence, of cooperation or of competition? Politics in the West is significantly Hobbsian to this day.

In his metaphysics, Hobbes was strongly materialist: reality consists only of matter, or matter in motion, as he put it. Like Descartes, he put forward an account of matter stripped of meaning and equated to brute extension. In his epistemology, Hobbes was strongly empiricist. At the intersection of metaphysics and

27 *Leviathan*, XIV, 8.
28 This is from *De Cive* ('bellum omnium contra omnes'). *Leviathan* XIV has 'warre of every one against every one'.

epistemology, he was strongly nominalist, which followed from his denial of anything but matter.

Locke

Whereas Hobbes was a royalist, John Locke (1632–1704) had opposed Charles II and James II. Like Hobbes, he turned to political philosophy (in his two *Treatises on Government*) out of political need, after training in other fields, including medicine. While Hobbes stressed the freedom of the sovereign authority to do almost as he wished in return for keeping the peace, Locke put forward a scheme of constitutional government that saw legitimacy as constantly bestowed by public consent, not given once for all in some aboriginal state. When the public withholds that consent, rebellion becomes licit. Overall, Locke's political scheme had a warmer view of the human situation than Hobbes', since the people transfer not only freedom to the governing power but also a sense of right and wrong, through natural law. This is not simply sacrificed by the populous, but rather achieves its potential to be impartial through civic exercise. Locke is also important for work on the virtue of toleration.

In his wider philosophy, Locke was – like Hobbes – strongly empiricist, a position he held in firm rejection of the more mind-focused scheme of Descartes. Particularly significant is Locke's distinction between the primary and secondary properties of things. A primary property belongs to the object itself, such as its solidity and motion. Other properties, called secondary, are not possessed by the object but only by the one who perceives it. Colour and taste are good examples. Solidity is in the object *and* the perceiving mind; colour is in the perceiving mind alone. Over primary properties, he lent towards realism; towards secondary properties, he leant in a nominalist or idealist direction.

Berkeley

Many important philosophers have been priests. Fewer have been bishops. (Albert the Great and Nicholas of Cusa are examples.)

The Anglican Churches since the Reformation have produced two notable bishop philosophers, Bishop Berkeley (1685–1753) and his contemporary Joseph Butler (1692–1752).

Berkeley presents us with quite a spectacle, working from what looks like a state of radical empiricism, he arrived at a position of radical idealism, which denied the existence of those things other than in the *mind*. He grounded his philosophy on what we perceive, like many an empiricist, but took this so far as to elevate the perception over that which is perceived. He was a strident critic of Locke, whose distinction of primary and secondary properties gives us a good way into Berkeley's thought. Locke said that some properties are in things, such as solidity, whereas other properties, such as colour, are only in the mind. Berkeley's philosophy denies the distinction. We have no reason, he supposed, to say that any property – solidity, motion or anything else – is other than in the mind. He collapsed everything about any object into the second of Locke's categories.

Descartes had turned to mind to shore up his confidence in reality ('I think therefore I am'). Berkeley equated mind with reality: 'to be is to be perceived', as he put it. Having said that, he then saw no value in supposing that there is a thing in itself behind our perceptions. This could lead to a position of thoroughgoing solipsism: the assumption that everything else and everyone else is a figment of my own imagination. Berkeley escaped this through his belief in God. A tree exists only in thought, but it continues to 'exist' when it is not in my mind because it is always in the mind of God. It springs from God's mind, not from my own.

It may be useful here to contrast Berkeley and Aquinas on being and knowing. For Aquinas, the world consists of matter and form. An apple is matter with the form of an apple. I have a form, which we also call a soul, and it is capable of receiving the appleness of the apple (the form of the apple) into itself, which is what we call knowing. Everything about the apple, and about me, is a gift from God, such that knowing the sustaining power of the apple constitutes some intimation of God as the one who sustains life. For Berkeley, in contrast, there are just spirits and ideas, which pass between spirits. Everything that I know comes to me directly, from God, as an idea. Rather like the Keanu Reeves character in *The Matrix*, who is plugged into a simulated reality, for Berkeley my soul is directly plugged into God. The apple comes to me from God, as it does in Aquinas, but without the mediation of a real material apple. This allowed Berkeley to by-pass all sorts of topics that were still philosophical problems in his time. He need not worry about the connection of the mind to the body, for instance, as there is no body. His scheme is almost occasionalist, in that when I choose to lift my hand God supplies the perception of my hand rising, except that, unlike for the real occasionalist, there is no material hand to rise.

Materialism, Idealism and Realism

Material things mediate, possess or exhibit spiritual realities such as beauty, truth, goodness and being. On the one hand, these examples show that the distinction made between material and spiritual (or 'abstract' or 'intellectual': the terminology is fraught) is real. Beauty is not something I can touch, but material things are beautiful; nor can I touch truth or goodness or being. 'Beauty', 'goodness', 'truth' and 'being' are abstract nouns, although they refer to concrete realities. On the other hand, to distinguish is not to separate. The chair is beautiful; it is the *chair* that is beautiful.

An idealist concentrates on the first of these ideas (that these realities are not material) and ignores or downplays the second (that it is material things that have these features). An idealist holds that reality is ultimately far more intellectual than material, such that the material is conditioned by the intellect, and may go so far as to suppose that only intellectual realities exist at all.

The materialist puts the emphasis the other way round, either claiming that existence cannot be attributed to anything other than that which is material, or at least that non-material concepts are only useful fictions or shorthands. The materialist would deny the claim made a couple of paragraphs before that non-material realities (being, goodness, truth) are just as real as material ones.

Opposed to both materialism and idealism is realism. Against materialism, the realist holds that there is something to material things, which we know, beyond their materiality. We have seen this aspect before: it is belief in form, the conviction that the appleness of the apple is something real. (The mediaeval nominalist, with which we contrasted this realism before, was not a materialist but we can see that materialism was the logic of his or her position.) Against idealism, the realist insists that thought rests on an external reality rather than externality resting on thought: a point made by Étienne Gilson. The truest philosophy is a fascination with a world that is given to us rather than with a mental universe we create: 'A philosopher talks about things, while a professor of philosophy talks about philosophy.'[29]

In the conclusion of his short book *Methodological Realism*, Gilson provides a 30-point programme for a realist revival in philosophy. He called it 'A Handbook for Beginning Realists'. The first paragraph confirms that this is not a cautious document. He proposes three first steps: first, 'recognize that one has always been a realist'; second, 'recognize that, however hard one tries to think differently, one will never manage to'; third, 'realize that those who claim they think differently, think as realists as soon as they forget to act a part. If one then asks oneself why, one's conversion to realism is all but complete.'[30]

Gilson's manifesto is magnificent for many reasons, not least because it embodies the principle of not arguing on one's 'opponents' terms. This involves being suspicious of even the mention of certain words. According to Gilson, we should distrust the term 'thought': 'the idealist thinks, whereas the realist knows': the realist is happy with thinking but it is never the start. Thinking involves 'organizing knowledge or reflecting on its content'.[31] Picking up the theme of gift, which became important in twentieth-century theology, Gilson suggests that the point is to recognize what sort of gift the world is: what we know is given to us 'in

29 *Methodological Realism*, Ignatius, 2011, p. 95.
30 *Realism*, p. 93.
31 *Realism*, p. 94.

thought', necessarily so, but we should suppose that means that it is given 'by thought'.[32] This is the idealist 'confusion'. In a pithy summary, Gilson writes that 'knowing is not apprehending a thing as it is in thought, but, in and through thought, apprehending the thing as it is'.[33] Gilson proposed that the truth of the matter lies in a position close to what would later be called 'critical realism'. We know real things out there in the world, although we can never know them more than partially: 'When we say that all knowledge consists in grasping the thing as it is, we are by no means saying that the intellect infallibly so grasps it.' Rather, 'What knowledge grasps in the object is something real, but reality is inexhaustible, and even if the intellect had discerned all its details, it would still be confounded by the mystery of its very existence.'[34]

Turning to the materialist, we might suppose that he finds his metaphysics as wearying in practice as Gilson suggests that the idealist must. All the time he uses words like 'beautiful', but all the time with a mental footnote: 'although, of course, there is no such thing as beauty, no realm of existence that encompasses *beauty*'.[35] The materialist is compelled by life to speak in ways that she holds to be deceptive. Now, of course, language *can* indeed be deceptive. The premise of this book is that mistaken philosophy – assumptions about what words mean and how to use them – can throw our thinking and judgements off course. However, to claim that *the whole of language*, with all its abstract nouns, in its most basic nuts and bolts, is somehow corrupt and misleading risks questioning the very possibility of rationality. One of the great questions in philosophy, and therefore in Christian apologetics, is whether the *common* use of language embodies metaphysical and spiritual truth. George Steiner wrote about this compellingly in *Real Presences*.[36] The philosophical, and more particularly *ontological* freight of language, with its theological entailments, is not – as

---

32 *Realism*, p. 95.

33 *Realism*, p. 96.

34 *Realism*, p. 102.

35 Or maybe not, but it would be weary in its own way never to talk or think about beauty.

36 George Steiner, *Real Presences*, London: Faber, 1989.

the materialist might claim – no more than some sort of vestigial throwback from less enlightened times.

Hume

On the face of it, David Hume (1711–76) is one of Christianity's most significant philosophical critics. This was a dangerous thing to be in the United Kingdom in the eighteenth century, for all his native Edinburgh was among the most rationalist parts of the realm. Hume was therefore careful to disperse his criticisms across his works. Justification of belief from standard natural theology is ridiculous, he writes in the *Dialogues concerning Natural Religion*, but the history of religion stands as another justification. In the *Natural History of Religion*, he attacked just this history, although natural theology could be thought to stand as an independent basis for faith. He attacked miracles in a different work, the *Enquiry concerning Human Understanding*.

Taking these works in order, the *Dialogues* take on a variety of arguments that proceed towards God from features in the universe: the 'arguments from design'. The background is of Christianity verging on deism, for which design is everything. Some of the criticisms do not work particularly well, such as the suggestion that there are other causes of order beside conscious design, including plant growth. The universe does not have the features of a vegetable. Others deserve a careful response, such as the presence of evil and suffering: if this universe is the product of a designer, one argument runs, then he is not a very good one. Another line anticipates late twentieth-century interest in 'multiverses': perhaps this universe has a certain fitness on the basis of an evolving pattern of successes and failures. Others still raise fundamental questions in philosophical theology that are more a matter of one's axioms than of argument: can we say anything about the significance of this universe being as it is, given that we have no access to 'other universes' to compare it with, for instance. Certainly given that this universe is 'all there is', at least materially and spatially, by definition it is all we have. Its features should probably strike us as significant, all the same – indeed all the more so.

The *Natural History of Religion* was significant in Hume's own biography for cementing his reputation for impiety but it need not concern us greatly. Hume had scant material to draw upon for a narrative of religious belief compared to contemporary scholarship. All the same, in the purported story he spells out, he was more concerned to insinuate that faith in his own time is irrational than he was to recount any particularly accurate account of the actual development of human religion.

Section 10 of the *Enquiry concerning Human Understanding* is often published on its own as 'On Miracles'. Hume suggests that we would always be more sensible to interpret an event as not miraculous than as a miracle. A miracle by his definition is 'a violation of the laws of nature' and, since we have established the accuracy of those laws to a high degree of certainty, it is always more likely that an event has a non-miraculous origin than a miraculous one. As an argument against miracles, Hume's position has problems from a theoretical view. For one thing, God stands above the laws of which he is the origin, so God can work outside the usual order of things without 'violating' the laws. For Christian orthodoxy, this definition of a miracle is mistaken. Even within Hume's own scheme, something is amiss, since he went out of his way to attack the very account of law that he seems to be invoking here. To explore that, we will need to turn to Hume's epistemology.

Hume was a thoroughgoing empiricist, one of the most thoroughgoing in philosophical history. He divided human consciousness into two categories: impressions, which are immediate apprehensions of the world, and ideas, which stand as the consequences of impressions at one remove. These and these alone are the legitimate objects of thought. Anything that cannot be traced back to an impression is to be discounted: the beginnings of the position known as 'positivism'. Among such fanciful notions ('speculations') are laws and causes (*First Enquiry*, 7). We never encounter a law, only isolated events that occur with regularity, and we never encounter the bond between a cause and an effect, only the effect. On that basis, talk of laws is redundant; there are only recurring patterns. Similarly, talk of causes is redundant; there are only conjoined events, even if they are 'constant conjunctions': I flick the light switch; the light comes on. There is serious room for disagreement with Hume here. For one thing, who is to say that my impression of the light switch event is not an impression of causation; for another, experience of patterns could well be experience of a law, especially if we allow for experience to be something that happens to a whole community of people over a centuries-long communal process.

We can see how Hume's invocation of laws of nature, violated or otherwise, in his argument against miracles is odd. He attacks precisely such a notion of laws of nature. That may, however, be a low swipe. Despite that invocation of laws of nature, he goes on to spell the argument out in terms of recurring patterns, which he does accept. Even on that account, however, even if a law is only a shorthand for a 'constant conjunction' (for instance between being dead and staying dead), Hume's account is still circular. It amounts to the claim that any empirical evidence that the dead can rise must be wrong because *empirically* the dead never rise.

Perhaps not: the dead do not usually rise, but neither is history full of figures like Jesus of Nazareth. What is more, we do not interpret events in isolation but in terms of an overarching whole. Hume lived within a world where miracles were never thought to happen. According to that world view, it may be reasonable to prefer another explanation when faced with your first seemingly miraculous event. Historically, however, most of the world's people have lived within a frame of reference within which miracles are thought to happen, with the fact that there is something rather than nothing topping the list, and the music of J. S. Bach (or whomever) not so far behind. Christians might be wrong to look at the world that way; we might not think so. Hume's argument is not going to convince us otherwise, if we do not accept the basic premise that miracles are something that never happen, or happen vanishingly infrequently, never mind the definition of a miracle as a *violation* of the laws of nature. Among the good reasons for inhabiting such an enchanted world view, as we have noted, is recognition of the act of creation, which is the primal and ever-repeated miracle: the supreme unexpected event, since 'prior' to creation there were no humans – or angels – to expect it, and which bucked every previous trend, in the sense that there were no previous trends to buck.

To be fair to Hume, he does have something to teach us here, namely not to accept miracles incredulously. The Scriptures were there already, however, not least with the injunction to test spirits (Deut. 18.22; Matt. 7.15; 1 Cor. 12.10; 1 John 4.1). The Church we are most likely to encounter that lives by miracles, the Roman Catholic Church, has detailed rules for judging any that are reported, including a very Humian insistence on asking what other explanations could also be given and taking them very seriously.

In the realm of moral philosophy, Hume is most well known for his attack on natural law, on the basis that statements about the properties of things (such as what benefits us) are one thing and statements about morality are another.[37] We cannot go from an 'is' to an 'ought': a move which G. E. Moore called the 'naturalistic fallacy' in his *Principia Ethica* (1903). The natural law enthusiast would reply that it all depends on whether one thinks that the nature of things and the nature of the moral good have a common origin in a creator.

In Hume's scheme, human sympathies carry much of the weight of morality and inter-human relations. This is not a realm for reason but for 'sentiment'. While that takes him a long way from the (Thomist) position that goodness is what well-informed reason would always choose, it leaves room for a moral sense to continue to function. More than that, it translates questions of ethics out of a clinical realm of duty or calculus (as with, respectively, Kant and the utilitarians, whom we will encounter below) and into the positively pastoral setting of one person's lived encounters with another. Hume's stress on sympathy, or fellow feeling, is underlined by contemporary neuroscience and the discovery of mirror neurones: the idea that our brains are wired to help us put ourselves in another's shoes.

---

37 *Treatise of Human Nature*, III.

The place of sympathy in Hume is an illustration of the principle that a scheme will often work in spite of itself. The truth is so true that even when a philosopher is on a hiding to nothing – such as Hume over morality as an irrational business – something will emerge that bears witness to that truth, even if, as in Hume's case, it means that an incongruous part of that scheme, such as sympathy, has to do more work than might otherwise reasonably be expected.

Reading On

Isaac Kramnick's anthology *The Portable Enlightenment Reader* (Penguin, 1995) provides an overview. Jonathan Israel's *Radical Enlightenment: Philosophy and the Making of Modernity, 1650–1750* (OUP, 2001) has been well received.

John Cottingham, Robert Stoothoff and Dugald Murdoch have translated *The Philosophical Writings of Descartes* (CUP, 1985–91). The best place to start is with the *Meditations*, found in both Penguin and Oxford World's Classics editions. Cottingham has written a basic introduction (*How to Read Descartes*, London: Granta, 2008) and a more detailed survey: *Descartes* (Blackwell, 1986).

Honor Levi translated Pascal's *Pensées* and various other works (OUP, 1995). The *Provincial Letters* were translated by A. J. Krailsheimer (Penguin, 1967).

Important works by Leibniz are collected as *Philosophical Texts*, translated by R. S. Woolhouse and Richard Francks (OUP, 1998). Two good overviews of his work are Maria Rosa Antognazza, *Leibniz: An Intellectual Biography* (CUP, 2011) and Nicholas Jolley, *Leibniz* (Routledge, 2005). Gilles Deleuze drew on Leibniz for the wildest possible postmodern metaphysics in *The Fold: Leibniz and the Baroque* (Minneapolis: University of Minnesota Press, 1993).

E. M. Curley translated Spinoza's *Ethics* for Penguin (1996). Discussions of his work include Stuart Hampshire's *Spinoza and Spinozism* (Oxford: Clarendon Press, 2005), which includes an introduction to Spinoza's philosophy previously published by

Penguin (1951), Richard Mason's *The God of Spinoza: A Philo-sophical Study* (CUP, 1997) and, from the postmodernist Gilles Deleuze, *Expressionism in Philosophy: Spinoza* (New York: Zone Books, 1990). The places to begin with Berkeley are his *Treatise Concerning the Principles of Human Knowledge* (1710) and *Three Dialogues between Hylas and Philonous* (1713), which appear in various modern editions. With Hume, students often begin with *Dialogues concerning Natural Religion* (1779) and *An Enquiry concerning Human Understanding* (1748, the 'first enquiry'), for the discussion of miracles and causation. For the human person and ethics, see his *Enquiry Concerning the Principles of Morals* (1751, the 'second enquiry').

12

Kant, Hegel and Romanticism

Immanuel Kant

As with Descartes, the work of Immanuel Kant (1724–1804) represents a turn inwards. Like any of the pivotal figures in the history of philosophy, Kant was concerned about foundations and, like Descartes, he proceeded by stripping away. Among his many works, Kant's project found its ultimate expression in three monumental works called 'Critiques': the *Critique of Pure Reason*, the *Critique of Practical Reason* and the *Critique of Judgement* (or *Critique of the Power of Judgement*). These are daunting works and it can be more manageable to start with some of Kant's helpfully cut-down parallel works: the *Prolegomena to Any Future Metaphysics* (for 'pure reason') and the *Groundwork for the Metaphysics of Morals* (for 'practical reason'). His *Religion within the Bounds of Mere Reason* does not relate in the same way to the third critique, but is worth reading.

Pure Reason

Philosophers can be as interested in how we know as in what we know. Kant is a perfect example. He was less concerned with the objects of thought than in how we conceptualize them and in where the limits lie as to what we could possibly know.

In Kant's own words, the provocation for his distinctive approach to philosophy came from reading David Hume. Hume, he wrote, 'woke me from my dogmatic slumbers'.[1] Kant had been exploring avenues for a new foundation to philosophy all his academic

---

1 *Prolegomena*, prologue.

life, and the three *Critiques* come relatively late. The earlier works had not been particularly effective and give the sense of someone looking for bearings, and even walking in circles.[2]

Causation has been a recurrent theme in this book and Hume was important for Kant because of his attack on the idea of causation. Kant valued an ordered world; stereotypes of eighteenth-century Prussia are not too far off the mark. He wondered what would be left of metaphysics if we were to jettison the principle of causation, or what would be left of ethics if the moral life were reduced to sentiment, as Hume also proposed.

Kant fought a rearguard action and, crucially, he did not start where previous Christian philosophers would have started: with God as the foundation of metaphysics and ethics. God was not evident enough for Kant, or a secure enough place to start. That Kant could think this, rests on the sort of Christian tradition to which he belonged and on what he was looking for in his philosophical quest. As a Lutheran, Kant was heir to a tradition of *pietism* that saw faith as going beyond reason, even as standing opposed to reason. Faith, on this view, was one thing and reason was another. Kant wanted a foundation for reason, so it could not rest on God, on transcendence, which belonged for Kant to the realm of faith. Notice that this approach is poles apart from various mediaeval accounts that each, in their way, *joined* faith and reason. It is far from recognizing that confidence in reason is, in the end, faith in reason, and that faith is reasonable only if God underwrites it. Kant's move also works with a very individualistic notion of faith. For all these reasons, nothing of faith can function as the sort of universal foundation that Kant sought. Later philosophy would line up with Christian theology in holding this to be wrong in two ways. First, reason is less universal than Kant understood and hoped it to be; there are no universal foundations for reason upon which all agree in a fashion independent of tradition. Second, faith is also less individual: it is something we inhabit as a member of some community or other.

---

2 For this, see the chapter of the *The Cambridge Companion to Kant*, ed. Paul Guyer, CUP, 1992, on his 'early' works.

Kant asked what basis we could possibly have for accepting causation. In doing so, he agreed with Hume that causation is a problem. Our observations show us events that we describe as causally related, but there is no empirical mantrap that will catch *causation* itself. For Hume, all we have are so many events to which we impute a relation. For theology of previous ages, causation was empirically obvious and yet so remarkable as to call upon God as its origin. Kant would not turn to God, for reasons we have just considered. With the transcendent debarred, Kant turned instead to the *transcendental*, which is to say, to the structures of human thought.

Kant decided that the only way in which something such as causation could be upheld was if it was always already there in the structure of reason, like a pre-existing channel in the bedrock of thought. Before we see, or feel, or in any way perceive anything, we have concepts into which any thought, feeling or perception would have to fit. To use a distinction we have already discussed, what matters is not what we observe a posteriori (*after* having 'turned to the world') but what makes observation possible a priori (*before* such a turn).[3] Causation is among these a priori concepts, or *categories*, as Kant called them. Existence is another, as are the ideas of necessity and possibility. 'Only by means' of these categories, wrote Kant, 'can any object of experience be thought at all.'[4] This Kant called his 'Copernican revolution'. Copernicus had shifted our ideas of what moves and what stays put. Kant proposed a similar revolution over the possibility of knowledge. Whereas for, say, Aquinas the 'knowability' of the world resided in things outside us, such as trees, stones and people, for Kant the secret of a thing being knowable lies in the mind. The tree, the stone and the person each receive their rationality, their truth, by the imposition of our categories.

---

3 This is sometimes expressed as a distinction between *synthetic* knowledge, where the truth of what is said resides in the terms themselves, and *analytic* knowledge, where the truth of what is said rests on observation.

4 *Critique of Pure Reason*, A93/B126. ('A' and 'B' refer to two different versions.)

Kant provided a complete and succinct table of the categories. We will not discuss them each in detail but the list is short enough to be reproduced here:

Quantity: unity, plurality, totality
Quality: reality, negation, limitation
Relation: inherence and subsistence (which relate to substance and accident), causality and dependence (cause and effect), community (reciprocity)
Modality: possibility, existence, necessity (and their opposites).

As a list of metaphysical categories, this takes some beating. For Kant, however, they are not metaphysical categories in any usual sense, which is to say relating to the structures of being. They are *transcendental*, they are within, structuring thought before we use them to structure reality.

This is Kant's transcendental method. We might call it a 'meta' method: not thinking about things but thinking about thinking about things. We could call Kant the father of this 'meta' move. We will also see it in his ethical writing: not thinking about right and wrong but thinking about thinking about right and wrong. In the twentieth century, this sort of move would dominate literary theory, which could spend more time thinking about thinking about texts than about the texts – novels and poems – themselves. The same could be said about almost every field of the arts and humanities, including music, history and geography. In moderation, it hones precision and lends sophistication. In excess, it misses the point. One role for theology, in response, is to advocate a return to the world, to creation and creativity.

Kant was disturbed by empiricism, since he could not see how it could provide the sort of foundations he wanted. He found those foundations in the realm of thought itself. Turning back to the world of objects, he continued to seek for the unchanging behind the changing and proposed that beneath what appears to us is a truer reality. *Phenomena* are available to us; *noumena* lie beyond us. We can talk of the *phenomenal* realm and the *noumenal* realm. On the face of it, this might remind us of Aristotle's distinction between substance and accidents. The comparison shows the peculiarity of Kant's scheme. For the scholastics, accidents reveal substance (Aquinas wrote that the substance 'shines forth' through the accidents).[5] For Kant, we have no access to noumena. For Aristotelians, substances exist in the world we recognize: in space and time. That cannot be said about Kant's noumena. Space and time are a priori categories, which *we* impose on what we observe. Noumena, the things themselves, somehow exist outside of space and time.[6] Whereas Berkeley rejected empiricism by turning to an idealism of perceptions alone, Kant rejected it with an idealism of unknowable *noumena* behind *phenomena*. Those *noumena* could perhaps also be said to exist in something like the world of spirit and ideas proposed by Berkeley.

Kant is a great thinker of limits. The noumenal lies beyond the limits of thought. This raises significant questions, however: can we really think a limit without thinking beyond it. Wittgenstein talked about thinking a limit from both sides and he may be on to something. For his part, Kant imagined a sound triggered whenever we go too far, when our thinking starts running into all sorts of trouble. In particular, we run into contradictions, which he called *antimonies*. There are four, and they each involve being able to prove that something is both true and false at the same time. (For this to be a problem, Kant obviously believes in the Law of Non-Contradiction, which we first encounter in Aristotle. Already, before Kant, philosophers had started to question it, or think beyond it. We have seen something of this in Nicholas of Cusa.) For instance, according to the first antinomy, we can prove that the world is both eternal and not eternal, or both finite and infinite in extent. This comes, in part, from speculating about what is neither a priori nor a possible object of a posteriori sense perception. Kant's position sounds proto-postmodern (and we will see how much Kant is a precursor of postmodern philosophy below): statements about certain sorts of subjects are not true but neither are they not

---

5 See W. Norris Clarke, *Person and Being*, Milwaukee: Marquette University Press, 1993, p. 90.
6 Kant is not always clear about this, but it is the logic of his position.

not-true. Like the characteristic bugbears of postmodernism, these non-entities are collections or wholes. We should leave off even trying to think about 'the whole universe' never mind how large or old it is: it is neither a priori nor is it something we could see. Just as 'causation' has never jumped at us from behind a bush, neither has 'the whole universe'. Kant, on this score, resembles his bête noir, David Hume. He too argued, in *Dialogues concerning Natural Religion*, that we have no place talking about design-like features in the universe as a whole, since the universe as a whole is not something to which we are privy. Kant saved causation (for all we only see 'causes' and 'effects' rather than 'causation' itself) by inscribing it in the transcendental realm. It is not clear why he could not save totality in the same way, since it is also one of his transcendental categories, alongside causation.

The most significant antinomy from a theological point of view is the fourth: that there both is and is not a necessary being. This makes God's existence, on this approach, beyond the bounds of knowledge.[7] Kant would provide a reason for believing in God, but it does not come from this 'theoretical' realm but rather from the practical or ethical realm, to which we turn.

Practical Reason

Kant had the same concerns in ethics as with metaphysics: to locate unshakable foundations. With metaphysics we are exploring 'pure' ('speculative') reason; with ethics we are exploring 'practical reason': the sort of reason we employ when we are thinking about how to get things done.

Philosophers around the time of Kant, and a little before, were starting to question the idea of an unassailable source telling us how to behave. The Reformation had dethroned church authority. That was the logic of the Reformation position, although at

---

7 Eric Alliez traces this back to Scotus, with Kant as 'the last Scotist', in *Capital Times: Tales from the Conquest of Time*, Minneapolis: University of Minnesota Press, 1996, p. 231. Cited by Gavin Hyman, *The Predicament of Postmodern Theology*, Louisville: Westminster John Knox Press, 2001, pp. 37–8.

first the Reformers held on to the sense that the Church could and should instruct people as to how to behave. That sat at odds with the theory they were expounding, and cracks were beginning to appear at that interface between theory and practice. At first, there had been a largely agreed sense of what the Bible required, but once Protestants began disagreeing about what the Bible meant, or demanded of us, there was no arbiter to turn to. Political power hitched itself to these disagreements. Hume, again, played his part in the sense of moral crisis. His attack on the so-called 'naturalistic fallacy', that 'you cannot get an *ought* from an *is*', rocked the authority of natural law approaches to ethics.

Kant sought a foundation for behaviour that was truly universal, and he found it in the same place as he did for pure reason: in what he proposed to be undeniable structures of thought. He wanted to know what must be true in the realm of ethics. For this he pushed beyond what he called the *hypothetical imperative* (were you to want A you would have to do B) to the *categorical imperative* (do B, no matter what). The business of 'doing B, no matter what' is the recognition of law. Such an approach to ethics, based on law or duty, is called *deontology* (from the Greek *deon*, 'necessity' or 'obligation'; it has nothing to do with *ontology*, despite the similarity of sound). The categorical imperative is that which is absolutely ('categorically') necessary for us to do in order to live ethically: it is written into the very *categories* of reason, and required by them.

Kant expressed the categorical imperative in three different ways, and even scholars of Kant admit that it is not entirely clear why he thought they were equivalent. Two concern 'maxims': the rules we apply in practice. Kant's big idea – his meta-rule we might say – is that we should formulate our maxims so that we would want them to be followed absolutely universally. A categorical imperative is one that can be rendered universal, so that everyone would obey it (the third formulation) without contradiction (the first formulation). For instance, Kant thought that there is a categorical imperative to tell the truth, because a rational person would always want that maxim to be followed by everyone. A prohibition on lying delivers its promise if everyone follows it. That makes it a categorical imperative. In Kant's favour, such rules about universality stand as the preconditions for sociability. Against Kant, the rules he wanted to be generalized look like ones that will uphold his eighteenth-century Prussian status quo. A Jew hiding in Germany in the middle of the twentieth century would not want a maxim about telling the truth to be held universally: certainly not by the family in whose house she was hiding, nor should she. Another formulation, which Kant claimed amounts to the same thing, is that people should always be treated as ends not means. Presumably the link is that this is a maxim which we would want to universalize.

God does not enter into this foundation for ethics. Rather, to speak roughly, ethics is the foundation for belief in God, not the other way round. Since we have by duty to attain to the highest good, we must be able to do so. (As Aristotle had said, what is necessary must be possible.) For Kant, this requires God, not least because goodness clearly does not always triumph in this life. We can invoke God to ensure that every wrong is punished in the end, and every right rewarded. There must be justice, and therefore there must be God, because God guarantees justice.

The 'good', for Kant, has nothing of the shimmering beauty that it has for Plato, none of the allure. Kant's ethics is all about the law and duty, while for Platonists such as Thomas, the Good is so compelling and desirable that duty is strictly secondary. If one perceives the Good, one runs after it. Augustine exemplified this approach when he wrote that we should love God and do what (as a result) we want:[8] get what you love right and the rest follows. At its best, and certainly for the holy person, ethics is immeasurably more about delight rather than duty. Kant, however, would have us seek the good purely 'for its own sake'. Any benefit that goodness might bring, personally or communally, is irrelevant at best and obstructive at worst, since it distracts the will from a pure decision for the good, abstracted from any reward. Again, the Platonist presents us with a different vision, according to which the good means all that it can mean in English: moral, excellent and beneficial. The Herculean effort to act without reference to

---

8 *Tractates on 1 John*, VII.8.

benefit and reward is unnecessary and perverse. That, however, is exactly what Kant would have us do, following here the Scotist legacy of separating the 'beneficial' from the 'just'. Kant goes so far, in *Religion within the Bounds of Mere Reason*, as to say that if we do the right or good thing, but out of self-interest – for instance if we refrain from cruelty because we were worried about our reputation – then it would not be a good act, because it is done out of self-interest and not out of obedience to duty. For Augustine or Aquinas, reputation is a good thing and a concern for it is one of the ways in which the good is mediated to us.

Religion

We have come to *Religion within the Bounds of Mere Reason*. This reasonably short work of Kant's is among the most easy to read. We find fairly extensive discussions of many of the main topics that we would expect in a theological work, such as sin, redemption, Christ, the Church. None of these ideas, however, is understood in a straightforwardly orthodox fashion.

As we might expect, Kant's account of 'religion' is largely concerned with ethics and duty. The picture is an individualistic one, at least for the philosopher aristocrat who can see the truth clearly. For them, the Church is not so much necessary as a useful site for the pooling of effort. The common person, however, may have need of the Church and its forms of life. Worship is strictly secondary. Even the Scriptures are simply useful aids for the ignorant, as even perhaps is the Incarnation, since Christ is cast as an exemplar, the best example of a general case. His earthly life is illustrative, and would be unhelpful if, attending to it, we allowed history to distract us from eternal truths. Kant's picture is basically Pelagian: the individual human being saves him- or herself through moral self-improvement; grace is a useful supplement. This takes sin insufficiently seriously. In another way, however, Kant placed too much emphasis on sin. With his notion of 'radical evil' sin receives a dualistic ultimacy that had been denied since the early Church.

Aesthetics

Kant's *Third Critique*, on the 'faculty of judgement', deals with two topics, aesthetics and teleology. It counts them more or less as two separate subjects, although for Kant they involve the same human faculty, namely judgement, which assigns individual things to their proper overarching categories.

Kant's aesthetics works with the categories of the 'beautiful' and the 'sublime'. He also mentions a third category, the 'agreeable', but not so as to give it an important place. That is itself a judgement, an assignment of something to a place within a larger category: in this case with the category of aesthetics, and to a low place within it. Western philosophy has a chequered history when it comes to judgements on 'low' culture. It goes alongside a certain denigration of the business of making, and of running down craft in comparison to art. Already in Aristotle we find a sharp distinction between *doing*, which was worthy of a free-born male, and *making*, which was the preserve only of slaves. We might think that Christianity would have a high view of making, given that God is 'the maker of heaven and earth', but this has not always been so. With characteristic force, John Milbank wishes to turn the tables on the art/craft hierarchy: art is low before it is high; it is public in the sense of being domestic, and in the town square, before it is public in the sense of being in the public art gallery. Milbank has place for high art, but he wishes to blur boundaries: there should be both making and doing, crafting and making beautiful, in 'all our handling of matter and all our speaking'.[9] Consequently, the fusion of art and craft is in

> architecture and house-decoration and gardening and tribute and commemorative portraiture and love-letters and hymns to the gods before it is novels and stage plays and contextless sculpture and the re-performance of old operas, etc.[10]

---

9 John Milbank, 'Scholasticism, Modernism and Modernity', *Modern Theology* 22 (2006), pp. 651–71, p. 665.

10 Milbank, 'Scholasticism', p. 665–6.

Kant placed disinterestedness at the heart of aesthetics, as with his ethics. Again, he stands opposed to the account of allure and involvement characteristic of a Platonist approach. Kant also held that in finding something beautiful one must expect that everyone else would also find it beautiful. Disinterestedness typically goes hand in hand in philosophy with universality. In contrast, for a Platonist account, it is sufficient for *this* thing to be the particular location for the mediation of divine beauty for me, at this time and in this place. Similarly, in the ethics of the Platonically inclined Augustine, we find an *ordo amoris*, an ordering of love, by which it is not only acceptably but constitutively human to love and care principally for those people to which providence has particularly bound us.

At the same time as beauty is given a universal quality in Kant, it is also rendered internal and subjective: there is no basis on which we can argue about why something is beautiful or it is not. Faced with something beautiful we are reduced to inarticulacy. Here aesthetics connects with teleology, the other part of the *Third Critique*, in that the beautiful object presents us with a sense of purpose that cannot be explained because it is a purposefulness without purpose. At best, Kant is pointing here to a rejoicing in the art work in its very existence. This sense of purposelessness, however, stands as a further dismissal of those forms of more practical art which are useful as well as beautiful, and exhibits a certain naivety about the ways in which all art, and especially 'high art', always serves an economic, social and political purpose, for good or ill.

In contrast to the beautiful, Kant's sublime concerns something like pleasure in the face of terror. We feel sublimity when we are faced with that which is overwhelming: in the realm of thought that might be the numerical infinite; in the realm of nature it might be a storm or thundering waves. The category of the sublime was to have a profound influence on the Romantic movement in painting (for instance in John Martin and Caspar David Friedrich), literature (from Wordsworth to science fiction), music

(Beethoven, and Slavoj Žižek argues for sublimity in both Rossini and Wagner[11]) and architecture (the skyscraper).

For Kant the feeling of the sublime rests on our sense of being mentally in control even when faced with overwhelming force since, for Kant, the world is always tempered to our mental faculties. Faced with an overwhelming situation, we recognize 'our physical powerlessness' as 'natural beings'. Simply to notice, however, that we are mental beings who can recognize,

> reveals a capacity for judging ourselves as independent of nature and a superiority over nature on which is grounded a self-preservation of quite another kind than that which can be threatened and endangered by nature outside us, whereby the humanity in our person remains undemeaned even though the human being must submit to that dominion.[12]

Little serves better to illustrate the priority of the mental over the material for Kant. If Kant were true to his scheme, he could stand on the deck of a sinking ship in the high seas not worrying about his doom but revelling in the self-preservation of the mind as 'independent' of nature, and superior to it.

Reception of Kant

Kant received a positive reception from some Protestants and fed into the growth of the growing liberal Protestant milieu, which rejected metaphysics, was distrustful of doctrine and put an emphasis on morality. He was generally rejected by Roman Catholics at first, but was later seen as the philosopher to deal with if one wanted to form a neo-Thomism respectable for the modern age, first by Joseph Maréchal (1878–1944) and then, all

---

11 The 'sublime excess of life is discernible in two main versions, Italian and German, Rossini and Wagner', *Journal of the Philosophy of Scripture* 2 (2004), pp. 18–30, p. 18.

12 Immanuel Kant, *Critique of the Power of Judgement*, trans. Eric Matthews, CUP, 2001, pp. 5:261–2.

the more, by Karl Rahner. Alongside Bernard Lonergan, Rahner produced a 'transcendental Thomism' where attention is given to the structure of human knowing. We will consider below the role of Kant in the construction of postmodern philosophy.

Hegel

Georg Wilhelm Friedrich Hegel (1770–1831) has influenced theology perhaps more than any other philosopher of the past half millennium. He has been influential because of the extent to which the great doctrines of the Christian faith figure in his system. They genuinely influenced the shape of this system. The similarities, however, only go so far. In Hegel's philosophy the various doctrines – creation, the Incarnation, the Trinity – are subsumed into his whole, and changed in the process. Few theologians have subsequently accepted that system entire, but his approach to the Christian faith has profoundly shaped the way it has been interpreted over the past two centuries.

Hegel saw the universe as proceeding from God, as in traditional Christian doctrine. However, he did not hold to the 'ontological distinction' between creatures and creator in anything like the same way. Aquinas would write that while the act of creation means everything for a creature, it does not change who God is. Hegel denied that. The act of creation for him was part of the story of God's 'development': an idea entirely alien to previous orthodoxy. 'God', Hegel could write, 'is not God without the World.'[13]

Creation therefore represents a sort of division of being. The totality of reality seen as including God becomes divided within itself. That division becomes more complete when creation arrives at self-awareness, expressed for Hegel in the Fall. In this way, the negative is also always positive. It is part of a process, and in particular part of the grand overarching process by which the ultimate underlying reality, which he calls 'Spirit' (*Geist*), comes

---

13 *Begriff der Religion*, ed. G. Lasson, Leipzig: Meiner, 1925, p. 148.

to self-awareness. Creation, the rise of human consciousness, religion, art and philosophy are all part of this development.[14]

Hegel's greatness was to see the significance of history for philosophy and theology and, in this, to see that the general is always revealed in the particular. Hegel helped Christians to see that God acts and that salvation is a drama. With this in mind, we can take the great metaphysical categories for being, which are perennially useful but risk a static interpretation, and provide what the Dominican Benedict Viviano calls 'a torque or twist which propels them spiralling forward in meaningful time'. With this, we can move beyond the 'mathematical' philosophy that often prevails today and does not understand 'human beings and their history' to a philosophy which operates in the 'salvation-historical mode, which prevails to a large extent in the Bible'.[15]

Hegel did not, however, see history as central to the created order alone. The climax of history was the period inaugurated by human self-awareness, and in this *God himself* has come to awareness. In technical terms, this makes Hegel both an idealist, since he counted Spirit (or Mind, *Geist*) as the ultimate reality, and a monist: he did not deny the reality of the material universe, but he subsumed it within the larger picture of a single reality (*monos* is Greek for 'alone'), the *Absolute*.[16] Thought parallels reality, or perhaps more accurately, reality parallels thought.

The relations here are complex, and the repercussions cut in more than one direction. Hegel elevated mind to the place of ultimate reality. In a sense, in doing so he also elevated materiality, since materiality is seen as part of the outworking of what is most real and significant. However, the Absolute is in a sense also reduced, since it now comes to include imperfection, and conflict is woven into ('ontologized') what is ultimate. According to Hegel, we should be aware that:

---

14 See the *Phenomenology of Spirit* and the later *Philosophy of History*.

15 Personal communication. Viviano points to Vico and Herder as important precursors for Hegel here, and to Schlegel as a Catholic rival for Hegel over the philosophy of history.

16 Diané Collinson, *Fifty Major Philosophers*, Routledge, 1988, p. 96.

the human, the finite, the weak, the negative, are themselves a moment of the divine, that they are within God himself, that finitude, negativity, otherness are not outside of God and do not, as otherness, hinder unity with God. Otherness, the negative, is known to be a moment of the divine nature itself. This involves the highest idea of spirit.[17]

Moreover, materiality is also devalued since it becomes only a passing moment in the history of the (fundamentally immaterial) infinite:

God has shown himself to be reconciled with the world [. . .] even the human is not something alien to him, but rather [. . .] this otherness, this self-distinguishing finitude as it is expressed, is a moment of God himself, although to be sure, it is a disappearing moment.[18]

All human life and history has become a 'disappearing moment' in God.

God works himself out through history: with this idea, Hegel was to be the father of the 'process theology' of the twentieth century. This put the emphasis on becoming rather than being, such that even God becomes a work in process. It did this by means of pantheism (God is equated with the world) or panentheism (the world is *part* of God). Process thought was proposed by Alfred North Whitehead, who opened our chapter on Plato. These distinctly heterodox notions have entered twentieth-century theology, even gaining acceptance in some parts of evangelicalism under the guise of 'open theism'.

Process theology represents one of the great wrong turns in the history of theology, selling out the doctrine of God for the sake of an anthropomorphic god supposedly found in the Bible. Along with panentheism and pantheism, process theology provides a

17 *Lectures on the Philosophy of Religion: Volume III – The Consummate Religion*, trans. Peter Hogdson, Oxford: Clarendon Press, 2007, p. 326.
18 *Philosophy of Religion*, III, p. 469.

good example of the need for attention to the meanings of words in theology. All speak of 'God'. That word, however, does not, and cannot, have anything like the same meaning as in traditional Christian theology.

Creation features prominently in Hegel's scheme, but it is not quite the Christian doctrine of creation. Rather, creation is a *necessary* part of the development, through self-estrangement, of *Spirit*. Since creation is necessary, it has nothing of the quality of gift and grace that marks the Christian account. As Charles Taylor puts it, '[i]n Hegel's system, God cannot give to man – neither in creation, nor in revelation, nor in salvation through sending his Son',[19] because all these are 'emanations of a necessity'. Similarly, the Incarnation becomes a necessary part of a larger scheme.[20] It is also more about awareness than redemption, and what there is of redemption is treated along the lines of early Greek Christian accounts, seeing the Incarnation itself as salvific, through the union of God and humanity, rather than focusing on the cross.

Hegel held that *Spirit* comes to fullest freedom, awareness and expressiveness in three dimensions of human life: art, religion and philosophy. They represent a progression, with philosophy in particular gathering up and surpassing what is valuable in art and religion. A threefold order emerges again and again in Hegel. In the *Logic* he described this recurring structure at the heart of things as *universality*, *particularity* and *individuality*.[21] With these and similar trios, Hegel circles round his own version of a familiar theme: dialectic. Previously we have seen dialectic as a process in thought. However, since for Hegel the whole of reality has the character of Spirit or *Mind*, now the whole of reality takes on a dialectic quality. His dialectic is sometimes expressed in terms of *thesis, antithesis* and *synthesis*. Hegel himself did not favour this formulation; it is more closely associated with his fellow German idealist, Johann Gottlieb Fichte (1762–1814). Nevertheless, it expresses something of Hegel's scheme. Indeed, such a scheme

---

19 Charles Taylor, *Hegel*, CUP, 1975, p. 493.
20 *Philosophy of Religion*, III, p. 313.
21 Hegel, *The Encyclopaedia Logic*, §163.

may come naturally to us today: a preacher might quite naturally structure a sermon along the lines of *one point*, followed by *its seeming opposite*, concluding with *their integration*. We should not be dismissive: it is a good scheme for a sermon, or an essay.

Dialectic in Hegel is practical. Not only must an idea be faced with its contrary, but every person and situation must pass through a history that will be an experience of trial and rupture, in order to grow to something greater and more complete. Hegel's word for the process is *Aufhebung*. This German word is often translated 'sublation'. It carries the meaning of raising up, of transcending, abolishing and preserving. The image is almost biological: that *within* any situation a partial negation already resides, out of which something else will arise. The idea of *Aufhebung* is a good way to see the usefulness of binary distinctions, and yet also to see beyond the division.

Care is needed here. As Agnes Arber wrote, it is 'fatally easy' to see process in Hegel as simply involving 'successive degrees, gradients, or levels, of truth or reality'. That, however, suggests that the conclusion *reabsorbs* both the beginning and its alienation. The beginning and the journey would then 'have no standing, except as parts of the synthesis'. This is not how Hegel sees it. Rather: 'The limited finite character of each of these three terms of the triad has itself a value, as being the necessary condition apart from which the special individuality of each would not exist.'[22]

In such terms, Hegel was able to give the doctrine of the Trinity an honoured place in his philosophical system. That doctrine belonged for him at the heart of Christianity and was part of what made Christianity the summit of human religious development: the 'Absolute Religion'. The Christian theologian might think 'so far, so good', but we should be cautious. A Christian may see an image of the Trinity in various threefold aspects of creation (past, present and future; three spatial dimensions; memory, intellect and will); Hegel was in danger of elevating a threefold pattern above even God, such that God becomes another, paradigmatic, example of a general structure. In God, for Hegel, we see first a distinction in the production of another, namely the Son, and

---

22 Agnes Arber, *The Manifold and the One*, London: J. Murray, 1957, p. 6.

then a return: 'God himself' is 'eternally triune. Spirit is this process, movement, life.' First there is a primordial differentiation involving the 'idea'. This distinction is 'sublated' and this process is nothing other than the Holy Spirit himself:

> That this is so is the Holy Spirit itself, or, expressed in the mode of sensibility, it is eternal love [. . .] For love is a distinguishing of two, who nevertheless are absolutely not distinguished for each other [. . .] This is love, and without knowing that love is both a distinguishing and the sublation of the distinction, one speaks emptily of it.[23]

Tragedy

Hegel was in danger of conforming his account of the Godhead to his principle of rupture and reintegration. That would lead later Christian Hegelians to interpret the Trinitarian processions, and especially the procession of the Son from the unity of the Father, in tragic terms: with the begetting of the Son, the Father sacrifices being all-in-all. From the perspective of earlier Christian theology, this is a horrific reading of the Trinitarian life. It demonstrates, however, that almost any dynamic that can be interpreted in terms of plenitude and donation can be interpreted, if we wish, in terms of privation and lack.

This observation introduces the topic of *tragedy*, which is one of the principal ways in which Hegel has influenced subsequent theology. We see it, and allied themes such as 'woundedness', in much theology, especially of the few decades from the 1960s onwards. In a recent book, for instance, Mary McClintock Fulkerson described theology as something that occurs 'at the scene of a wound'.[24]

Tragedy, like good theology and pastoral practice, takes suffering seriously. We are reminded that redemption does not deny

---

23 *Philosophy of Religion*, III, p. 418.
24 Mary McClintock Fulkerson, *Places of Redemption: Theology for a Worldly Church*, OUP, 2007, pp. 12–18.

that the human situation can be terrible, nor promise to remove human suffering as if by magic. Tragedy, in the words of Giles Waller, 'resists the move to philosophical abstraction and bids us attend to the ambiguities of concrete life'.[25] A sense of tragedy is therefore important in a utilitarian age, when untold suffering can be written off as 'collateral damage', and in an optimistic age, when almost anything and anyone can be sacrificed for the sake of progress. The turn to tragedy was particularly strong among left-wing theologians and philosophers, and this could well be seen as a way to disavow the statist sacrifices of Stalin (who represents another side of Hegel: a sense of the relentless march forwards). Tragedy keeps us focused on the contingencies of life, the missed opportunities, the fragility of history. Tragedy can, however, only take us so far. The Christian story is ultimately a comedy, in the sense of it being a story where things get worse than they were but end up far better.

History

Towards the beginning of this book we observed several reasons why an attempt at theology without attention to philosophical questions and categories is naive. One reason is that theology involves texts, and what we are doing when we read, or write, a text throws up all sorts of 'philosophical' questions. Another reason is that theology is concerned with history, both through the discipline found within a theology department called 'Church history' or, more generally, simply because we are concerned with things that happened in the past. Like literature, history is by no means philosophically innocent.[26]

Historians are concerned with 'what happened'. This immediately raises questions about truth, objectivity and subjectivity, and

---

25 Giles Waller, 'Freedom, Fate and Sin in Donald MacKinnon's Use of Tragedy', in *Christian Theology and Tragedy*, ed. Giles Waller and Kevin Taylor, Aldershot: Ashgate, 2011, pp. 101–48, p. 103.

26 I have found an article by Daniel Little useful: http://plato.stanford.edu/archives/win2012/entries/history/.

about certainty and ambiguity. Historians do not seek to recount a series of isolated facts; they want to put them within a bigger picture, to tell a story, and that will involve a sense of how events are related and – in some way – what caused what. That we tell history as a story is significant. Stories that wander aimlessly are not usually very good stories (unless we have a taste for the postmodern avant garde in fiction). To read history as having a direction is an interpretive decision, a matter of one's fundamental philosophy or world view. Such a decision has often had theological roots, as with Hegel, who saw history as the master theological category in which universal Spirit works out its development.[27]

Christians, we might think, are committed to reading some sort of meaning in history, not least because they see it as a story with a beginning and an end. A sense of story and meaning does not necessarily mean a sense of progress however. Biblical accounts of the end, after all, tend to fall into the category of the *apocalyptic*. While that means, literally, a 'revealing' – and an ending that reveals meaning implies meaning in what it brings to a close – it has the more popular meaning of 'catastrophe', and not without good reason. In 1992, Francis Fukuyama declared that capitalism had reached a position of stability and global domination, which marked 'the end of history'.[28] History was kickstarted by 9/11 and Fukuyama subsequently admitted that he was wrong.

Lessing and Novalis

If history has been central to theology and philosophy, it has been disparaged by others. Where history has been rejected, Christianity has often been rejected along with it. G. E. Lessing (1729–81) stands as a particularly strident and influential thinker, who argued that 'if no historical truth can be demonstrated, then nothing can be demonstrated by means of historical truths'. As he put it, '[a]ccidental truths of history can never become the proof of

---

27 Many other philosophers have written on history, including Kant and Hume.
28 In Francis Fukuyama, *The End of History and the Last Man*, New York: Free Press, 1992.

necessary truths of reason'. For him, this amounted to an 'ugly, broad ditch which I cannot get across, however often and however earnestly I have tried to make a leap'.[29]

The point is not whether events in 'theological history' happened: Lessing writes, unconvincingly, that he does not 'for one moment deny that Christ did miracles', for instance. The point is whether any 'historical' knowledge could have the sort of authority that would make us change our lives. Who, Lessing asked, 'would risk anything of great permanent worth, the loss of which would be irreparable' on 'historical truth'?[30]

In line with this, some have turned from history to aesthetics. In a poem about a Greek statue, Rainer Maria Rilke (1875–1926) argued that although the statue does not present us with something we can 'know' – we cannot know the model 'historically' – there is a communication at the level of the statue as an object, as a work of art. The poem concludes: 'You must change your life.'[31] The Christian claim about Christ might combine the two: the coming of the Son among us was 'in human form', and that 'form' was historical but it is also a form in the sense of the form of a work of art. Christ echoes down history through literature and art, not least that of the written Gospels.

With Hegel and Lessing we have been introduced to a disparate but important broad school of philosophy and art called Romanticism. As a further example we might conisder Georg Friedrich Philipp von Hardenberg (1772–1801), who wrote under the name 'Novalis'. His philosophical writing was for the most part expressed through a particular form or genre, the *fragment*. Kristin Gjesdal has pointed to the significance of this means of expression: with its 'broken form and literary style' Novalis was criticizing the sense that literature was one thing and philosophical writing another, as had for instance been assumed by Kant or Fichte.[32] Novalis's

29 Gotthold Ephraim Lessing, *Lessing's Theological Writings: Selections in Translation*, trans. Henry Chadwick, Stanford University Press, 1957, pp. 53, 55.
30 *Writings*, p. 54.
31 'Archaic Torso of Apollo'.
32 'Georg Friedrich Philipp von Hardenberg [Novalis]', *The Stanford Encyclopedia of Philosophy*, http://plato.stanford.edu/archives/fall2009/entries/novalis/.

work was 'an attempt, from within the realm of critical reason, to explore a reality whose complex nature cannot be captured by the work of a narrowly oriented rationality'. Other philosophers of this period and sensibility, such as Schelling and Hegel, had a similar desire to give philosophy the widest possible embrace and subject matter but Novalis stands out, even among this group, for resisting any urge to build an overarching philosophical system. For Novalis, philosophy ought to be 'open-ended', as Gjesdal puts it, 'forever on its way and thoroughly inductively minded'. That last point is important. The contrast is between *inductive* and *deductive* reasoning. Induction proceeds from many specific and concrete examples to some guessed-at truth, perhaps from many examples of love to some statement about the nature of love itself. Deduction proceeds by means of logic from one general and abstract statement to another: love is madness, a sensible person rejects madness, therefore a sensible person rejects love, as an example. This is an intimation of a later divide: induction aligns with 'Continental' philosophy today, and deduction with 'analytic' philosophy. We have seen that Lessing argued against historical sources for philosophy, or theology, on the basis that 'Accidental truths of history can never become the proof of necessary truths of reason'. Historical arguments are not deductive, which is why they are to be rejected. (That is not to say that Lessing was a cold rationalist on that basis: in fact, with history ruled out, his religious impulses became rather more based on pure subjectivity.) For Novalis, in contrast, something precisely like history – in all its specificity and human involvement – is always going to be the proper basis for philosophy: at least when philosophy is concerned about the areas of life that really matter.

Philosophy and Language

The twentieth century was to see such an interest in language of such magnitude among philosophers that historians of philosophy talk of a 'linguistic turn'. Even definitive moments have precedents, however, and in another romantic philosopher, Johann

Herder (1744–1803), we encounter significant attention to the relation between language and thought, and the relation of language to culture and common identity. The topic was taken up by Wilhelm von Humboldt (1767–1835), founder of the University of Berlin, in his *The Heterogeneity of Language and its Influence on the Intellectual Development of Mankind*, published posthumously in 1836. As we can guess from the title, he credited language as having a strongly determinative effect on the thought of the speaker. This position is sometimes called 'linguistic relativism'. To this day, two interwoven points are disputed: whether there is any sense in which we could know something without, or prior, to language, and whether the particular language (or languages) that one speaks has a strong influence on how one thinks. The predominant view among linguists today is to down-play the effect of linguistic differences on thought, led by the American linguist and philosopher Noam Chomsky (1928–), who nonetheless builds upon Humbolt's insight that language is based on rules.

In the twentieth century, Ludwig Wittgenstein was to argue that the meanings of words is bound up with forms of life and traditions of practice. This opened the way for many theologians to argue for a strong and necessary connection between Christian ideas and Christian practices, not least when it comes to teaching and learning the faith. Important examples from recent decades include George Lindbeck and Stanley Hauerwas.[33] A recent defence of moderate linguistic relativism comes from Guy Deutscher in *Through the Language Glass: Why the World Looks Different in Other Languages*.[34] He gives the example of the Matsés tribe in the Amazonian rain forest. Their language requires the speaker to stipulate with extreme precision not only when something happened but the means and surety with which you know it: rather, as Deutscher has it, as if they were continuously under questioning from the 'finickiest of lawyers'.[35] It is not that the Matsés think

---

33 I have applied these ideas in the opening chapter of *For the Parish: A Critique of Fresh Expressions*, which I wrote with Alison Milbank (SCM Press, 2010).

34 Guy Deutscher, *Through the Language Glass: Why the World Looks Different in Other Languages*, London: Arrow, 2011.

35 *Glass*, p. 153.

things that we cannot think, or vice versa, but that their language puts a different emphasis on what is important than would naturally occur for an English speaker.

Philosophy and Grammar

Language is one reason we cannot escape from philosophy. The structure of language itself is replete with philosophical categories. The tense of a verb, for instance, brings in time, one of the most philosophical of all concepts. Most languages complicate tense with the idea of aspect, which refers to completion or incompletion, span and instant. Nor can we avoid the distinction between the one and the many, another warhorse of philosophy, with the singular and plural. Then we have *case*. Among other options, case distinguishes between someone doing, done to, done with, and done for. Some of the most basic philosophical concepts are at play here, including agency, possession and instrumentality, and the distinction between subject and object. Some languages also allow for a mixing of subject and object, where the one doing is also done to. We find this in the so-called 'middle voice': I sacrificed a goat, but it was for my advantage. Classical Mongolian, for instance, sees five distinct ways in which this dynamic can be worked out. Or consider fact, opinion and argument: in Croatian, for instance, a speaker indicates, when making a comment, whether an explanation can be given.

Some languages hold inclusion and exclusion always before speaker and hearer, with two forms of the first person plural: a 'we' that includes the hearer and one that does not. The relationship between the universal and the particular is present to some degree in the distinction between 'house', 'the house' and 'a house' in English. This discussion could carry on at length. Consider 'mirativity', an inflection to show that something is surprising. Even English has the exclamation mark. Or consider mood. English does not have many moods, but in other languages even everyday speech considers the relation of events (the condition), hope (the optative), emotion (the subjunctive), and desire and pleading (the jussive).

Lakoff and Johnson have demonstrated that metaphor is constitutive of language. Spatial metaphors are particularly foundational: up, down, within, without, backwards, forwards. This is illustrated by the grammatical 'cases' we have already considered, which distinguish *at, within, into, by, to, by means of,* and so on, as fundamental categories. We see an example in Christian thinking about war, itself developing earlier classical ideas: the criteria for a just war. The terminology distinguishes between two senses of the word 'in': one meaning 'into' (implying motion) and another meaning 'within' as already being inside. These have different cases in Latin, so that we distinguish between *jus ad bellum* and *jus in bello*: the criteria for a just entry into war and the criteria for just conduct when one is already at war. This pseudo-spatial language of into and within is unavoidable, and points to a *structure* to being. Language has emerged to explore the metaphysical features of reality. Not every language explores all features, or all features to the same degree. This is rather like evolution, no one creature has emerged to explore all of what a creature can explore of ways to exist.

Both the spatial reference (for example into or within a box) and this conceptual reference (into or within war) rest on the even more fundamental metaphysical truth of two ideas: one associated with embrace or containment, the other with motion. This is not surprising, since we find both in God. The Patristic notion of *perichoresis* finds both ideas in the relation of the Persons of the Trinity. The Persons interpenetrate one another (the 'within' idea). As the Son says, 'I am in the Father and the Father is in me.' We have seen from John 1.18 that this is dynamic rather than static: the Greek suggests that the Son is 'into' the Father's bosom.

Reading On

The simpler works of Kant, recommended above, have been translated in the *Cambridge Texts in the History of Philosophy* series, published by CUP, which is also producing the complete *Edition of the Works of Immanuel Kant*. The first and third *Critiques* are to be found in this series. Allen Wood's *Basic Writings of Kant* (New York: Modern Library, 2001) is a good anthology and Morris Stockhammer produced one of his remarkable collections of quotations in the *Kant Dictionary* (New York: Philosophical Library, 1972).

On the overlap between Kant's philosophy and theology, Allen Wood provides a thorough treatment of the most obvious dimensions in *Kant's Rational Theology* (Ithaca: Cornell University Press, 2009). Chris Firestone and Stephen Palmquist have collected evangelical essays on Kant in *Kant and the New Philosophy of Religion* (Bloomington: Indiana University Press, 2006). Chrisopher Insole's *Kant and the Creation of Freedom: A Theological Problem* (OUP, 2013) paints an arresting new picture of Kant, as cast at sea with Thomist longings but without knowledge of Thomas himself as a compass.

Around the same time as Kant's *Third Critique*, the Englishman Edmund Burke wrote a treatment of some similar topics in *A Philosophical Enquiry into the Origin of Our Ideas of the Sublime and Beautiful* (OUP, 2008).

Peter Hodgson compiled and translated a selection of texts by Hegel that bear directly upon theology in *G. W. F. Hegel: Theologian of the Spirit* (Minneapolis: Fortress Press, 1997). Among works of Hegel, a good place to start is with the *Phenomenology of Spirit*, as translated, for instance, by Arnold Miller (Oxford: Clarendon Press, 1977). The monumental recent study of Hegel by a Christian writer is Charles Taylor's *Hegel* (CUP, 1975).

Terry Eagleton has written a dramatic introduction to the philosophy of tragedy in *Sweet Violence: A Study of the Tragic* (Blackwell, 2002). Kevin Taylor and Giles Waller collected essays as *Christian Theology and Tragedy* (Aldershot: Ashgate, 2011).

On history, see M. C. Lemon, *Philosophy of History: A Guide for Students* (Routledge, 2003) and on language, George Lakoff, *Women, Fire and Dangerous Things: What Categories Reveal about the Mind* and (with Mark Johnson) *Metaphors We Live By* (both University of Chicago Press, 1987 and 2003).

13

The Nineteenth Century and the 'Masters of Suspicion'

In his 1970 work *Freud and Philosophy: An Essay on Interpretation*,[1] the French philosopher Paul Ricœur, a Reformed Christian, named three 'masters of suspicion': Karl Marx (1818–83), Friederich Nietzsche (1844–1900) and Sigmund Freud (1856–1939). Ludwig Feuerbach (1804–72) is often added to this list, as he will be here. They each practised a 'hermeneutics of suspicion':[2] hermeneutic, in that they each offered 'an art of interpreting'. Their text was nothing less than society itself. In the words of Gabriel Josipovici, these masters of suspicion

> revealed that what we had taken to be natural, a 'given' was in fact man-made [. . .] thus Marx laid bare the workings of capital, Nietzsche the workings of morality, Freud the workings of sexuality. [. . . They explored] the secret histories [. . .] of morals and social institutions, with the aim of freeing men from bonds to which they did not even know they were subject.[3]

The masters of suspicion hold a common position that they know what is really going on, indeed that they have unmasked some fundamental dynamic to life and thought for the first time. Whatever any person, or community, might say about his or her reason

---

1 Paul Ricœur, *Freud and Philosophy: An Essay on Interpretation*, New Haven: Yale University Press.

2 Ricœur, *Freud*, p. 33.

3 Gabriel Josipovici, *On Trust: Art and the Temptations of Suspicion*, New Haven: Yale University Press, 1999, p. 8.

for thinking or acting this way or that, these writers know what really drives people. Religion lies at the centre of this exposé: you might think that you do this, or think that, for theological reasons; in fact you are being driven by a far larger story, which amounts to a quest for power (according to Nietzsche), or for money (for Marx) or for sex (for Freud – although the picture is more complicated for Freud, who has us running away from things as much as straining towards others).

The masters of suspicion were reductionists: each says, in one way or another, x is really only about y. The word 'only' here is important. To say that one thing is about another is not necessarily a reductionist move. The Christian will say that everything is about God, and will not imagine that this statement *reduces* anything: the relation of things to God gives things their being and freedom, rather than removing them; the logic of human life still makes sense, and still has explanatory power, on its own terms. Similarly, a quantum mechanical account of why a pigment is a certain colour does not reduce or invalidate a painter's description of what that colour means to her and why she uses it. To say, however, that Christian accounts of marriage are really about property transfers or, for that matter, that altruism is only about the propagation of genes, is reductionism. In this, thinkers as seemingly unscientific as Marx or Freud are in the same camp as the supposedly scientific New Atheists, and vice versa.

Hegel set the scene for Marxism in his emphasis on history, estrangement and alienation. This was mediated through a group called the 'Young Hegelians', among whom we find Feuerbach. They are important because they took the scheme of Hegel, the idealist for whom everything is about Spirit, including matter, and switched this around. For Hegel the 'higher' principle of Spirit sets the running; for the Young Hegelians it is the 'lower' principle of matter. The history of the world becomes a story to be told about matter, giving us that most prevalent, and most obviously incorrect, form of reductionism, namely materialism.

Feuerbach was a leader among these Young Hegelians. He was close to Auguste Compte in performing an 'empirical turn': all that can be known is what is empirically obvious to the senses. Since we cannot apprehend God in this way, Feuerbach denied a place for God in thought. His critique of Christianity was published in 1841 as the *Essence of Christianity*. He claimed that religion works on the basis of *projection*: God is something about humanity written large and 'projected' as something external to us. This theme was to be taken up by others, including Freud. For Freud, the image we cast on a wall and call 'God' is composed of some fairly unpleasant parts of us. Feuerbach was generally more positive: God is the sum of our unrealized hopes and aspirations. We are forever 'placing [our] being outside [ourselves]', 'ensouling' the world with our own sighs because we cannot believe the world to be 'feelingless'.[4] The *effect* of that projection, however, is not at all positive. In what was to become a common criticism of Christianity, Feuerbach held that expectations among Christians of redress in a future world led to stunted politics in the present world (which for him was the only one).

Among those in the immediate slipstream of Hegel, Marx has been even more influential. He pressed the 'Young Hegelian' shift from mind to matter to great lengths, presenting it in terms of the drama of history, a frame of reference inherited from Hegel himself. For Marx, history is marked by a dialectic swing, with each triumph containing the seeds of its own destruction. This process unfolds with a certain inevitability. He put these ideas to economic and political use. Every society contains, and tends towards, the forces that will destroy it, producing, for Marx, politics focused on revolution.

Marx's sense of the importance of material conditions, along with much of his terminology and emphases – labour and capital, alienation and others – continues to exercise a profound influence on contemporary thought. Even if few today are paid-up Marxists in a technical sense, little of scholarly thought in the twenty-first century has not been touched by his analysis and, after the financial collapse, it is clear that Marx was right about

---

4 *The Essence of Religion*, §32. Translation from Van Harvey, *Feuerbach and the Interpretation of Religion*, CUP, 1997, p. 165.

capitalism bearing within itself the seeds of its own destruction, even if he was wrong about the prospect of a communist alternative.

Nietzsche

Frederich Nietzsche is one of the most exultant of philosophers, and at the same time one of the most depressing. This sense of a dichotomy runs through his work. It is there in his distinction between the ordered and the untamed, the slave and the master, the heroic and the tragic, the superman and the *untermensch* ('under-man'). Like Freud after him, Nietzsche paid attention to what we suppress. Whereas Freud's psychoanalysis might, potentially, offer therapy for all, Nietzsche's philosophy saw inequality as inherent and good. His message was of enjoyment and affirmation, of life and of power, at least for those who could throw off old prohibitions, at the expense of those who could not.

Nietzsche's first book, *The Birth of Tragedy* (1872), introduced his interest in ancient Greek philosophy and culture, and this was to remain foundational. In that first book, he contrasted the love of order and restraint, associated with Apollo (god of light and poetry), with an unrestrained expression of life, associated with Dionysus (god of wine and revels). Nietzsche respected Greek tragedy for combining these two tendencies but considered the West to have turned away from that balance in favour of order alone since the time of Socrates. Nietzsche did not call for an *exclusive* celebration of the Dionysian, but against the backdrop of what he took to be a frigid rationalism, his philosophy certainly looks like a Dionysian intervention. We have already seen him attacking Plato for preferring 'cobwebs' over reality (pp. 26–7).

Nietzsche's works are full of criticisms of Christianity. In his collection of aphorisms, *Human, All Too Human*, for instance, he denounces the faith as having 'crushed and shattered man completely, and submerged him as if in deep mire', this being the prelude to 'stunning' him with a ray of 'divine compassion' which aroused a 'sick excess of feeling' and the 'deep corruption of head and heart'.[5] We can analyse this accusation in terms of his Apollonian/Dionysian distinction. Christianity involves restraint, but the wrong kind of restraint, and 'intoxication', but the wrong sort of intoxication: it is 'barbaric, Asiatic, ignoble, un-Greek'. Nietzsche called the resulting Christian situation one of a 'slave morality'. In contrast, those few who could come to their senses – the powerful and enlightened – would live by the 'master morality' of action, effectiveness and their own account of what counts as noble.[6]

Slaves may not enjoy economic or political power, but slave morality is not without power dynamics of its own, exercised either by collusion with the powerful or by poisoning (as Nietzsche saw it) the idea of noble power. The weak, as much as the strong, are driven by what became Nietzsche's master category: the 'will to power', as first expounded systematically in *Thus Spoke Zarathustra* (1883). The masters (who are few and called *Übermensch* – 'over-men' or 'supermen') express the will to power in one way, slaves (who are many and called *Untermensch* – 'under-men' or 'sub-human') in the other. The ubiquity of the will to power is Nietzsche's key for unmasking what is going on: it is the main principle of 'suspicion' for this 'master of suspicion'. So, for instance, if people become religious, they do it for their own advantage. They choose to be Christian and 'servile' because they can do no better; it serves them well.[7]

While 'supermen' set their own standards and are active, 'under-men' are defined by others. These *Untermenschen* may take pride in their morality, seeing it as setting them, ethically, above those who have power over them, but even here they are slaves, since that morality is reactive, the result of being positioned by others. This dynamic, and the feelings it produces, Nietzsche called *ressentiment* (borrowed from the French, with a French pronunciation). It continues to be an important concept in Marxist-inspired social criticism and found parallels in

---

5 Friedrich Nietzsche, *Human, All Too Human*, trans. Helen Zimmern, London: Allen & Unwin, 1909, §114.

6 In *The Genealogy of Morals*.

7 *Human*, §115.

twentieth-century French existentialist thought as 'bad faith' or *mauvaise foi*.

Nietzsche's call for his readers to overthrow the claims of the Christian scheme came in his *Gay Science* (1882), with its announcement that 'God is dead', subverting the theme of a Lutheran chorale for Good Friday. In this work, we also find the idea of 'eternal recurrence'. It is not clear whether Nietzsche meant this to be taken as a metaphysical reality or whether it functions simply to illustrate the superiority of the master over the slave: the slave, the typical Christian, wishes for a world beyond this one; the master, however, can bring himself to revel in this world, and this world alone, for all eternity.

The figure and works of Nietzsche remain important for Christian thinkers, since his legacy is a principal continuing source for the criticism of Christianity. Some theologians look upon this Nietzsche as principally someone to be refuted; for others it is a provocation to meditative self-criticism. Among those who have taken that second track, some have seen Nietzsche's accusations as cutting at the heart of the historic Christian message, for instance in the claim that traditional Christianity is constitutively world-hating. This produced a significant strand of liberal Christian thought, or even 'post-Christian thought'. Don Cupitt and the 'Sea of Faith' movement, founded in 1984, are a prime example. Others look to Nietzsche's criticisms to play a more constructive role. For instance, his comment that Christianity disparages the created world and human society – Christianity 'is all hatred of the intellect, of pride, of courage, of freedom, of intellectual libertinage; Christian is all hatred of the senses, of joy in the senses, of joy in general'[8] – would be seen as indicative of how Christians have failed to live up to the logic of their faith. We can also note that Nietzsche was scandalized by much that *is* truly scandalous about Christianity. He despised glory in the cross of Christ as the 'revolt of all creatures that creep on the ground against everything that is lofty: the gospel of the "lowly" lowers'.[9] Nietzsche was

---

8 *Antichrist*, §21, trans. H. L. Mencken, New York: Alfred A. Knopf, 1918.
9 *Antichrist*, §43.

right; Christians do place a man upon a cross above the emperor, humility above pride, the 'foolishness of God' above 'human wisdom'.

Nietzsche was to have a terrible influence on later history as an important influence on Nazism, both in its general ideology (think of his 'will to power' and the Nazi exultation in the 'triumph of the will') and in the details: Nietzsche was anti-Semitic, and Nazi disgust at Christ upon the cross and the image of the Lamb of God (they wished these images to be taken down from German homes)[10] finds its roots in Nietzsche.

Other Reductionist Approaches

Turning to England, Jeremy Bentham (1748–1832) worked unflaggingly to popularize an approach to ethics and law known as utilitarianism. His governing principle, however, he took from Joseph Priestly, a scientist and founder of British Unitarianism: 'the greatest happiness of the greatest number'.

Bentham accepted the Aristotlian and scholastic maxim that people act so as to seek their own happiness. Utilitarianism urges them to bear in mind the happiness of others, and in this there is little to find objectionable. Problems emerge, however, when it comes to *gauging* happiness. The paradigm is basically quantitative and for that to work, happiness must be *reduced* to a single variable for means of comparison: what he called the 'felicity calculus'. This does not distinguish between 'higher' or 'lower' forms of happiness.

Bentham was a colleague of John Stuart Mill (1806–73), whose rallying cry for freedom echoed, for instance, in his book *On Liberty*. Mill attempted to add sophistication to Bentham's picture with his *Utilitarianism* of 1861, which *did* distinguish between higher and lower pleasures, although it did not succeed in justifying this distinction on its own terms.

---

10 As, for instance, in Alfred Rosenberg's grotesque *The Myth of the Twentieth Century*.

Utilitarianism has also fallen into disrepute in recent decades among Christian writers. There has been a widespread revival of interest in the *virtue* ethics of Aristotle and Aquinas. After that, utilitarianism seems one dimensional, since it concentrates only on the consequences of actions, not on the character of the people performing them. Utilitarianism is also open to abuse and injustices: the ends eventually justify the means. Why should we not forcibly remove all of someone's organs if that saves the lives of many people? To be fair, the anti-utilitarian instinct may be a little too keen to keep its moral hands absolutely clean. In a fallen world, we have sometimes to make a tragic choice between actions we do not find entirely palatable, or choose not to act, which is a choice of its own.

A certain thread connects the utilitarian and virtue approaches, namely a concern for fulfilment and happiness. The virtue ethicist has no more problem than the utilitarian does with people wanting to be happy. In this, she sides with the utilitarian against the *deontologist* or ethicist of duty. The virtue ethicist simply insists on a particular, and particularly elevated, sense of where true happiness lies. Happiness is closer to the heart of the God to whom we are drawn than is duty. In the end, even justice turns out to be happiness in God.

With Auguste Compte (1798–1857) we come to the father of 'positivism': the attempt to put thought on the same footing as natural science, indeed, of a caricatured natural science pretending to be mathematics. Compte wanted to reinvent reason along the lines of the natural sciences so conceived. For him, the only valid basis for knowledge was direct observation. Alongside biology, physics and so on, he wanted to erect a series of new, 'social' sciences, working with what he saw as the same necessary rigour. In some ways this was a continuation of the Enlightenment project, involving the triumph of reason over belief and the disenchantment of the world, but in other ways it was not. Compte contrasted three ages: not only the 'age of theology' (from pre-history to the French Revolution) and the 'age of metaphysics' (from the Revolution to his own day) but also the new 'age of science', which he was going to play a part in inaugurating. The Enlightenment 'age of reason' was still too literary, too tradition-based for him, compared to the 'age of science'. It still dealt too much with abstract ideas, especially in Continental writing, with which he tried to dispense.

On the questions of politics that continued to concern philosophers throughout these centuries, Compte took a distinctive, chilling and somewhat prescient position: he hoped for government by autocratic managers. The shape of his epistemology and of his social project come together in the title of his 1822 work *Plan for the Scientific Works Necessary for the Reorganisation of Society*. The democratic ideals of the Enlightenment, he thought, put too much confidence in the people, unschooled as they were in the techniques of the new social sciences. Government in a true 'age of science' would fall to those who had mastered those techniques. Compte's aims were often noble: the material betterment of his fellow human beings through increased efficiency. This has indeed been achieved, to the material advantage of many. However, it has also become clear that the words of Christ apply at a social as well as an individual level: it is possible to gain the whole world but loose ones own soul (Mark 8.36).

Schleiermacher and Kierkegaard

Friedrich Schleiermacher (1768–1834) has been called the father of liberal Protestantism. In the early twentieth century, Karl Barth traced much of what he found wanting in Christianity to Schleiermacher's door, yet also acknowledged his greatness.

Schleiermacher is principally remembered for the role he gave to experience within Christian thought. The foundation of his scheme was the *feeling of absolute dependence*. This is the 'consciousness that the whole of our spontaneous activity comes from a source outside of us [. . . this source] is not the world, in the sense of the totality of temporal existence, and still less is it any single part of the world'.[11]

---

11 *The Christian Faith*, §4, trans. H. R. Mackintosh and J. S. Stewart, T&T Clark, 2008.

Schleiermacher has been pilloried by later philosophical theologians for this emphasis on experience, as have those who followed him in this, such as William James in his *Varieties of Religious Experience* (1902). The accusations are serious ones: religious experience is incommunicable and therefore very difficult to discuss; it is frequently conceived as something entirely individual and therefore fails to take into account the communal dimension of faith; it works with a problematic sense of derivative and generic 'religion'; if seen as somehow intrinsically otherworldly, then religious experiences are threatened by attempts to explain them from psychology or neuroscience. Whatever later writers may have held, however, it is not clear that Schleiermacher stands entirely guilty as charged. For one thing, his *feeling of absolute dependence* proposes an idea that can be taken into thought, rather than standing over and against it. What is more, he held that this 'feeling' is to be interpreted within the broader contours of common life, whether in the sweep of Church history (as in *The Christian Faith* of 1821) or in a family, with one generation teaching another about the faith (as in his short Christmas theological story, *Christmas Eve: A Dialogue on the Celebration of Christmas,* of 1806).

Schleiermacher was also right to hold that reason means more than the cold, analytic process it was increasingly coming to mean in Europe. The sort of reason we might apply to theological questions, as to other topics of the first importance, will involve imagination and instinct, for all it will not let go of logic. It will be reason that knows that it cannot be separated from love. For Schleiermacher, 'A true appropriation of Christian dogmas cannot be brought about by any scientific means and thus lies outside the realm of reason': at least if 'reason' is defined in that limited way, we might add. An appropriation, he goes on, 'can only be brought about through each man willing to have the experience for himself as indeed it is true of everything individual and characteristic, that it can only be apprehended by the love which wills to perceive'.[12]

12 *On Religion: Speeches to its Cultured Despisers,* trans. Richard Crouter, CUP, 1988, p. 22.

In the twentieth century, the Italian Luigi Giussani was to see this with particular clarity. The truth of theology, like the truth of love, is not something we can discern from a side seat: we have to stake something. In Giussani's words, we have to take a 'risk'. Indeed, any education worth the name involves this sort of investment of the self.[13] Schleiermacher and Giussani were pastors as well as theologians, and from them comes a vision of faith that takes reason seriously (although we might think that Schleiermacher's intervention was a little too drastic) while also expecting that faith makes some sort of difference to life. Otherwise, the traditions from which they come (one was a Protestant, the other a Roman Catholic) were in danger either of judging faith simply to be a set of ideas, or to be a state in which one simply happens to stand, or not, in a fashion that makes no tangible difference.[14]

Søren Kierkegaard (1813–55, his surname is sometimes pronounced in English as it looks, and sometimes as in Danish: Keer-kuh-gor) is among the most influential of nineteenth-century philosopher–theologians. A key to understanding Kierkegaard is as a fierce critic of Hegel. He particularly rejected the sense of comprehension that we find in Hegel's thought. For Kierkegaard, this was a recipe for complacency and, in any case, thoroughly mistaken: we cannot sit in a position of airy ease and survey the whole. We must make choices while still in darkness; things – particular things, not general things – happen to us that are beyond our control. Neither repose nor synthesis is usually to hand.

Kierkegaard stands as the father of 'existentialism': an approach to philosophy that places an emphasis on human choice and the potentially overwhelming freedom that accompanies it, on the concrete over the general and on the sense that human beings find themselves 'thrown' into the midst of these concrete particularities. The name 'existentialism' refers to what is sometimes called the 'priority of existence over essence': existence being particular and essence general, existence lining up with verbs and

---

13 Luigi Giussani, *The Risk of Education*, New York: Crossroad, 2001.
14 I am grateful to John Milbank for making this point.

action, and essence with nouns and thought. Almost as soon as existentialism flourished after Kierkegaard, it began to lose its Christian character, such that the principal later existentialist philosophers tended to be antagonistic towards Christianity, or at least definitely not Christians: Sartre, Camus and Heidegger, for instance. The existentialism that was later to return to theology (for instance in Rudolf Bultmann or Paul Tillich) was mediated via these non-Christian sources. Kierkegaard, however, was influential on some later theologians such as Karl Barth and Dietrich Bonhoeffer.

In Kierkegaard, we find a Lutheran emphasis on sacrifice and the cross of Christ as a paradox that confounds reason. He explored this in terms of three ways of life. The first is *aesthetic*: living for beauty and pleasure. When explored, however, this can lead to a crisis, the sense that 'there must be more to life than this'. That can lead people to the second way of life, which is *ethical*, and represented, for Kierkegaard, by the figure of Socrates, for whom Kierkegaard had great respect. (These two approaches were contrasted in *Either/Or*, published in 1843.) That stage can also, however, lead to a crisis, when we recognize an impossibility to ethical demands, and a sense of our own sin. This he characterized as 'anxiety', a sort of dread in face of our own freedom (discussed in *The Concept of Anxiety* of 1844). Such realization can be crippling, but it can also urge us on to the third, *religious*, approach. Here, the human being, standing alone before God, comes to risk everything for God's sake. Kierkegaard's paradigm here was Abraham and his willingness to sacrifice his son, Isaac (as explored in *Fear and Trembling* in 1843, written under a pseudonym, Johannes de silentio, or 'John the Silent', as many of his works were). This willingness to sacrifice one's child stands as the perfect example of the 'religious' transcending the 'ethical'. Such willingness to risk everything Kierkegaard called the *leap of faith*. His writings have been a way to faith for many, and a way to preserve faith for others. In this he serves the Church perennially. Such a remedy always exacts some cost, however, not perhaps to the individual, but for the whole, nudging faith a little further in the direction of fideism: faith in spite of reason.

THE NINETEENTH CENTURY AND THE 'MASTERS OF SUSPICION'

We find an emphasis on inwardness in Kierkegaard and a certain sense of disjunction between one person and another. That is part of his rejection of Hegel, for whom the individual was always subsumed within some larger scheme. If Kierkegaard was right to reject this, he was also in danger of falling into a not-fully-Christian individualism as a consequence. The other part of this individualism is Kierkegaard's dismissal of cultural Christianity. One is a Christian, for him, only by virtue of a direct act of faith, and not by virtue of being a Dane (or English or American, for that matter). This note was to be influential on subsequent thinkers, mainly Protestant, such as Karl Barth (whose will it steeled to resist Nazi assimilation of Christianity in Germany) or Stanley Hauerwas. However, in rejecting Christendom, Kierkegaard (though not all of his followers in this respect) was in danger of rejecting the very biblical notion that salvation involves, and indeed comes through, incorporation into the Body of Christ. We might also ask whether Kierkegaard had a sufficient grasp of the grace of God as central to everything, and whether his emphasis can turn faith into a work. The Danish bourgeoisie may have failed to grasp that Christ came 'to bring fire to the earth' (Luke 12.49) and that only those who lose their lives will keep them (Luke 17.33), but their cheerful happiness may point to the quality of the life of the world to come in a way that Kierkegaard could not comprehend. For a different presentation of the value of action, sacrifice and excess, from another Dane, we might consider the short story 'Babette's Feast' by Karen von Blixen-Finecke (writing as Isak Dinesen).[15] There has, perhaps, been no more perfect exploration of grace in literature.

Reading On

Principal works are collected in the following readers: *The Portable Karl Marx*, edited and translated by Eugene Kamenka (Penguin, 1983); *The Freud Reader*, edited and translated by Peter Gay (New York: Vintage, 1995); *A Nietzsche Reader*, translated

---

15 In *Anecdotes of Destiny*, London: Michael Joseph, 1958.

and edited thematically by R. J. Hollingdale (Penguin, 2004); *The Portable Nietzsche*, translated and arranged by work, some in full, by Walter Kaufmann (Penguin, 1994); *The Fiery Brook: Selected Writings* [of Ludwig Feuerbach], translated by Zawar Hanfi (Verso, 2013). On Nietzsche, see Craig Hovey, *Nietzsche and Theology* (T&T Clark, 2008).

George Pattison has collected an anthology of texts by Kierkegaard on 'spiritual' themes: *Spiritual Writings: A New Translation and Selection* (New York: HarperPerennial, 2010). Among the secondary literature, Murray Rae's *Kierkegaard and Theology* (T&T Clark, 2010) covers a wide variety of topics admirably. Schleiermacher's great work is *The Christian Faith* (published, for instance, by T&T Clark, 1999) but his most philosophical works are collected in *Schleiermacher: Hermeneutics and Criticism: And Other Writings*, translated by Andrew Bowie (CUP, 1998).

14

The Early Twentieth Century

Pragmatism

Among the schools of philosophy to have grown up in North America, *pragmatism* is particularly emblematic. As its name suggests, this school placed the emphasis in philosophical matters on what any idea or scheme could achieve, or what difference it made. The proof, even truth, of an idea lay in its consequences. Representatives included Charles Sanders Pierce (1839–1914), William James (1842–1910) and John Dewey (1859–1952). These pragmatists held that metaphysical ideas and categories had no discernible consequences and that, on that account, metaphysical discussions were worthless. Here, the pragmatist school stands diametrically opposed to the thesis of this book, which is that often the most seemingly abstract philosophical positions have profound practical consequences. Nietzsche and Hitler, Aquinas and Mother Teresa, Marx and Stalin, Ayn Rand and Margaret Thatcher all worked from metaphysical commitments, acknowledged or unacknowledged, concerning such topics as life and the will to power, competition and cooperation, freedom and solidarity. These commitments made a difference.

Pierce is important for his work on the philosophy of signs, or 'semiotics', of which he is often considered the father. A sign can be related to what it signifies in a variety of ways; Pierce bequeathed a thought-provoking analysis of the options. He distinguishes between a symbol, an index and an icon, according to the relationship of the sign to what it represents. With a symbol, the relation is of human construction. Little reason can be given why a warning sign should be triangular, or that the letters S-T-O-P, written underneath it, should have the meanings that they do. Such relations are conventional. With an index, the relation is stronger without direct likeness. A raised temperature is an 'index' of an infection, as is the level of the liquid in the thermometer that tells my temperature. An icon stands at the opposite extreme to a symbol, bearing a direct likeness to what it signifies, as with a photograph or a non-abstract painting.

Theorists of semiotics have also written in a more ebullient mood than Pierce, claiming everything for their discipline: everything is a sign. We might agree, in that there is no getting beyond language, which works with signs. The theologian can go further, claiming that everything is also sign in the sense that everything comes from God and is therefore a sign of God, even if, in this world, it may signify in part what it means to deny one's origin in God.

We only get to God through created things as signs, not least through the material signs on paper, or a screen, of the Bible. That does not subordinate God to signs, since it turns out that signification 'pre-dates' created things. Eternally, in the Godhead, the Son is the Word: the Son is eternally the Sign of the Father; the whole substance of the Son is to be the Sign of the Father. Our world of signs exists only as the sign of the Sign.

Vitalism

Vitalism, a small but significant philosophical school associated with France, took life as its starting point, rather than matter, being or mind. The principal representative is Henri Bergson (1859–1941), whose work stands as a sharp rebuttal of materialism. Whereas the American pragmatists, Bergson's contemporaries, claimed that their rejection of metaphysics was 'common sense', a vitalist could equally well claim that life at its most metaphysical is the 'common sense' place for the philosopher to begin, since life is what most of all grabs the attention of thinking beings. Bergson pointed to life as the most significant feature of the universe as a whole, and therefore took life as the interpretive key to the whole: the history of the universe is a history of the progress of the *élan vital* or life-urge. This resembles Hegelianism, but with life replacing thought. It is also heavily indebted to Darwin, as well as to Bergson's wider interest in the biological sciences of his day.

Bergson's work is a reminder of how different philosophy could be on the Continent from that in the Anglo-Saxon world, where discussion of the history of the universe in terms of a life-urge would be anathema. For his part, Bergson quite consciously rejected the sort of objectivity for which that analytic tradition strove. Philosophy for him should deal with the world as it is perceived from the inside of a human life. As an example in relation to time, he put the emphasis on *dureé*, which denotes 'real' or 'lived' time, rather than the abstraction of 'clock time', which proceeds in isolation from human experience. Vitalism was to be taken up with an even stronger emphasis on evolution by the French Jesuit Teilhard de Chardin, and it finds something of a parallel in pantheist approaches such as the process theology of Whitehead.

Not the least achievement of Bergson was to have given grounds for living to a significant twentieth-century philosophical theologian and his wife, Jacques and Raïssa Maritain. As atheists, they had agreed to kill themselves unless, by a certain date, they could understand the world as more than a meaningless shift of matter. Bergson's work provided the momentum for that shift: not necessarily, as MacIntyre puts it, because it presented good answers but because it posed questions to materialism that materialism could not answer.[1] One of the principal Thomists of the twentieth century, Maritain worked in many fields. His writings on theology and art, the Church and the world, and the common good are particularly important.[2] He was the French Ambassador to the Vatican between 1944 and 1948 and played an instrumental role in drafting the *Universal Declaration of Human Rights* of 1948.

---

1 Alasdair MacIntyre, *God, Philosophy, Universities: A Selective History of the Catholic Philosophical Tradition*, Lanham: Rowman & Littlefield, 2009, p. 155.

2 See, for instance, *Art and Scholasticism* and *Integral Humanism*, both trans. Joseph Evans, New York: Charles Scribner's Sons, 1962 and 1968 and *The Person and the Common Good*, trans. John J. Fitzgerald, New York: Charles Scribner's Sons, 1947.

Structuralism

With structuralism we encounter another enormously important intellectual outlook, also with strongly French (or French-speaking) roots. A plausible genealogy would begin with the Swiss French linguist Ferdinand de Saussure and his ground-breaking *Course in General Linguistics*. His influence spread to anthropology, in the work, for instance, of Claude Lévi-Strauss.

Saussure's insight was to claim as misguided any attempt to study individual elements of language in isolation. Each part only means anything on account of its relation to the rest. In particular, he contended that words only have meanings on the basis of the way in which they contrast with others. With this move, Saussure was to shift the emphasis from individual parts (which he called *parole*) to the structure as a whole (which he called *langue*). As an example, consider that the word 'meat' means different things depending on which system or structure of other words it has a place within. In the English of the Prayer Book, the line 'He gave them their meat in due season' refers to food in general. A different, more restricted meaning, is sought in the title of *The River Cottage Meat Book*. Its author, Fearnley-Whittingstall, means meat in contrast to vegetables; the Prayer Book means food in contrast to other human necessities. As an example of how these meanings emerge by contrasts, look at a good dictionary of antonyms, or opposites. 'Original' belongs either with 'newfangled' or with 'unimaginative'. In one pairing, it means something old, in the other, it means almost the opposite.

Saussure turned our attention away from individual elements of language towards the study of the way in which the structure as a whole is the necessary condition for language to mean anything. He allowed us to see the part that our language (and culture) plays in the production of much of what we mean. Previous thinking had supposed that we work from what we mean to its expression in language, in an uncomplicated manner. He was also important in shifting emphasis away from seeing meaning in the history of a word (*diachronic*: over time) to the meaning in the culture where it is used at the time it is used (*synchronic*: at a particular time).

Etymology can be wonderfully illuminating, and a helpful way to illustrate an idea, but the meaning of a word is determined by the place it has in the current day.

Wittgenstein

Ludwig Wittgenstein (1889–1951) is one of the most significant philosophers of the twentieth century, not least for theologians. His output is dominated by an early and a posthumous work, the *Tractatus Logico-philosophicus,* and the *Philosophical Investigations.* Concern with words binds his work together. Wittgenstein was at the forefront of the so-called *linguistic turn* in twentieth-century philosophy.

The *Tractatus* looks fearsome on the page. Here Wittgenstein argued on the basis that words are stable signs that correspond to items in the world and that both words and items can clearly be demarked. The structure of language maps on to the structure of the world. This cannot be demonstrated logically, he thinks, only illustrated: his task is not to prove but to show, which is a useful distinction for Christian apologetics.

In the *Tractatus,* Wittgenstein's rallying cry was that 'Everything that can be thought at all can be thought clearly. Everything that can be put into words can be put clearly' (4.116) and therefore that 'What we cannot speak about we must pass over in silence' (7).[3] Interpreters from a more analytic perspective, and certainly his atheist followers, have taken this comment as a dismissal of theological subjects. Certainly, Wittgenstein thought that he was ruling out metaphysical statements (they are not to be 'solved' but 'dissolved', as MacIntrye puts it).[4] He was not, however, necessarily dismissing all that cannot be said clearly. He was denying it as subject matter for philosophy, as he understood philosophy. 'There are, indeed, things that cannot be put into words', as he put it. 'They make themselves manifest. They are what is mystical' (6.522). The *Tractatus* has seven sections and the comments about

---

3 Trans. David Pears and Brian McGuinness, Routledge, 2001.
4 *God,* p. 160.

silence come in the seventh. It amounts to only eleven words in English translation, words that we have already noted: 'What we cannot speak about we must pass over in silence' (§7). As Bruce Kawin notes, we have here a sabbath for speech that does not represent rejection of the religious or the mystical in its own terms.[5] Wittgenstein and his family were intensely musical for example. Perhaps music, or the liturgy for that matter, can address that which philosophy – according to Wittgenstein – cannot.

Wittgenstein's posthumously published *Philosophical Investigations* were written after a period of doubt and withdrawal, during which he reassessed his philosophical scheme. As he thought further about language, he decided that the rigours of the *Tractatus* could not be upheld since there is, after all, no uncomplicated and one-to-one mapping between words and meanings. Instead, he came to understand the meaning of a word to be inseparable from the context in which it is being used: what is often called the 'game' in which that language applies. The point is a confirmation of Sausurre's structuralism. Any given word will have an entire family of uses, and while there will be an overlap of meanings and intentions from one setting to another, there may well not be a single meaning or intention that applies in every case. This suggests that we should not expect to teach the Christian faith without inviting people into the experience of the Christian community, as I have argued elsewhere.[6]

Throughout his life, Wittgenstein was concerned with the limits of thought, and on preventing the transgression of philosophy into territory where it over-stretches itself and becomes meaningless. In his later work, his message was that human language is up to the tasks it fulfils in everyday life, but that we get into increasing trouble the further its application gets from those settings.

Theologians have been particularly interested in Wittgenstein's link between meanings and practices, and specifically the

---

5 Bruce Kawin, *The Mind of the Novel: Reflexive Fiction and the Ineffable*, Champaign: Dalkey Archive, 2006, p. 98.

6 Andrew Davison, 'Christian Reason and Christain Community', in Andrew Davison (ed.), *Imaginative Apologetics: Theology, Philosophy and the Catholic Tradition*, SCM Press, 2011, pp. 12–28.

inter-related practices that he called 'forms of life'. Putting this insight to work has been a definitive mark of the post-Liberal school associated with figures such as George Lindbeck and Stanley Hauerwas.[7] Lindbeck made complementarity with practice one arbiter of truth in *The Nature of Doctrine*;[8] Hauerwas stresses the formation of individual and community in virtues that align with Christian doctrine across many of his writings.

Heidegger, Existentialism and Phenomenology

Among twentieth-century philosophers, Martin Heidegger (1889–1976) has exercised a particularly significant influence on subsequent theology. He is also among the last century's most impenetrable writers, as exemplified by his long book *Being and Time* of 1927, which was taken up by the 'existentialist' theologians of the mid-twentieth century.[9]

Philosophical schools are often diffuse; the term existentialism is to be applied with a particularly broad brush. Common to Heidegger and other existentialists was a sense that philosophy should proceed from attention to existence as we experience it. We have already seen this in Kierkegaard, and his rejection of the comfort of the overarching scheme and sense of communal belonging, in favour of an emphasis on the individual, who finds him- or herself in a position of inescapable choice. Human freedom is hemmed in on every side by anxiety, a favourite existential word. For Kierkegaard, this calls for a leap into the arms of God. Non-Christian existentialists, such as Heidegger and Jean-Paul Sartre (1905–80), instead favoured a clear-headed acknowledgement that the world *cannot* be understood in relation to God. For Heidegger, this casts the human being as 'being-towards-death'; Sartre placed freedom centre stage, as both absolute and yet absurd. It is absurd because,

---

7 I have drawn upon it in the first chapter of *For the Parish: A Critique of Fresh Expressions*, SCM Press, 2010.

8 George Lindbeck, *The Nature of Doctrine*, Philadelphia: Westminster Press, 1984.

9 Trans. John Macquarrie and Edward Robinson, Blackwell, 1962.

without a creator, there are no rules, and no metaphysical contours to give a steer. Sartre called that metaphysical shape (non-existent, to his mind) by its mediaeval name – 'essence'. To say that there are no essences to guide us is to say, in Sartre's words, that 'existence precedes essence'.[10] The Christian, in response, might hold to the characterfulness of things, however naive that might sound to the philosopher.

In his most influential middle period, the period of *Being and Time*, Heidegger was not as entirely gloomy as Sartre, whose philosophical novels bear titles such as *Nausea*, *The Flies* and *No Exit*. Chastened by his enthusiasm for National Socialism in Germany, Heidegger's late works took a more mystical and ethical route. Unlike *Being and Time*, they are typically short essays, often focused on a particular practical object or situation (such as a jug, a pair of boots or the rise of technology). Although dense, these pieces have the appeal of mysticism. They are the best place to start.[11] In them, we notice a shift in attention from 'being' to 'dwelling': to having a place in the world, among other people and among objects. This 'dwelling' takes the shape of a disposition of wonder and reception from a world that 'gives' itself'.

Turning back to *Being and Time*, we find Heidegger arguing, or asserting, that the history of philosophy has wandered down a blind alley since at least the time of Plato. It has been, for Heidegger, 'forgetful' of being. His account is complex and contested, but one important dimension was to stress the peculiar state of being proper to humans. Heidegger's criticism is that philosophers had talked about being with neutral indifference, not with the authentic response of care or concern (*Sorge* in German). Heidegger sought a characterization of being where such concern was constitutive, not incidental: being is involving; it is gracious; it bestows itself (an insight that made Heidegger a founder of *phenomenology*).

10 *Existentialism and Humanism*, trans. Philip Mairet, London: Methuen, 1948, p. 27.

11 For instance, 'Building Dwelling Thinking', 'The Origin of the Work of Art' and 'The Question Concerning Technology' in *Basic Writings*, ed. David Farrell Krell, San Francisco: Harper, 1993 and 'The Thing' in *Poetry, Language, Thought*, trans. Albert Hofstadter, New York: Harper & Row, 1971.

According to Heidegger, Plato was an important perpetrator of this mistake. He accused Plato of identifying objects with our conceptions of them. Everything here revolves around whether Plato was right or not. If Plato was wrong, then his Forms are no more than human ideas, and things in the world are indeed being subordinated to our ideas about them: the world becomes a shadow of an idea. If, however, Plato was right, and things are what they are by some donation from a plenitudinous source (which he did not call God, but we will), then Plato was *not* identifying reality with *our* idea of it. He was doing the opposite: our knowledge of the thing, like the thing itself rests upon a reality that is denser still, not more rarefied. Part of the problem here is in translating Plato's word for the Forms (*eidos*) as 'idea' (not least because it sounds like *eidos*). True, in Christian thought the forms were rehabilitated as 'ideas in the mind of God', but God is so perfectly real that even ideas in his mind enjoy an abundance of reality.

Heidegger characterized human particularity as one of 'thrownness' in that we cannot separate ourselves from where and how we find ourselves to be at this moment. Significantly, that includes our mood: our mood is not incidental to the character of the world. Awareness of death therefore becomes important. Being is always perceived in a particular way and for human beings little is more important than that it is framed by a 'horizon' of death.

We are involved with particular things and particulars are what we care for. Heidegger had a horror of confusing being-as-such with individual beings, but also wanted to focus on particular objects and situations. As an example, in a later essay, he suggested that we could best learn what 'nearness' means not by thinking of nearness in the abstract but 'rather by attending to what is near'.[12] He immediately presents us with an example, a jug, and from that point on the essay becomes a meditation on that object.

Heidegger's later writing can sound like New Age esotericism, although of a literary superior sort. There can be something pseudo-scriptural to the ring of it. Depending on one's perspective, it stands

---

12 'The Thing'.

as a rival to Christian faith, as an ally, or as a poor imitation. He is closest to Christian philosophy in his sense of wonder, and much of his terminology reflects his exposure to Christian philosophy as a Roman Catholic seminarian (which cannot have been philosophy of the best sort if he could later characterize the Christian position as presenting us with being in neutral indifference). Among this terminology, 'nothingness' plays an important role: too important, the Christian might think. Heidegger can read like an endless elaboration of the gloomier parts of Ecclesiastes: as an example, that jug, for Heidegger, ultimately comes down to the void it encloses.

His writing comes closest to a revivified paganism in an essay such as *Building Dwelling Thinking*. There he analysed the situation in which the human being finds him- or herself in terms of a 'fourfold' of earth, sky, divinities, mortals. There is that which supports us, that which lies over us, that which beckons us, and that which we are. The earth has a solidity but also bears life; the sky is characterized by light, movement and the passage of time; the divinities are manifestations of a 'godhead' that is also concealed; human beings are characterized by the fact that they die: they are passing and finite. The human task is to 'dwell': to 'save the earth', 'to receive the sky', 'to await the divinities', 'to use and practice' their state as mortal 'so that there may be a good death'. His characterization of humanity is in terms of death – we are 'mortals' – but while that is central, we cannot understand ourselves fully other than in relation to the earth, sky and the divinities. The ethical concerns of this later writing can chime with Christian perspectives, for instance in his worry about technology as divesting us of an 'authentic' connection to the world in which we live.

We have already seen that Heidegger sought an account of being that rang true to human experience. This was the part of his quest for an authentic way of living in the world that made him a phenomenologist. He sought an account of subjectivity that allows us to attend to the way things are in themselves: 'to let that which shows itself be seen from itself in the very way in which it shows itself from itself'.[13] To return to the jug, for Heidegger it emerges as

---

13 *Being and Time*, p. 58.

so much more than something we might depict casually in a photograph or label with a word. It is only properly known through its function: when it is used. Then, it 'gives' something to us; pouring out the wine, it pours out a gift from its own self. This sort of attention to the way things are for, with or to us is the foundation of phenomenology.

'Phenomenology' describes both a school of philosophy (that of the 'phenomenologists') and a broader philosophical approach or set of concerns. The principle is to proceed on the basis of phenomena or, even more accurately, on the basis of their *appearing*. (The Greek *phainomenon* means 'what appears'.) Phenomenologists urge a return to human experience as the basis for philosophy, potentially experience at its most 'everyday', and yet they have also produced some of the most complicated prose of the past century.[14] The founder is usually taken as Edmund Husserl, although Hegel had written a treatise in 1807 entitled *The Phenomenology of Spirit* and Franz Brentano (1838–1917) had also stressed the centrality of 'intentionality' for philosophy, or a directionality of thought, which bears upon some phenomenon, object or action.

Phenomenology is not quite concerned with phenomena. It is most of all concerned with the ways in which phenomena appear to us and what that reveals about the structures of perception, thought, consciousness and the world. The foundations of phenomenology are closer to philosophy of mind and knowledge (epistemology) than to ontology (a consideration of the being of things as things), which is to say, it is more about the appearing of the phenomenon than it is about that of which something is a phenomenon.

Phenomenology is built from answering the question of what it is like to perceive phenomena, explored in the context of everything that goes along with that, such as memory, desire, the relation of the person to his or her own self, or the situation of being

---

14 I have drawn on David Woodruff Smith, 'Phenomenology', *The Stanford Encyclopedia of Philosophy*, http://plato.stanford.edu/archives/fall2011/entries/phenomenology/.

open to that which is other than ourselves. This is home ground for literature, especially in the twentieth century, as in the 'stream of consciousness' novels of Virginia Woolf or the minute dissection of memory in Marcel Proust's *Remembrance of Things Past*. Although this can begin to sound rather inward and self-obsessed, phenomenology is broadened by consideration of what it is about the world, and our place in it, that provides a structure within which attending to appearances is possible. Such an investigation of what we might call 'the conditions for the possibility of the appearance of that which is apprehended' might seem very abstract, but it can and should include plenty of physical and communal aspects. On this basis, phenomenology has produced some particularly perceptive accounts of bodiliness. Maurice Merleau-Ponty (1908–61) is an important writer in this respect.

Philosophically minded readers may occasionally have undertaken the exercises of trying to observe themselves thinking. We are likely to encounter something elusive. The act of thinking, at its most living and intimate, seems impossible to grasp other than as an echo. I cannot observe what I am thinking right now in the same way that I can be aware of what I was thinking a moment ago. What I was thinking a moment ago is sufficiently finished to be an object of thought, whereas what I am thinking right now cannot be considered in this same moment: it is not an object of thought but thought itself, not something to be considered but consideration itself. That which is most radically first-person (of the pronoun 'I') is what is closest to me, but for that reason it is also extremely difficult to think about. Phenomenology stands four-square in the tradition of finding ways to characterize this experience.

Husserl went so far as to ask us to suspend judgement about the object of perception, even about its very existence, in order to attend only to the appearing of the object as internally apprehended. Husserl called this the discipline of 'bracketing'. It is sometimes given the Greek name of *epoché*, meaning 'suspension'. For Husserl this was simply a technique; the existence of the external world was not in doubt. Later writers have reacted in various ways. Some have wanted to move in a non-realist direction, by which ontological questions about the reality of the world beyond are, at best, beside the point. Others, seeing this as a danger inherent in the business of 'bracketing' from the beginning, have had less time for this cultivation of a studied distance from the reality of what we perceive.

Phenomenology has something in common with Descartes' rationalist philosophy in that it maintains a first-person perspective. It also has something in common with the empiricism that grew up as a reaction to Descartes. Phenomenology also has something in common with Kant, not least in its interest in the preconditions for perception and knowledge. In its existentialist variety, phenomenology pays particular attention to what it means to be free and choosing. Other forms are closer to hermeneutics, and are concerned with what it means to be able to understand. Among the philosophers influenced by phenomenology that a theologian is most likely to encounter, the Jewish philosopher–theologian–ethicist Emmanuel Lévinas (1906–95) is particularly significant. He placed his emphasis not so much on perception as on encounter, and principally the encounter with another human being. While traditional phenomenology can risk putting the subject, perceiver or agent centre stage, and wrapping the world around this first-person 'I', Lévinas stressed the other person and their address, which calls to us to go beyond ourselves, and presents us with demands. The danger is in going too far in the other direction: this human 'other' can be so magnified as to appear almost as an idol, to whom anything and everything is due by way of sacrifice, and to function so strongly as an 'other' that his or her own subjectivity comes to be beside the point.

The 'I' of traditional phenomenology required both a supplement of 'you' (this 'you', or 'thou', being the concern not only of Lévinas, but also of his fellow Jew, Martin Buber) and of the third-person 'he–she–it' of Thomism.[15] The emphasis on interiority was also helpfully supplemented by Edith Stein (1891–1942), perhaps the greatest of Christian phenomenologists, who was to die in

---

15 The point is MacIntryre's, *God*, pp. 158–9.

Auschwitz for her Jewish heritage.[16] As MacIntrye comments, she stressed that 'feelings and thoughts are characteristically expressed' in and through the body and its gestures. (Wittgenstein made similar comments at a similar time.) Thoughts are not immaterial and bodies are not reducible to materiality and its motions. Stein had worked closely with Martin Heidegger. She took his thought in new, theological directions. That rests on her faith, not only in the abstract but also as practically applied. Her writing on death, for instance in *Finite and Eternal Being*, was informed by her work as a nurse during the First World War (before her conversion to Christianity). It stands in marked contrast to Heidegger, who constantly invoked death but had infrequently experienced it first hand, if at all.[17]

Outside the ranks of strict phenomenologists, we can call an approach broadly phenomenological when it works by paying attention to the ways in which we perceive something. So, for instance, someone who said that she was concerned with a 'phenomenological study of worship' would not likely mean a study conducted according to the method of Husserl and his followers, but a study based on the way in which worshippers perceive what they are doing.

In the late twentieth century, something unexpected happened to phenomenology, especially in France: it became theological. This shift was noted in a now famous essay by Dominique Janicaud in 1991. Since then, it has been called the 'theological turn' in French phenomenology. A 'second generation' of French phenomenologists (figures such as Lévinas, Jean-Luc Marion, Jean-Louis Chrétien, Michel Henri and Jean-Yves Lacoste) not only mentioned God, they made God central to their schemes. Janicaud was horrified, seeing it as a betrayal of phenomenological principles: 'phenomenology and theology make two', he wrote; they are two distinct things, not to be combined.[18] God, however,

---

16 MacIntyre, *God*, p. 160.

17 I am grateful to James Orr for this point.

18 Dominique Janicaud, 'The Theological Turn of French Phenomenology', in Dominique Janicaud (ed.), *Phenomenology and the 'Theological Turn': The French Debate*, New York: Fordham University Press, 2000, pp. 3–103, pp. 99–103.

has not gone away. Some later twentieth-century phenomenologists were drawn to frame their philosophy in theological terms, because phenomenology attends to the way in which the world gives itself, and a gift implies a giver. G. K. Chesterton had said something similar in *Orthodoxy*.[19] The new phenomenologists were insisting on a place for 'transcendence' in their accounts, as the source of what is perceived and as what those things point to beyond themselves. Here they stand not only in the tradition of Edith Stein but also of Dietrich von Hildebrand (1889–1977).

Reading On

Phenomenology constitutes an important source for twenty-first-century theology. On the twentieth century as a whole, John Lechte's *Fifty Key Contemporary Thinkers: From Structuralism to Poststructuralism* (Routledge, 2007) is as good an introduction as one could want. The first edition (1994) contains some entries ousted by more recent figures in the second.

Before attempting works by Wittgenstein, the reader may appreciate starting with Fergus Kerr's *Theology After Wittgenstein* (SPCK, 1997), which is a highly significant work in its own right. D. Z. Phillips, Mario von der Ruhr and Rush Rhees edited a collection of essays, *Religion and Wittgenstein's Legacy* (Aldershot, Ashgate, 2005). Tim Labron discusses Wittgenstein from a Lutheran perspective in *Wittgenstein and Theology* (London: Bloomsbury, 2009).

With Heidegger, start with the shorter essays. Details are given in footnote 11 (p. 248) above. For the brave, *Being and Time* was translated by the theologian John Macquarrie and Edward Robinson (New York: Harper & Row, 1962).

Two excellent anthologies of existentialist writings are Walter Kaufmann's *Existentialism: from Dostoevsky to Sartre* (New York: Plume, 2004) and Gordon Daniel Marino's *Basic Writings of Existentialism* (New York: Modern Library, 2004). We see existentialism applied to theology in John Macquarrie's *Existentialist*

---

19 Chapter 4.

Theology (SCM Press, 1955) and the *Handbook of Christian Theology*, edited by Marvin Halverson and Arthur Allen Cohen (London: Collins, 1960).

Robert Sokolowski has written an excellent introduction to phenomenology in his *Introduction to Phenomenology* (CUP, 1999). Merleau-Ponty's most famous work is his *Phenomenology of Perception*. A more accessible, though still difficult, place to start is *The Visible and the Invisible,* translated by Claude Lefort (Evanston: Northwestern University Press, 1968). Alasdair MacIntyre has written an excellent introduction to the work of Edith Stein in *Edith Stein: A Philosophical Prologue* (Continuum, 2006).

15

Literary Theory

Among the fruits of twentieth-century thought, the theologian is likely to come across little with more impact upon his or her thought than literary theory. An encounter with literary theory may represent the first time that a student comes across philosophy that seems to bear directly upon the work of theology, and indeed on many aspects of everyday life.

Literary theory is the business of attending to texts and how they function. Although people have thought about such questions as long as tales have been told, the discipline rose to a new seriousness of purpose in the nineteenth century. It continues to unfold, as a tale of its own, through the twentieth century and into our own.[1] From the early twentieth century onwards, literary theory became inseparable from strands of thought discussed elsewhere in this volume, such as structuralism, post-structuralism and semiotics.

Over the course of the later twentieth century, ideas that had grown up in literary theory came to be applied to an ever wider range of parallel disciplines, including the study of film, architecture and music. This wider phenomenon was sometimes called 'critical theory' and, on other occasions, simply 'theory'. For a while, 'theory' seemed to be all of the foreground of many humanities disciplines. Today it tends to find its place as a constitutive part of the background.

---

1 For a historical account, see the first half of Hans Berten's *Literary Theory: The Basics*, Routledge, 2008.

The Turn to the Text

One conviction lying at the heart of literary theory is its attention to the text rather than the author (and an assessment of his or her putative intentions or mental states). We see this emphasis in the 'New Criticism' associated with figures such as T. S. Eliot. A text has to stand on its own two feet; the 'intention' of the author is either obscure, irrelevant or impossible to gauge, depending on one's approach. To think otherwise, these theorists wrote, would be to commit the 'Intentional Fallacy'. Roland Barthes called this 'the death of the author'. We encountered this question in the chapter on Plato: it is one thing to ask what Plato said and another to ask what can be said on account of reading Plato; it is one thing to ask what Plato 'meant' and another to ask what meanings we want to advance having read Plato.

This can be, and has been, exaggerated, but in another sense it chimes with a certain degree of common sense and human practice. When a law is ambiguous, the courts may pay attention to sources that elucidate what the framers of the law intended (such as parliamentary transcripts) but that only goes so far. If, for example, a statute clearly creates a tax loophole, then that loophole stands, even if it seems obvious that parliament 'intended' to raise taxes rather than let them go. The proper response is new and better-drafted legislation.

As an example of the 'sovereignty' of the text over the author, consider John Henry Newman's reinterpretation of the *Thirty-Nine Articles of Religion* of the Church of England in a catholic direction. A hundred years before trendy literary developments, we see him applying the principle that the text says what the text says. Article 31 condemns the idea that in the 'sacrifices of Masses' the priest offers Christ to the Father. Newman takes the article at face value, and in particular that plural: sacrifices. The text condemns the idea that the priest offers new and independent sacrifices; that does not condemn what Newman took to be the correct view, that the priest presents before the Father the one sacrifice of Christ upon the cross. Article 25 points out that 'the Sacraments were not ordained of Christ to be gazed upon, or to be carried about, but that we should duly use them'. Quite so, replies Newman. The Eucharist was not instituted for the purpose of processions or adoration of the Blessed Sacrament; it was instituted for the purpose of Holy Communion. The force of the article is to remind us of this, and that reminder was necessary in the sixteenth century. It does not rule out eucharistic devotions (with processions and gazing upon) that serve to focus our meditation on the Communion.

Newman's interpretations are proto-postmodern in their playfulness, even wilfulness. They demonstrate that the postmodern concentration on the text above the imagined or reconstructed inner life of the author is not so new. Cranmer, Parker, Elizabeth I, and the others involved in writing the articles chose their words carefully: 'sacrifices', for instance, not 'sacrifice'.

If attention is placed on the text, it is also placed on the reader, especially in what are called 'reader response' approaches to criticism. This takes us into the territory of 'hermeneutics', a word often veiled in confusion or even obfuscation but which simply means the practice of determining meaning. The towering figures here are Hans-Georg Gadamer (with *Truth and Method*) and Paul Ricœur (with works such as *Interpretation Theory: Discourse and the Surplus of Meaning* and *Time and Narrative*). In broad terms, the realization is that reading is a partnership between text and reader. A text is incomprehensible without all that the reader brings. No text can provide the complete basis for its own intelligibility. Thinking about the process of language acquisition helps here, as it does surprisingly often. A text presupposes that you can read; it does not teach you to read (although, perhaps we could say of the very best texts that we come away from one with the conviction that it has, in some fashion, 'taught us how to read'). There is also our knowledge of conventions about how a book works, for instance that a preface functions differently from an introduction, or about how a particular genre functions, ranging to subtle dimensions of how one form of poetry, or prose, differs from another. In any text, but perhaps especially in a novel, relevant social conventions have to be understood. As confirmation of this, if we read a novel set in an unfamiliar context, it can seem largely opaque to us. Texts, in summary, are unreadable without what the reader brings. Different readers, however, bring something different. On that account, *Hamlet* is innumerably many different plays.

In any of these considerations it is possible to place undue emphasis on the reader as an isolated individual. We do not read texts in quite this way, but as members of one community or other, perhaps of many. In fact, one of the things that gets close to the heart of defining a given community is a commonality of outlook in the way in which we approach texts. All being concerned with the same, or associated, texts, is also often constitutive. We will return to this below in the form of the 'canon' and to these themes more widely in the section on narrative theology. Putting the communal aspect back into the interpretation of texts is one of the ways in which twentieth-century cultural theory can sometimes seem like simply catching up with what the Church has always known. Similarly, the insight that authors write, and communities interpret, texts with reference to other texts, which is sometimes called 'intertextuality', has been part of the Church's life from the beginning. The liturgy is an 'intertextual' edifice woven out of the Bible; plainsong themes have permeated church music for a millennium.

For some, the suggestion that arriving at a meaning for a text might be a complicated matter at all is a cause of worry. Even more so is the sense that this meaning might not entirely be determined in advance. Anxieties become most acute of all when it comes to the Bible, and yet it may be our experience of reading the Bible that can begin to allay these very fears. Most Christians, of any tradition, will attest to the sense that the Bible 'speaks to them'. They may even say that 'the Bible speaks to me', with an emphasis on 'me'. In other words, this book, or collection of books, can be read by a million different people, even in exactly the same translation, and yet 'speak' to each individually. We bring all that we are and have experienced to this text and it addresses us in precisely that situation. So, while the radically postmodern theorist of hermeneutics might propose that no text has any stable meaning at all, we do not need to go that far. We should not, however, run so far from this extreme as to betray our experience of a text, especially the biblical text, speaking to us in our own, particular situation. Those who believe in God, and see God as the source and foundation of truth, are in a strong position to allow texts to be open-ended, especially the Scriptures, without resorting to complete relativism. Because of their grounding in God, that text, and indeed any bearer of truth, will convey truth inexhaustibly.

To arrive at that point, it may be useful to make a detour back, once again, to our discussion of Plato in Chapter 2. There we came across the distinction between arguments based on situations in the world and arguments made in more absolute terms: between *a posteriori* and *a priori*. We noted that, although we can make this distinction, it stands more as a recognition of two tendencies or directions in thought than as a hard and fast division. The two notions bleed into one another. Recognizing this points us to a characteristic insight of the twentieth century over what is called the *situatedness of knowledge*.

As we have just seen, any act of understanding is also an act of investment: we have to invest ourselves with some degree of creativity, and draw upon what we already know, in order to understand any text laid before us. Our experiences, and view on the world, are what allow us to make sense of other people, of texts and situations; they also mean that such understanding will always be coloured by those experiences and preconceptions. Even over something as seemingly settled as, for instance, mathematics, complete objectivity cannot be attained, since there are significant areas where the axioms are contested: what is taken for granted, the position from which we argue. Even here, and all the more in the humanities, there is – to use Thomas Nagel's phrase – no view from nowhere.[2]

This view contrasts with previous visions of philosophy, where completely settled, inarguable – and therefore common – foundations were thought to be freely available. All 'sensible people' started that way, which was a good way to brand as insensible those who disagreed. The legacy of the twentieth century is to

---

2 Thomas Nagel, *The View from Nowhere*, OUP, 1989.

THE LOVE OF WISDOM

be generally 'anti-foundationalist', which is to say, not supposing that there are common foundations upon which everyone agrees alike, and from which any two people can begin a conversation in an uncomplicated way. There is a 'committedness' to knowledge: we all have prior intellectual commitments (which will also be commitments 'of the heart') that shape what we think. The fact of the committedness of knowledge does not undo our sense of value, or the struggle for a proper objectivity. There is no view from nowhere, but that does not mean we cannot try to be fair. Indeed, appreciating the sense in which the whole of our person and background is involved in the search for truth – our outlook, even our mood on a given day – should help us, rather than hinder us, in that quest for fairness.

Anti-foundationalism may seem to place a question mark over the possibility of knowledge, and of truth. It might do so justly for the person who supposes that truth is only in the mind. For the robust realist, however, who sees the truth as undergirded by the reality of the world, and more ultimately still by the reality of God, we need not be so disturbed. The realist can trust that truth will look after itself, and might be modest enough to suppose that we have only half a handle on the truth in any case. Mature realism like this is sometimes called 'critical realism'. We encountered it in Chapter 11 in a discussion of Gilson: we know real things, out there in the world, but we can never know them more than partially. As Gilson put it, '[w]hat knowledge grasps in the object is something real, but reality is inexhaustible, and even if the intellect had discerned all its details, it would still be confounded by the mystery of its very existence'.[3] One way to say this is that the truth outstrips our grasp, and that we can get to it only through images, through models and metaphors. On that account, the very things that allow us to speak and know – those models or metaphors – are also what mean that we do not know exhaustively, what hold the truth from us at arm's length. To put it in knotty fashion, the conditions for the possibility of

3 *Methodological Realism: A Handbook for Beginning Realists*, San Francisco: Ignatius, 2011, p. 102.

knowledge are also what make the incompleteness of knowledge constitutive.

Narrative and Narrative Theology

The later twentieth century saw the retrieval of the importance of *narrative* as a category of thought within Christian theology. To a large degree, that came as part of a certain 'post-liberal' return to the Bible as the source and norm for Christian theology, often associated with the Yale School and theologians such as George Lindbeck and Hans Frei. Whereas the Enlightenment liberal approach to religion would treat the narrative, and poetic, form of much of the Bible as something less than fully rational, the post-liberal 'narrative turn' took those features, and especially the narrative element, as central to how the Bible exercises its authority.[4]

Little is more central to our sense of our own identity than the stories we tell about ourselves. Asked to give an account of ourselves, most of us will tell a story about ourselves before we are long into the exercise, whether that puts the stress on our origins, or on a move beyond our origins, whether it is simple or complex, long or short. The post-liberals recognized that personal and cultural transformation is not all about adopting new concepts. Just as important, perhaps more so, is the adoption of a new story. Consequently, adopting and living a Christian identity is pivotally about situating, and integrating, our story within that of the Bible. The use of the Old Testament by the writers of the New Testament is the paradigmatic example.

At its best, this approach to the importance of story and history offers enormous gains. It explains the ancient wisdom of spending so much time in church listening, thanks to a lectionary, to readings from all of the Bible. It suggests that apologetics need

---

4 Attention to how narratives work is also illuminating for theology, both for biblical studies and pastoral theology. See, for instance, Christopher Booker, *The Seven Basic Plots: Why We Tell Stories*, Continuum, 2004, as well as the many excellent introductions to narrative theory now published.

not simply be worked out as a clash of concepts, but can usefully involve telling a story, whether that is the story of Christ or of the saints, or an alternative, Christian, trajectory to the story of human thought and culture.

This approach also supports a historical approach to teaching theology, or any other discipline. This, after all, is often the way that these disciplines, even the sciences, *are* taught. It helps us to appreciate the extent to which even the seemingly most objective of human enterprises, the natural sciences for instance, are embedded in human culture, and social and political history. This narrative and historical approach starts to become more foe than friend, however, if we suppose that it provides a complete account of these disciplines, as if science, for instance, is no more than a story about science, and perhaps its economic entanglements, or when theology is seen as no more than a story about theology, perhaps with political explanations ousting any sense of there being truth to its claims. The 1970s accounts of Constantine and the Council of Nicaea did that with Christology, just as Thomas Kuhn's remarkable and enormously important book *The Structure of Scientific Revolutions* (1962) risks doing it with natural science.[5] In his excellent introduction to narrative theology *Telling God's Story*,[6] Gerard Loughlin presents the science of the premodern world, and that of the present day, as being fundamentally no more different than alternative stories we tell ourselves about the world. The narrative element is crucial, as Kuhn showed, but if the Babylonians could predict an eclipse to the accuracy of a day, then contemporary quantum electrodynamics can predict the magnetic properties of an electron (for instance its 'anomalous magnetic dipole moment') to one part in a hundred million. In a certain, largely non-narrative sense, quantum mechanics is not simply an alternative to Babylonian science; it is better.

---

5 Thomas Kuhn, *The Structure of Scientific Revolutions*, University of Chicago Press.
6 Gerard Loughlin, *Telling God's Story*, CUP, 1999.

Reading On

Two good introductions to literary theory are Jonathan Culler's
Literary Theory: A Very Short Introduction (OUP, 1997) and
Hans Bertens's *Literary Theory: The Basics* (Routledge, 2008).
Terry Eagleton criticizes the discipline he did much to develop in
After Theory (Penguin, 2004). On narrative theory, see Gerard
Gennette, *Narrative Discourse: An Essay in Method*, translated
by Jane Lewin (Ithaca: Cornell University Press, 1983), James
Phelan and Peter Rabinowitz (eds), *A Companion to Narrative
Theory* (Blackwell, 2008) and the suggestions on tragedy on
p. 226. Gerard Loughlin's *Telling God's Story* is a good way into nar-
rative theology (CUP, 1999), as is the anthology *Why Narrative?:
Readings in Narrative Theology*, edited by Stanley Hauerwas
and L. Gregory Jones (Eugene: Wipf and Stock, 1997). F. LeRon
Shults has written about theology after foundationalism in *The
Postfoundationalist Task of Theology* (Eerdmans, 1999), as have
Stanley Grenz and John Franke in *Beyond Foundationalism: Shaping Theology in a Postmodern Context* (Louisville: Westminster
John Knox Press, 2001). Grenz and Franke give a particularly
good account of how both conservative and liberal theologians
have been shaped by a contrasting, but ultimately shared, appeal
to foundations.

16

Postmodernism

For a definition of postmodernism we can turn to Terry Eagleton. It is a movement born in the second half of the twentieth century, which 'rejects totalities, universal values, grand historical narratives, solid foundations to human existence and the possibility of objective knowledge'. It 'is sceptical of truth, unity and progress, opposes what is seen as elitism in culture, tends towards cultural relativism, and celebrates pluralism, discontinuity and heterogeneity'.[1] Particularly central is the sense that no overall story could any more be told that would gather up the pieces. This is the 'end of meta-narratives' described by Jean-François Lyotard (1979) in his report, then book, *The Postmodern Condition*.[2]

Postmodern writers have managed to combine startling insights with much that is preposterous. They are worth reading for the sake of those insights, which means putting up with the excesses. They are also worth reading because the culture on which they are commenting is our own. Whereas scholars of the analytic school aim for an approach to philosophy that is often outside of history and the concerns of the moment, postmodern thinkers are fully immersed, and often quite deliberately consider a culture at its most ephemeral. Their danger is therefore the opposite of that for the analytic school: blink and the fashion about which they are writing may have passed.

We will get the most out of reading postmodern philosophy, and not sustain too many mental injuries in the process, if we approach these authors with a sense of their literary style. Post-

---

1 *After Theory*, Penguin, 2004, p. 13, n. 1.

2 Jean-François Lyotard, *The Postmodern Condition*, Manchester University Press, 1979.

modern philosophy typically reads like prose poetry. Given that these authors are interested in texts, it is no surprise that the texts they produce should be highly charged. Here is philosophy that recognizes the problems associated with the expression of meaning. Those problems are expressed in the density of the writing. As such, it often stands on the boundary between profundity and an Emperor's New Clothes vapidity. Postmodern writing can even strike us as an assault upon reason itself. Classically, theology was thought to rest on three legs: Scripture, tradition and reason. The Reformation questioned tradition, often letting it go; the Enlightenment questioned Scripture, often letting it go. With postmodernism, the same dynamic was applied to reason.

This style of writing calls for its own style of reading. We cannot wait until we have understood one sentence fully before we move on to the next. Adopt that approach and you might not get beyond the first sentence. The measure of what might count as comprehension resembles more that for poetry than that for prose. What any particular line means is likely to be unveiled by what comes next, at least in part. (This observation might apply beyond postmodern philosophy. In general, half of what we do not understand on one page will be filled in by the next, and half of what still remains by the rest of the chapter.)

Put another way, postmodern philosophy can be secular mysticism, especially mysticism of the 'negative' or 'apophatic' form, which stresses the unknowability of what most matters. These writers sometimes approach that unknowability with a masochistic attachment to emptiness. That, however, is not entirely without its parallels in Christian spirituality either.

Whereas analytic writing can fail through a quest for the objectivity of mathematics, postmodern philosophers risk seeming whimsical or looking like brute assertion. Little could stand as a clearer expression than this of the divergent assumptions of these schools over the limits and methods of reason.

Postmodernism, Modernity and Postmodernity

Discuss postmodern philosophy and we are invited to consider questions of relation: between postmodernity and modernity, and between postmodernism and postmodernity. Few questions are of greater significance than the former: how does postmodernity stand in relation to modernity? By 'modernity' we mean a period, stretching from at least the sixteenth century, characterized by confidence in reason, universality and progress. For some commentators, postmodernism obviously marks a profound break: from unswerving confidence in objectivity to doubts over its possibility, or from a narrative of incessant and inevitable progress to the idea that not only progress, but history itself, has come to an end.

For others, postmodernity is fundamentally continuous with modernity. Modernity gave prominence to capital, for instance, and capital is already proto-postmodern in the elevation of an abstraction over concrete reality. In postmodernity, such abstractions are simply intensified or consummated. Still other commentators combine elements of both continuity and disparity in their analysis: postmodernity is an unmasking or an intensification that leads to collapse. Modernity, for instance, proposed a vision of reason newly severed from tradition. In postmodernity, this was reversed (with the sense that there can be no tradition- or context-less reason), and yet, in a sense, this severing was also intensified: modernity rejected reason-within-tradition as lacking universality; although postmodernity accepted the *ubiquity* of tradition, it upheld the judgement that this precludes universality, fragmenting knowledge, and celebrating its fragmentation.

We have every reason to suppose that the truth about the relation of postmodernity to what went before will be complicated, and that it might vary across disciplines. Postmodern literature will have a different relation to modern (or modernist) literature than postmodern architecture has to its particular history. Mention of architecture is significant: it was an important, even trailblazing, arena for the development of postmodernism. It was also short lived: full-blown postmodernism architecture looks more dated today than that from the 1950s: as unforgivable as leotards in primary colours, from the same period, and buccaneer shirts.

The second contrast is between postmodern*ity* and postmodern*ism*. Graham Ward has written perceptively about this in the introduction to the *Blackwell Companion to Postmodern Theology*.[3] Postmodernity is our cultural condition; postmodernism is a more intellectual affair. Postmodernity is the age and world in which we live (unless, perhaps, we have already moved on); it characterizes the way you visit the cinema, and what is depicted in the films you see there, whether you take a step back to think about it critically or not. Postmodernism is a school of philosophy, or of cultural analysis; it is a mode of thinking and writing taken up by many philosophers and critics of culture (including critics of those films and those visits to the cinema).

Ward approaches the distinction between postmodernity and postmodernism in terms of where theology stands. His suggestion is that our times are postmodern, and that postmodernism does a good job at describing them. On the other hand, postmodern thought is less successful at teaching us how to respond. If postmodernity is a time of spiritual poverty, postmodernism can highlight that situation but not offer much by way of a constructive remedy.

The Political Edge and its Blunting

Postmodernism has been better at describing the ethical, political and economic condition than it has been at transforming it. That is significant. From its inception, postmodern philosophy has been thoroughly political, which is to say usually Marxist. If it cannot effect political and economic transformation, then it fails on its own terms, as well as those of anyone else. Terry Eagleton, earlier a great exponent of postmodern methods in literary theory, has been blunt about these failings. His *After Theory* is particularly significant. Over the postmodern celebration of flux, for instance, over what is stable, Eagleton wrote that 'Those for whom "dynamic" is always a positive term' might care to consider the effects of capitalism, which he describes as 'the most dynamically destructive system of production which humanity has ever

---

3 Graham Ward, 'Introduction: "Where We Stand"', in Graham Ward (ed.), *The Blackwell Companion to Postmodern Theology*, Blackwell, 2005, pp. xii–xxvii.

seen', a system which at present offers a 'brutally quickened [. . .] melt-down, with the tearing up of traditional communities, the breaking down of national barriers, the generating of great tidal waves of migration'.[4]

The prominent postmodern philosophers were heirs to the 'masters of suspicion': Nietzsche, Feuerbach, Marx, Freud. The other all-important addition to this mix was feminist thought, and to a lesser extent the perspective of post-colonialism. At root lies Nietzsche's assumption that the dynamo for human action, including human culture, is the 'will to power'. The result was a *hermeneutic of suspicion*. No text or other aspect of culture was considered for long without voicing certain questions: Who profits? What values are assumed and reinforced? Whose perspective is overlooked? A good example, drawn from literary theory, is the idea of 'the canon of literature'. This is the list of works considered definitive: the works which, if we have not read them, define us as less than perfectly literate. Literary theory asked, with postmodern vigour, questions such as 'Who draws up the list?' and '*Whose* canon are we talking about?' Any such list serves certain interests including, but by no means limited to, the economic interests of publishers. Recognizing this has been liberating for many. Women, non-whites, gay people and speakers of minority languages have been disadvantaged by the standard canon. Now, they can have canons of their own. Then, within each such group, different sub-groups can have a canon of *their* own. The consensus fragments. Much is gained, and we let go of much that we should not lament. All the same, there are losses. It is now far less likely that a person in her twenties will have novels to discuss with her grandparents, or for that matter with her neighbour.

The hermeneutic of suspicion looks below the surface in a move that is entirely characteristic of postmodernism. The emphasis shifts from what is said, done or thought to the preconditions (in thought and action) that make it possible for them to be said, done or thought. This level, call it higher or lower as you wish, is the pre-eminent domain of postmodern thinkers. Michel Foucault

---

4 *After Theory*, p. 50.

was a particular master at this sort of excavation. He called it the *archeology of thought*.[5]

This approach as been taken up by theologians and activists concerned with justice, and it is not difficult to see why. The focus is shifted from individual situations (this injustice, or that) to the underlying structures that made such injustices possible. Here, however, postmodernism has been better at diagnosis than repair, and at pulling down than at pulling up. The risk, perhaps unintended, is that it will corrode whatever it touches. Structural injustices and inequalities are unmasked but trust is the victim. Trust is at a chronic low in Western societies and this rests to no small degree on postmodern thought in this 'critical theory' mood; the etymological relation between crisis and criticism is not accidental. A second consequence is a shift from acting to writing. Shift our understanding of the nature of mental illness, as Michel Foucault certainly did, and, at best, you change the life of hundreds of thousands of people for the better. The jury must be out over how much good his body of theory has in fact achieved on that score. He spent a great deal more time writing about the underlying structures of thought and behaviour that underwrite our attitudes to mental health than he did working with those afflicted. We can put it this way: nuns with a postmodern outlook are more likely to be writing books than their sisters with a pre-modern outlook. The paleo-nuns may be too busy running hospitals in Zambia.

We can propose two routes into postmodern thought. We might call them East Coast and West Coast, with an American reference, or the Left and Right Bank approaches, if we prefer Paris. With an East Coast route, you argue yourself, carefully, out of earlier cut-and-dried confidence. In this way, Wittgenstein emerges as a key proto-postmodern figure. The traditional story, however, starts with Saussure and the structuralist idea that any category makes sense through its place in a web of relations. Notice that this web extends for ever, and we have jumped from structuralism to postmodern *post-structuralism*. Jacques Derrida (1930–2004) used the French term *différance* here, which has notes of both

---

5 For instance *The Order of Things* and *The Archeology of Thought*.

difference and deferral: difference because, in good structuralist fashion, differences are the basis for meaning; deferral because one contrasting difference opens to another and another, so that the meaning of a word is never entirely settled. Approached another way, a text takes its meaning in part from its relation to other texts, but the number of comparisons that could be made is endless. A complete grasp of meaning is endlessly deferred. This seemed terribly racy at the time, as if meaning were unravelling. With the benefit of a couple of decades, it appears important but not so groundbreaking: good poets had been exploiting ambiguity for centuries but that had not prevented meaningful exchange at the grocer's shop.

Alongside *différance*, Derrida's other enduring theme was 'deconstruction'. This aligns with the project of 'suspicion' we have already discussed. It is an approach to texts that looks for gaps or slips (sometimes named from the Greek, *aporia*) where the text 'gets into trouble'. Here the author betrays some unconfessed project, which might be her own or might, indeed, be the 'project' of a whole culture. (Other post-structuralist writers, such as Lacan, would latch on to the psychoanalytic possibilities of a statement such as this.) An *aporia* is like a ruck in the carpet; deconstructionists were adept at tripping over them. Here *différance* and deconstruction line up: slippage is inevitable; it is a consequence of trying to write or 'inscribe' the boundlessness of meaning in a finite mode. Derrida wrote about writing as an attempt to leave a 'trace' on the void (or *chora*). Also in this 'suspicious' or deconstructive style is the postmodern tradition of 'readings', as in 'N will provide a reading of *x*', where *x* might be a text or an aspect of culture. Proficiency in this approach usually involves a combination of laying bare inner workings and assumptions, and a certain degree of reading 'against the grain', in a fashion that underlines that interpretation is itself creative and that every such 'reading' is also a 'writing'. The French critic Roland Barthes produced particularly celebrated readings of contemporary culture in his *Mythologies* of 1957, right at the start of this trend.

Returning to Derrida, he wrote about aspects of human life that he thought illustrated *aporia*. They are useful reading for Christian theologians, for the sake of contrast with the Gospels. What philosophy makes complicated and conveniently impossible, Jesus made possible: often inconveniently so. For instance, Derrida suggested that forgiveness is impossible because it leaves the one who is forgiven in debt to the one who forgives. The Christian might reply that bonds are no bad thing, that we are all in debt to one another anyway, and that, most important of all, any human forgiveness takes place against the backdrop of divine forgiveness, and it is no debt to be 'in debt' to the one who gives, and loves, without need. Derrida also wrote about the tragic impossibility of love to fulfil itself, on the basis that the person who loves cats, for instance, cannot love every single individual cat. Again, the reader of the Gospels can reply that it is not necessary to love every last instance in order to love. It is sufficient to love one's neighbour; it is sufficient to care for the person in front of you who is hungry, thirsty, naked, sick, imprisoned or homeless. The idea of loving all remains safely abstract;[6] we are to love in particular, and that is enough.

The 'East Coast' route takes structuralism seriously and carefully pushes it to its limits. The West Coast route throws care and caution to the wind and dances in the void. At the origin of this trajectory we might place the oh-so-sober Kant; a principal postmodern example might be Gilles Deleuze (1925–95). Kant had said that we only have access to phenomena; the noumena, although what is most real about something, are beyond access. The late twentieth-century twist on this was to say 'here are the phenomena, and who cares about the noumena? After all, no one claims to have seen one for a few hundred years (if we're good Kantians).' We go from perceiving surfaces, behind which lie hidden depths, to saying that there are only surfaces.

Another Kantian lineage involves freedom, which for Kant was a value of ultimate worth. Freedom is, in Kantian language, 'sublime': Kant's version of the sacred. Make freedom an absolute,

---

6 In an episode of the British comedy series *Little Britain* a woman has filled her house with depictions of frogs, upon which she dotes in general. When, however, a real frog appears in her garden, she abhors it and brutally clubs it to death. She loves all frogs in abstract but not in particularity.

however, and it eventually becomes absolutely debased: freedom to shop, freedom to have a tattoo, freedom to pretend that we can all do what we want. Consumerism is no debasement of Kantian philosophy but rather its perfectly consistent and sensible development and expression.[7] Since the end of the twentieth century, theorists have told us that appearances, surfaces and freedom are all that matter; architects and creative people of various stripes have danced to that tune.

In one more way, postmodernism was Kantian. It took Kant's insistence that people are ends, not means, and pushed it all the way. Each person was to determine his or her purpose absolutely, for him- or herself. Since formal and final causes are related – nature and destiny – this led to massively exaggerated postmodern notions of the human being as plastic and self-determining of their essence as well as their purpose. Here we might contrast Augustine who, in very un-Kantian terms, referred to people as means: means in the sense that only God is ultimate, and people attain their meaning in relation to God.[8] That can sound chilling, but his principal point was that people are *for God*, and because of that, for each other. God is the end, and our end. God has drawn us into a great project where God condescends, remarkably, for us to assist him. The paradox is that we achieve greater dignity as means (co-workers with God), and have a more glorious end (as children of God and members of the redeemed society), than if we were pure ends. If I am a pure end, I have no reference beyond myself. Make me an end, and only an end, and I have a certain ultimacy. This is profoundly bad news because, with no source and destiny beyond myself, I am ultimately nothing.

An Example: Jean Baudrillard

The French philosopher Jean Baudrillard (1929–2007) was a master at dreaming up titles for books. He gave us *For a Critique of the Political Economy of the Sign* (1972), *Symbolic Exchange*

---

7 I am grateful to John Milbank for this point.
8 *On Christian Doctrine*, early chapters of book I.

and Death (1976) and *Simulacra and Simulation* (1981). The last of these has a walk-on part in *The Matrix*, a film as impressively philosophical as its two sequels are disappointing. Towards the start, Neo, the hero, hides his contraband computer programme on a disk concealed within a hollowed-out copy of *Simulacra and Simulation*.

Baudrillard's early work grew out of his doctoral research with Henri Lefebvre, a thinker whose work spanned sociology, philosophy and politics in a way that is frequently highly instructive. Lefebvre was particularly interested in 'everyday life', and the meanings and values that inhere in the ways we deal with everyday rituals and the 'space' in which we live, most particularly the urban landscape.[9] From his supervisor, Baudrillard gained, and never lost, a fascination with everyday objects and rituals. 'Low' culture captivated him more than 'high'.

Baudrillard's earlier writings show the strongest signs of his Marxist involvement, although even then he wanted to add philosophical sophistication. In these works, Baudrillard made points that have since become commonplace (although he was not the only person to be working along these lines at the time). He stressed, for instance, the significance of consumer goods as *signs*: with a piece of clothing or a car we are as much buying a sign as a physical object. His later works were highly political, discussing the involvement of the media in war, for instance, but in a manner so individual and provocative as to move beyond conventional politics. In his early works, Baudrillard urged active resistance to the trends he observed; in the later works he simply observed. Indeed, inasmuch as he was clearly *fascinated* by the quirks of late capitalism, there is a sense in which he did not want it to go away.

Baudrillard's point was that we have lost touch with reality. He never quite *celebrates* this but his rapt attention to the phenomenon is telling. A zoologist might think it unscientific to write even a single sentence in *praise* of the butterfly, but turn out such

---

9 Particularly recommended is Henri Lefebvre, *The Production of Space*, Blackwell, 1991.

a succession of careful studies of every aspect of the butterfly that his work could only be called celebration. Baudrillard feels the same. As with other postmodern writers, Baudrillard is therefore more significant for what he sees, and points out to us, than for his judgements about what is welcome or unwelcome.

From his middle works onwards, Baudrillard became fascinated with *simulation*, and the idea that a copy is in a sense less than what it represents, and in a sense more. His subjects for investigation were cinema, cyberspace and all that is made of plastic. Simulation emerges as being as much definitive of postmodernity as production and consumption were of modernity. (All, in their way, are concerned with a sort of repetition.)

In good French postmodern style, Baudrillard gave the name of 'the *real*' to common or garden, old-fashioned reality. In contrast, he thought, human life has now become virtual reality: augmented, manipulated and, to use a good English word, spun. 'Everything is destined to reappear as simulation', he wrote, 'Landscapes as photography, [. . .] thoughts as writing, [. . .] events as television.'[10] This simulation or *simulacrum* he called the hyper-real; it is 'repetition *as something more real*',[11] such that mediaeval altarpieces, presentations of native cultures, or the history of evolution become more real in a museum than they would be outside. The *real* has been eclipsed by the *hyper-real*: the constructions of the media and advertising, of fantasy and aspiration, of technology and science. We are no longer concerned with our families: we have more lurid, colourful households to watch on *Big Brother* and its progeny. In his later work, Baudrillard went so far as to proclaim 'the destruction of the real', although the forces that have destroyed it keep an illusion of the real in play. Along these lines, he surpassed even his most provocative previous writing with *The Gulf War Did Not Take Place* (published in 1991). Baudrillard's point, made in stark hyperbole, is twofold. First, that war coverage comes to us so completely through the filter of media organizations (and before that, through the filter of the public relations

---

10 *America*, Verso, 1988, p. 32.
11 *America*, p. 42, emphasis in original.

wing of the armed forces) that what we see ('The Gulf War') bears little relation to what happens on the ground. Second, that even in the combat itself, this was a hyper-real war, not a real one: it was waged in the simulated realm of cruise missiles launched and tracked on computer screens. The title of the book was callous in humanitarian terms, but it had a humanitarian point. That said, technology was soon to move us to a new stage. In these days of Twitter feeds and camera phones, we are catapulted into a *more direct* contact with the face of war than ever before.

The theme of reality and simulation is familiar from the Old Testament: 'Why do you spend your money for that which is not bread, and your labour for that which does not satisfy?' (Isa. 55.2) and 'Thus they turned their glory: into the similitude of a calf that eateth hay' (Ps. 106.20 in Coverdale's matchless version). And God, as the Dominican Cornelius Ernst put it, is 'the ultimately really real'.[12]

Baudrillard was particularly fascinated with America, as the home of the hyper-real. His philosophical travelogue, *America*, remains one of the most accessible ways into his work. America is 'hyper-reality': dream become reality while still remaining dream.[13] While writing this book, I had a road trip in the USA. On the outskirts of New Orleans, I got out of the car for a coffee. My feet alighted on a grass verge with the broadest and deepest of blades. As they sank, as one would sink into a feather mattress, I found myself thinking, 'This grass is so good, it could almost be fake.' This is the hyper-real.

Reading On

From Routledge we have an anthology, a collection of essays, and a reference work: Michael Drolet (ed.), *The Postmodernism Reader: Foundational Texts* (2003), Stuart Sim (ed.), *The Routledge Companion to Postmodernism* (2011), and Victor E. Taylor and Charles E. Winquist (eds), *Encyclopedia of Postmodernism*

---

12 *Multiple Echo*, London: Darton, Longman & Todd, 1979, p. 73.
13 *America*, p. 28.

(2003). Among Jean Baudrillard's works, good places to start are *Selected Writings*, translated by Mark Poster (Oxford: Polity Press, 2001), *America* (Verso, 1988) and *Cool Memories* (Verso, 1990). The last of these is a collection of autobiography and aphorism, followed by four further volumes, numbered 'II' to 'V' (1996, 1997, 2003 and 2006). James Walters has given us a terrific discussion entitled *Baudrillard and Theology* (T&T Clark, 2012).

On the theological response of theology to postmodernism, Graham Ward edited two collections. The first is more of a response and the second more a collection of sources, but the distinction is not absolute: *The Blackwell Companion to Postmodern Theology* (Blackwell, 2001) and *The Postmodern God: A Theological Reader* (Blackwell, 1997). As an introduction, see his essay 'Postmodern Theology', in David Ford and Rachel Muers (eds), *The Modern Theologians* (Blackwell, 2005). Kevin Vanhoozer's *The Cambridge Companion to Postmodern Theology* (CUP, 2003) is excellent. From a Reformed perspective we have James K. A. Smith, *Who's Afraid of Postmodernism?: Taking Derrida, Lyotard, and Foucault to Church* (Grand Rapids: Baker, 2006). A. K. A. Adam has produced a number of works on postmodern biblical scholarship including *What Is Postmodern Biblical Criticism?* (Minneapolis: Augsburg Fortress, 1995) and *Postmodern Interpretations of the Bible: A Reader* (St Louis: Chalice Press, 2001). Benno van den Toren tackles apologetics in a postmodern context in *Christian Apologetics as Cross-Cultural Dialogue* (T&T Clark, 2011).

17

Theology and Philosophy in the Present Day

This book might start in earnest at this point, with the previous chapters serving only as an introduction to a discussion of philosophy newly minted in the present day. Instead, however, with this chapter it draws to a close. It does so for three reasons. First, the philosophy that is most influential on contemporary theology is not that which is being proposed afresh at this moment; it is philosophy that has had time to be disseminated and assimilated. Second, any presentation of the history of philosophy is already something contemporary, since it cannot but be relayed on the basis of contemporary concerns. It does not only begin to be contemporary when our history reaches the present day. Finally, the contemporary philosophical traditions upon which today's theologians are drawing are particularly eclectic. Indeed, eclecticism is a defining character of the present attitude towards philosophy. Given this eclecticism, an attempt at an exhaustive survey would also be exhausting.

Eclecticism

This eclecticism manifests itself in at least two ways. First, that there is no one dominant philosophical tradition among theologians today, nothing parallel to the position of idealism in the early twentieth century nor even of a Marxist-postmodern-suspicion perspective at that century's close. Since the theological tradition is a broad and disputed one, it would be naive to suppose that theologians had ever danced to the beat of a single drum. All the same, diversity is particularly notable today. Among graduate students in my own university, I encounter those who want to work out theology in dialogue with Aquinas, in either a more Platonic or more Aristotelian mould, or with Deleuze, or Kant, Derrida or the German Romantic philosophers, to name only a few.

Theologians are also eclectic today in the sense that any individual theologian is likely to look to a wide variety of influences. This is perhaps particularly the case in the United Kingdom, where the still-strong presence of theology in mainstream universities – despite many pressures to the contrary – ensures that theologians are exposed to other disciplines, and because theology there remains a thoroughgoing ecumenical endeavour. As never before, it is possible to be a Thomist for whom Barth is important, who delights in the early Fathers and is inclined to think that Schleiermacher is undervalued or, in philosophy, to be a Platonist for whom Aristotle makes all the difference, to think that the post-structuralists are over-rated but indispensible, and to hold fast to Wittgenstein as having said things that needed to be said.

Such eclecticism might make for fuzziness, but it need not do so. Indeed, eclecticism today can be a corollary of confidence, and often is. One can all the more easily be a philosophical magpie when firmly nested in the theological tree. We see this confidence in contemporary interactions with philosophy, and with science, that bear a far greater sense of a theological logic than in previous decades. After all this patting of ourselves on the back, however, we might also note a certain listlessness. Theology has turned a corner and is both confident and productive. All the same, theologians may not be quite sure how to inhabit, or move on, in this new, less timid situation. Philosophically, the ground seemed to shift after the death of Derrida, the last of the pioneering post-structuralists. We find ourselves in a position of post-postmodernism, and it is not quite clear what that will mean.

Theology among the (Political) Philosophers

In the public arena, much of the noise in the interaction between theology and philosophy comes from New Atheist attacks, albeit from writers who are either not philosophers (such as Richard Dawkins) or who have largely given up philosophical research for the sake of polemic. More quietly, however, and in a more specialist register, another interaction is worth noting: an interest in theology, and the practices of religion, by a constellation of atheist philosophers, initially from the political hard left but now joined by Alain de Botton, who has not made politics part of his platform, and Roger Scruton, from the right. (While perhaps not fully paid up over Christian metaphysics, Scruton no longer describes himself as an atheist today.)

This new, political, interest in theology and religion among political philosophers began with Continental work on the Epistles of Paul. The principal figures are Agamben, Badiou and Žižek. They were interested in Paul's eschatology and the possibility of total change or transformation: what they called 'the event' and allied with revolution. Of these writers, Žižek– the nearest thing to a media celebrity among current Continental philosophers – has shown the widest-ranging engagement with theology.[1] For their part, theologians show a significant interest in politics, and therefore in political philosophy, whether within the burgeoning discipline known as political theology or within a wider penumbra.[2] This is often rooted in a post-liberal, Wittgensteinian, concern for the connections between theology and corresponding 'forms of life'. Recently, both Simon Critchley and Alain de Botton have given philosophical reasons for wanting a recovery of religious (or quasi-religious) *practices* even against a

---

1 Giorgio Agamben, *The Time that Remains: A Commentary on the Letter to the Romans*, trans. Patricia Dailey, Stanford University Press, 2005; Alain Badiou, *Saint Paul: The Foundation of Universalism*, trans. Ray Brassier, Stanford University Press, 2003; Slavoj Žižek, *The Sublime Object of Ideology*, London: Verso Books, 1989, for Pascal; *The Monstrosity of Christ*, with John Milbank, ed. Creston Davis, Cambridge, MA: MIT Press, 2009, for Chesterton.

2 See the 'Reading On' section below.

strictly atheistic backdrop,[3] as Critchley put it, seeking not the faith without religion of Bonhoeffer but, rather, religion without faith.

Mindset in Philosophy and Theology

Philosophy today comes in two varieties, 'analytic' and 'Continential'. To a large degree, so do philosophers and philosophy departments. The lineaments of this distinction have been sketched in previous chapters. As an overall approximation, analytic philosophers pride themselves in speaking with the utmost clarity, and for that reason avoid questions that will not yield clear answers. Continental philosophers pride themselves on their bravery and breadth. No topic is too grand or involved, nor too vague and unlikely to yield an answer. Analytic philosophy is principally defined by its method; Continental philosophy is principally defined by its subject matter, although it does have distinctive approaches, such as commentary (and commentary on commentary). We only just trespass on parody to say that analytic philosophers give precise answers to questions that do not particularly matter while Continentals obfuscate over questions that do; analytic philosophers may devote their lives to the nuances of the word 'if' and Continental philosophers may write impenetrably about the meaning of being in relation to death.

From another angle, we could say that analytic philosophy is the philosophy of minima and Continental philosophy the philosophy of maxima. Analytic philosophy is a search for the absolutely secure grasp of reality that no one can gainsay. Life may offer considerably more than understanding the meaning of the word 'if', but a philosopher of certain mentality will rejoice that this, at least, has been established securely. Continental philosophers address all that is most significant for the human being, but risk speaking so grandly, so boldly, as not to speak meaningfully

---

3 Respectively, Simon Critchley, *The Faith of the Faithless: Experiments in Political Theology*, London: Verso, 2012 and Alain de Botton, *Religion for Atheists: A Non-believer's Guide to the Uses of Religion*, Penguin, 2012.

at all. Additionally, analytic philosophy tends to see philosophy as a very narrow field, whereas Continental philosophers give philosophy extensive and porous boundaries, and frequently write with reference to literature, film and art, politics, psychology and psychotherapy.

We find a link between these approaches and the countries in which, by and large, they grew up. Analytic philosophy is the product of an environment that is largely Protestant, or at least Anglican. It is in the first place Anglo-Saxon, or North Atlantic, and largely Anglophone. Its early champions were largely hostile to theology. Theologians who have later applied it to theology are more often Protestants than Catholics. Continental philosophy, in contrast, was initially largely German and French, and theology was at least in the margins from the start. Among theologians, Roman Catholics are the most steeped in Continental thought. This makes sense: since the beginning, Protestant theology has sought for minima: *sola scriptura* (by Scripture alone), *sola fide* (by faith alone), churches without images, the cross without the body. The Catholic impulse, as even the word itself suggests, is towards maxima: Scripture *and* tradition, faith necessarily expressed in works, churches full of images, the crucifix – body and all. As to piety and practice, the Protestant will say that invocation of saints and ritual can be unhelpful, and will therefore avoid the former and minimize the latter; the Catholic will say that invocation of saints and ritual can be helpful, and will therefore have them both.

Much is to be said in favour of precision; it is one of the reasons a theologian might concern herself with philosophy. We may, however, seek for precision where it cannot be found, for instance by treating God and divine things with a rationality appropriate only to things in general, ignoring the fact that God is not a thing in general or, indeed, even a 'thing' at all. That has been a danger in the discipline called 'philosophy of religion'. This has been a largely 'analytic' endeavour, and has often constrained theology to the inflexible rules of that approach. Alternatively, we may choose to ignore or discount aspects of thought where the desired precision is not possible, theology among them. For much of the twentieth century, mention of God in analytic philosophy was forbidden, ruled out of court, laughed away. From a yet further perspective, we might worry that analytic philosophy of religion is *not analytic enough*, nor sufficiently precise. We can imagine an argument entirely characteristic of this school: 'Persons are entities in time, God is a person, and therefore God is in time.' Faced with such a statement, the demand should be for *more* analysis and precision, not less. The tradition has not let such definitions stand unchecked but has gone on to ask questions such as 'Are all persons entities in time?' and 'What does it mean, and what does it not mean, for God to be a person?' Indeed, from the first days that 'person' was used of God, theologians have acknowledged that the answers to questions such as these would not be the same as we would give for the persons we more commonly know.

The theologian has much to gain from familiarity with the largely Anglo-Saxon school of analytic philosophy, but his or her more natural partner is likely to be Continental philosophy. Its strength, as we have seen, is the breadth of its interests. It delights in all the topics that an analytic philosopher tries his hardest to avoid, among which we might list love and death (the subject matter of Continental philosophy often resembling the subject matter of a good opera or a gripping biography), while the analytic philosopher might prefer logic and possibility. Some topics are held in common between the two approaches, such as time and being, although the approach will be different. The Continental throws herself upon them, willing to be consumed by them; the analytic braces herself for combat, like a soldier putting on a flak jacket, her colleagues squeezing her shoulder, wishing her luck, urging her to come back safely. A danger with Continental philosophy is the flip side of its strength. It aspires to the same breadth of interest and concern as theology itself, such that it can become a substitute theology. The theologian who roams in Continental territories should be aware of going native.

In both cases, obscurity is another danger, although of two very different sorts. The analytic philosopher aspires to the purity of mathematics. His writing can easily leave any semblance of everyday speech behind, preferring formal logic and its specialist symbolism. This may be incomprehensible not only to a general audience but even to other theologians. The danger for Continental philosophy, and the theology that draws upon it, is, at best, poetic obscurity and, at worst, the impenetrability of invented words and grammar strained to breaking point.

As a suggestion, we might consider the proposal that theology often thrives on Continental sources, while the life of the Church would often be served by a little more analytic rigour. Such rigour might be deployed to chasten sloppy thinking and help the Church to live more consistently by the logic of its theological message.

Two Attitudes to Mathematics

The distinction between analytic and Continental philosophy can be illustrated by looking at two approaches to mathematics. Links between theology, philosophy and mathematics have turned up across this volume, whether in Pythagoras, Plato, the late scholastics (and their turn to quantity), Descartes or Pascal. In recent philosophy, interest in mathematics has often been in infinitude.[4] An entire sub-discipline, transfinite mathematics, began with the ground-breaking work of a devout Italian Roman Catholic mathematician, Georg Cantor (1845–1918), who showed that we can distinguish between different 'sizes' or orders of infinitude.

Analytic philosophy can be seen as an attempt to provide philosophy with the precision of mathematics, even if that comes at the cost of discounting subject matter that cannot be treated that way. On the page it can look as much like mathematics as prose, with ideas treated with the procedures, and symbols, of formal logic.

The analytic philosopher might look to mathematics, and especially to logic, in order to escape from questions of metaphysics. In contrast, the Continental perspective is often to see mathematics as among the most metaphysical areas of human thought. Currently, a clutch of contemporary philosophers are seizing upon

---

4 A particularly forceful account of the relation between mathematics and theology comes in the work of Brian Rotman, although in his case he wishes to exorcise the theology. See, for instance, *Taking God Out of Mathematics and Putting the Body Back In: An Essay in Corporeal Semiotics*, Stanford University Press, 1993.

transfinite mathematics as a foundation for philosophy, most prominently Alain Badiou and Quentin Meillassoux.[5] Both are tremendously difficult philosophers to understand. We may think that they totter on the edge of being meaningful at all (or even fall over the edge). Transfinite mathematics appeals, among other reasons, for its ability to construct itself 'out of nothing', or a least out of 'the empty set': the set of things distinguished by being the only set to contain nothing. For the secular philosopher, wanting to find a foundation for philosophy other than God, building up from the empty set can look like a seductive analogy to pursue. Although some philosophers, and some theologians, sense the beginning of a significant 'turn to mathematics', it remains to be seen if this will amount to anything significant.

Philosophy of Religion or Philosophical Theology (and Literature)

Today we are likely to come across two approaches to explicating a link between theology and philosophy: 'philosophy of religion' and 'philosophical theology'. The identity of the noun in each of these descriptions matters, since it indicates what is likely to set the running. As we have just seen, philosophy of religion often falls foul of the charge laid against the Fathers (although incorrectly, in their case) that philosophy bends theology into new shapes. The noun in 'philosophy of religion' is *philosophy*, and its norms are philosophical. Philosophy of religion risks being a 'procrustean bed', named after Procrustes, a figure in Greek mythology, who stretched his guests to fit a bed, or cut off limbs. In contrast, the noun in 'philosophical theology' is *theology*. By and large, those who favour this title want to take theology as their starting point, honouring revelation. Their philosophical interests are in exploring theology using philosophical tools, and in forging a philosophical world view on the basis of Christian doctrine.

---

5 Respectively *Number and Numbers*, trans. Robin Mackay, Cambridge: Polity Press, 2008 and *After Finitude: An Essay on the Necessity of Contingency*, trans. Ray Brassier, Continuum, 2010.

It will be clear that this book advocates philosophical theology over philosophy of religion. We might, however, note a criticism even of this approach, levelled by John Milbank in one of his most important, and accessible, essays: that 'philosophical theology' is 'a wholly redundant term', for two reasons.[6] First, all theology is 'philosophical' in that it involves 'discursive reflection' and cannot avoid appeal to 'traditions of philosophical reflection'. Second, there is no sub-discipline of theology (such as the problem of evil or the divine attributes) that is so philosophical as to be beyond the norms of doctrine based on revelation.[7] All theology involves philosophy but no questions are entirely philosophical. Milbank suggests a third, alternative configuration: 'Faith, Reason and Imagination', where 'imagination' refers principally to literature. Both theology and philosophy, he argues, 'also exist in poetic and narrative modes of representation'. Indeed, since 'the Romantic reaction to the Enlightenment these have often proved to be the most important idioms for the defence and development of Orthodox doctrine'.[8]

The task, in other words, of taking 'every thought captive to obey Christ' (2 Cor. 10.5) and of the 'renewing of [our] minds' (Rom. 12.2), is theological and philosophical, and its scope is nothing less than the whole of human life: all that proceeds from human reason and desire, imagination and creativity.[9] Its goal is not only that our worship may be 'rational' (Rom. 12.1) but also that our reason may be worshipful, forever rejoicing in God as reason's origin and goal.

Reading On

Excellent introductions to Christian political theology are Elizabeth Phillip's *Political Theology: A Guide for the Perplexed* (T&T Clark, 2012), *The Blackwell Companion to Political Theology,*

---

6 'Faith, Reason and Imagination: The Study of Theology and Philosophy in the Twenty-First Century', in *The Future of Love*, SCM Press, 2009, pp. 316–34.

7 Milbank, 'Faith', p. 320.

8 Milbank, 'Faith', p. 319.

9 This breadth is explored in my *Imaginative Apologetics*, SCM Press, 2011.

edited by Peter Scott and William Cavanaugh (Wiley-Blackwell, 2006) and the anthology *An Eerdmans Reader in Contemporary Political Theology* (Eerdmans, 2011), edited by William Cavanaugh, Jeffrey Bailey and Craig Hoveyr. For the application of ideas in political theology on practical Christian concerns see James K. A. Smith, *Desiring the Kingdom: Worship, Worldview, and Cultural Formation* (Baker, 2009) and William T. Cavanaugh, *Being Consumed: Economics and Christian Desire* (Eerdmans, 2008).

Simon Critchley's *Very Short Introduction* to Continental philosophy is an excellent place to start (OUP, 2001). Examples of Continental philosophy are given in other 'Reading On' sections. Nick Trakakis discusses Continental and analytic approaches to philosophy in theology, and the weakness of the analytic approach, in Chapters 2 and 3 of *The End of Philosophy of Religion* (Continuum, 2008).

The best of what analytic 'clear thinking' has to offer is represented in Anthony Weston's *Rulebook for Arguments* (Hackett, 2009), although much that is presented here goes back as far as Aristotle. The 'analytic theology' tradition is sufficiently prominent today to deserve a mention, for all its method and output are by and large antithetical to the vision outlined in this book. Michael C. Rea has edited several collections: *Oxford Readings in Philosophical Theology*, 2 volumes (OUP, 2009); *Analytic Theology: New Essays in the Philosophy of Theology* (with Oliver Crisp, OUP, 2011) and *The Oxford Handbook of Philosophical Theology* (with Thomas Flint, OUP, 2011), which is remarkable for representing 'philosophical theology' in general within the *Handbooks* series while giving hardly a suggestion of philosophical theology outside the analytic approach. Helen Beebee, Nikk Effingham and Philip Goff provide an excellent and accessible introduction to metaphysics from an analytic perspective in *Metaphysics: The Key Concepts* (Routledge, 2010).

Biblical Index

Index of Names

Knowles, David 106, 110 n. 18, 115 n. 24
Kramnick, Isaac 199
Kuhn, Thomas 264

Labron, Tim 255
Lacan, Jacques 272
Lacoste, Jean-Yves xvii, 254
Lakoff, George 226
Lechte, John 255
Lefebvre, Henri 274
Lemon, M. C. 226
Leo the Great 75, 161
Leo XIII, Pope 127, 129
Lessing, G. E. 220–2
Lévi-Strauss, Claude 244
Lévinas, Emmanuel 56, 253
Lewis, Clive Staples 88, 101, 109
Lewis, David 181 n. 18
Liebniz, Gottfried Wilhelm 179, 181–3, 185, 199
Lindbeck, George 223, 247, 263
Lints, Richard xvii
Little, Daniel 219 n. 26
Locke, John 188, 190, 191
Lombard, Peter 112–13, 120
Lonergan, Bernard 213
Loughlin, Gerard 264, 265
Louth, Andrew 100
Lubac, Henri de 27 n. 27, 129, 149
Lucretius 82 n. 21
Luther, Martin 56, 164, 169–72, 173 n. 3, 202, 232, 238, 255
Lyotard, Jean-François 266, 278

MacIntrye, Alasdair 51, 103, 108 n. 10, 132, 174, 179 n. 13, 181 n. 17, 243, 245, 253 n. 15
Mackenzie, Jon 170 n. 17, 171
Macquarrie, John 255
Malebranche, Nicolas 176–9, 181, 183

Malherbe, Abraham 60–1, 62 n. 28, 63, 72
Marcus Aurelius 71–2
Maréchal, Joseph 212
Marenbon, John 99
Marino, Gordon Daniel 255
Marion, Jean-Luc 254
Maritain, Jacques 171, 243
Maritain, Raïssa 243
Martin, John 211
Marx, Karl 227–9, 231–2, 239, 241, 269, 270, 275, 279
Mary, the Blessed Virgin 22
Masaccio 160 n. 1, 167
Mascall, Eric 170
Mason, Richard 199
Maximus the Confessor 67, 94–6, 99, 104–5, 161–2
McCabe, Herbert 88, 165
McClintock Fulkerson, Mary 218
McDermott, Timothy 142
McKeon, Richard 52
McMullin, Ernan 83
Meillassoux, Quentin 286
Menander 63
Meredith, Anthony 7, 8, 12 n. 5, 53 n. 1, 63 n. 30, 65, 66 n. 40, 69–70, 71 n. 53, 73, 75 n. 4, 76 n. 6, 79, 81, 82 n. 19, 84, 85 n. 2, 91
Merleau-Ponty, Maurice 252, 256
Messiaen, Olivier 87
Meuthen, Erich 172
Midgley, Mary 36
Milbank, Alison 223 n. 33
Milbank, John 28, 147 n. 4, 148 n. 5, 173–4, 210–11, 237 n. 14, 274 n. 7, 281 n. 1, 287
Mill, John Stuart ix, 233–4
Mirandola, Giovanni Pico della 166
Monica 14
Montaigne, Michel de 168
Moore, G. E. 198

Index of Subjects

INDEX OF SUBJECTS

bracketing
  as *epoché* 252–3
  of God with world 47, 165,
    182–6, 214–15
Buddhism 86
Byzantine Empire 95

Cambridge Platonists 16
canon 161, 260, 270
capitalism 64 n. 34, 220, 227,
    229–30, 268–70, 275
casuistry 138
categories
  Aristotelian 44, 89
  discovered or imposed 42
  Kantian 203–6, 210
catholicism 127, 129, 131–2, 160,
    165, 167, 170, 198, 212, 214
    n. 15, 237, 250, 258, 283, 285
causation ix, 20, 140–1, 155 n. 12,
    196–7, 200, 202–7, 212, 220
  efficient, 35, 38, 46, 152, 155 n. 12
  final 35, 38, 46, 155 n. 12, 274,
    see also teleology
  formal 35, 152, 155 n. 12, 158,
    274, *see also* form
  four causes 35–9, 47, 124, 134,
    152, 178
  material 35, *see also* matter,
    materiality
  secondary 39, 135, 177–9
change 17, 36–8, 43, 204
Christianity as true philosophy 75,
    77
Christology 40, 73, 74–5, 79–80,
    162, 264, *see also* Jesus Christ,
    Incarnation
Church 61, 133, 171, 209, 239,
    243
  as interpreter 57 n. 13
cinema xiii, 257, 269–70, 275, 276,
    283
clarity, desire for 48, 245, 282–3

Cloud of Unknowing 97
common good 243, *see also*
  community, cooperation and
  competition
community 40, 127, 171, 202,
    204, 236
  significance for philosophy, 4,
    13–14, 24, 71, 103, 106, 174,
    196–7, 246, 260, *see also* forms
    of life
competition and cooperation 178,
    189, 241
complete system
  absent in Aquinas 131–2
  present in Neoscholasticism 131–2
  rejected by Kierkegaard 247
  rejected by Novalis 222
Continental philosophy *see*
  philosophy, Continental
cooperation, *see* competition and
  cooperation
council of the Church 79
  of Chalcedon 75, 80, 161
  Lateran IV 132, 164
  Nicea II 161
courage xv, 52
creation 12, 17, 21, 25, 26, 35, 47,
    53, 61, 68, 91, 107–8, 124, 140,
    148, 155, 157, 162, 170 n. 17, 171,
    197, 210, 213–14, 216, 242, 248
  as emanation 82, 88, 90–2, 216
  out of nothing 35, 47, 67, 82–3,
    90, 170 n. 17, 186, 286
creeds 79–80, 126
critical theory 257
crucifixion 43, 116, 125, 169,
    232–3, 238, 283
culture ix, xii, 1, 21, 55, 62, 65,
    74, 76, 86, 95, 125, 145, 160,
    161, 171, 210, 223, 230, 244,
    264, 266, 269–70, 272, 276
  low and high 210, 226, 275
Cynics 60, 63

301

openness of 39
situatedness of 261–2, *see also*
    reason

language x–xi, 18, 20, 29, 42,
    56–8, 62, 75, 96–7, 101,
    138–42, 151–2, 164, 194, 216,
    222–5, 244, 225–6, 242, 244–7,
    259, 262–3, 270
as game 246
everyday 48, 164, 224, 284
langue and *parole* 244
laughter 88
law 104, 109, 114, 130–1, 133, 148,
    181, 196–7, 207–8, 233, 258
English 130–1
international 111, 163
Napoleonic 130–1
natural 59, 63, 130, 146–7, 150,
    163, 190, 198, 207
of Moses 13, 56, 59
of nature 184, 186, 188, 196–7
of non-contradiction 205
positive 130–1
letters, exchange of 16, 72, 174
lev as mind or heart 58
life 45, 230, 242–3
and movement 50
and soul 36
as crown of universe 45
literary form 58, 63, 106–7, 130,
    221, 248, 259–60, 266–7, 285,
    see also dialogue
literary theory 32, 62, 204, 257–65
literature xiii, 87, 160, 211, 219,
    220, 221, 239, 248, 252, 268,
    270, 283, 287
liturgy 64, 85, 97, 106, 125–6,
    129–30, 166, 180, 246, 260, *see
    also* Eucharist
logic 32, 48–50, 92, 95, 116, 117,
    169, 222, 236, 284
modal *see* possible worlds

Logos
as 'spermatic' 76, 78, 90
in Christian theology xiv, 5, 9,
    47, 53, 61, 72, 76, 78, 94,
    242
in Greek philosophy 5, 53, 72,
    89–90
in Philo 67–9, *see also* Jesus
    Christ
love xiv, 23, 52, 97, 218, 236, 273,
    284, *see also* desire, eros

magic 85, 166,
making 37–8, 42, 155, 187
materialism 8, 29, 154, 184, 189–90,
    192–5, 228–9, 243
materiality as arena for spiritual
    23–4, 28–9, 50, 92–3, 155,
    214–15, 228
mathematics 3–4, 6, 19–21, 23,
    56, 93, 155, 158, 174, 176, 180,
    181, 185, 188, 214, 234, 261,
    267, 284, 285–6
transfinite 285–6
matter 3, 6, 8, 19, 29, 35–8, 40,
    45, 47, 50, 53, 72, 82–3, 89, 92,
    101, 124–5, 134–5, 155, 175,
    179, 189–91, 191, 210, 214–15,
    228–9, 242–3
as mysterious 175
prime 134
maxima and minima 165, 282–3
maxims, Kantian 207–8
means *see* ends and means
measurement 39, 233
mediation 92, 150–1, 161, 192,
    209, 211, 274
meta-narratives 266
metaphor 56–8, 97, 118, 225, 226,
    262–3
metaphysics x, 32, 40, 56, 62, 70,
    116, 135–6, 202, 212, 241, 245,
    251, 285

INDEX OF SUBJECTS

open theism 215, *see also* theology,
   process
order 6, 17, 20, 49–50, 53–4, 59,
   61, 68 n. 46, 72, 144–9, 151,
   156, 176–7, 185, 189, 195–6,
   202, 211, 214, 216, 230, 244,
   271 n. 5, 285
ordo amoris 211, 273
Organon 48

panentheism 215–16
pantheism 162, 167, 184–8, 215,
   243
   and definition of substance 184
paradox 6
participation 22, 26, 28–9, 47, 90,
   94, 132, 136, 138–42, 145, 152,
   158, 170 n. 17, 175, 178, 191,
   228, 242, *see also* relation of
   world to God
particularity and generality 40,
   171, 237
passion, category of 44
Perfect Being Theology 107–8
perfection *see* excellence
person, definition of 94
personhood 8, 43, 48–9, 62, 75,
   80–1, 94, 134, 137–8, 140, 188,
   200, 208, 255, 243 n. 2, 251–3,
   262, 274, 284
phenomena and noumena 204–5,
   212, 273
phenomenology 248, 250–5, 256
philosophy
   after postmodernism 269, 280
   analytic xii, 56, 222, 236, 243,
      245, 266–7, 282–5, 288
   as framework 54, *see also*
      philosophy, ubiquity of
   as preparation for gospel 77
   Continental xii, 56, 130, 222,
      235, 243, 281–6, 288
   dangers of ix–xi, xv, 64–70, 74–6,

78–83, 95, 166–7, 169–71,
   194, 217, 283, 286
   in Old Testament 56
   independence of 91–2, 104, 119,
      126, 145–51, 154, *see also*
      secularity
   of religion 182, 283–4, 286–7
   postmodern *see* postmodern
      philosophy
   relation to theology xi, 91–2, 126,
      144–5, 154, 173, 287
   transformed by theology xiii, 24,
      40, 47, 65, 77–9, 82, 86, 122,
      135, 286
   ubiquity of ix, 28–9, 40, 49, 154,
      165–6, 174, 220, 241, 286
physics 40, 117
place 39, 44–5, 170 n. 17,
   175, 183, 248, 252, *see also*
   extension, space
plenitude 42, 66, 162, 165, 218,
   249, of a text 165, 168, 260–1
poetry 58
politics 8, 27–9, 40, 56, 91, 96,
   102, 117, 163, 172, 188–90,
   207, 211, 229, 231, 235, 264,
   269–71, 275, 281–3, 287–8, *see
   also* theology, political
Port-Royal 178–80
position 44
positivism 60, 196, 234–5
possibility and necessity *see*
   necessity and contingency
possible worlds 181–3
post-liberalism 247, 263, 281
post-structuralism 257, 271–4, 280
postmodern philosophy 8, 205–6,
   213, 266–78
   'East Coast' route 271–3
   Kant at origin of 205–6, 274–5
   'West Coast route' 273–4
postmodernism *see* postmodern
   philosophy

307

Printed in the USA
CPSIA information can be obtained
at www.ICGtesting.com
JSHW062235041124
72817JS00040B/795

9 780334 043843